This book may be kept

The Story of the Trapp Family Singers

The Story of the
Trapp Family
Singers

MARIA AUGUSTA TRAPP

Drawings by Agathe and Martina Trapp

J. B. LIPPINCOTT COMPANY
Philadelphia   New York

st. Fr.

CONTENTS

PART I

PART II

ILLUSTRATIONS

The Chapter Before the First

TO BE quite honest, this really is a foreword or an introduction, but I'm so afraid that if I say so, you won't read it, as I never read forewords, and being so anxious that you do listen to what I want to tell you about the book before it starts, I ask you, foreword or no foreword, please read it just the same.

About fifteen years ago my family and I were visiting in Tirol. Our hostess was a famous writer.

"Isn't it funny," she said one day, "I never wrote a word in my life until after I was forty!"

"That's quite incredible," we mused.

The next day we all went into a picturesque valley. On the way we saw a chapel greeting us from one of the wooded slopes.

"Let's climb up there," said our hostess. "That's an interesting place." And so it was. The ancient building was of quaint architecture. Through the roof came a rope dangling down, which belonged to the bell in the little steeple. Playfully I took the rope to try out the sound of the bell.

Looking at our friend, I said: "I wish I could become a writer, too, after I'm forty!" I meant that as a joke, and felt a little embarrassed when she didn't smile.

She looked at me rather queerly and said: "Did you know the story?"

I let the rope go and asked: "Which story?"

"Well," she said, "the people say that once in a hundred years it happens if someone rings this bell while pronouncing a wish, that wish, whatever it may be, will come true, provided the person is unaware of the legend. The people of this valley call it the 'wishing bell.'"

"No—I didn't know this story," said I.

This was fifteen years ago.

7

While working on this book and writing down the memories of a family, it astonished, amazed, almost overwhelmed me to see how much love—genuine, real love—was stored up in one short lifetime: first, God's love for us His children, the leading, guiding, protecting love of a Father; and as every real love calls forth love in return, it couldn't be any different here.

As we are singers, this story turned into a song, a canticle. "Cantate Domino canticum novum," sings King David in one of his Psalms: "Sing unto the Lord a new song." God has become for our age the great Unknown One. Things are blamed on the weather, on politics, on circumstances, on lack of vitamins, on inheritance; but they are rarely attributed to their one source. "The Story of the Trapp Family Singers" wants to be a canticle of love and gratitude to the Heavenly Father in His Divine Providence.

Cor Unum
Stowe, Vermont
Pentecost Sunday, 1949

Part One

Just Loaned

SOMEBODY tapped me on the shoulder. I looked up from the workbooks of my fifth graders, which I was just correcting, into the lined, old face of a little lay sister, every wrinkle radiating kindliness.

"Reverend Mother Abbess expects you in her private parlor," she whispered.

Before I could close my mouth, which had opened in astonishment, the door shut behind the small figure. Lay sisters were not supposed to converse with candidates for the novitiate.

I could hardly believe my ears. We candidates saw Reverend Mother Abbess only from afar in choir. We were the lowest of the low, living on the outskirts of the novitiate, wearing our black mantillas, waiting with eager anticipation for our reception into the sacred walls of the novitiate. I had just finished the State Teachers' College for Progressive Education in Vienna and had to get my Master of Education degree before the heavy doors of the enclosure would shut behind me—forever.

It was unheard of that Reverend Mother Abbess should call for a candidate. What might this mean? Her private parlor was far at the other end of the old Abbey, and I chose the longest detour to go there, in order to gain time for examining my conscience. I was the black sheep of the community; there was no doubt about that. I never meant anything bad, but my upbringing had been more that of a wild boy than that of a young lady. Time and again I had been warned by the Mistress of Novices that I could not race over the staircase like that, taking two and three steps at a time; that I definitely could not slide down the banister; that whistling, even the whistling of sacred tunes, had never been heard in these venerable rooms before; that jumping over the chimneys on the flat roof of the school wing was not fitting for an aspirant to the novitiate of the holy Order of Saint Benedict. I agreed wholeheartedly each time, but the trouble was, there were so many *new* trespasses occurring every day.

What was the matter now, I thought, slowly winding my way down the two flights of old, worn steps, through the ancient cobblestoned kitchen yard, where the huge Crucifix greets one from the wall, and where the statue of Saint Erentrudis, founder of our dear old Abbey, rises above a fountain. Slowly I entered the cloister walk on the other side of the kitchen court.

Troubled as I was, searching through my laden conscience, I still felt again the magic of the supernatural beauty of this most beautiful place on earth. Twelve hundred years had worked and helped to make Nonnberg, the first Abbey of Benedictine Nuns north of the Alps, a place of unearthly beauty. For a moment I had to pause and glance again over the gray, eighth-century cloister wall before I ascended the spiral stairway leading to the quarters of Reverend Mother Abbess.

Shyly I knocked on the heavy oaken door, which was so thick that I could hear only faintly the "Ave," Benedictine equivalent of the American, "Hello, come in."

It was the first time I had been in this part of the Abbey. The massive door opened into a big room with an arched ceiling; the one column in the middle had beautifully simple lines. Almost all the rooms in this wonderful Abbey were arched, the ceilings carried by columns; the windows were made of stained glass, even in the school wing. Near this window there was a large desk, from which rose a delicate, small figure, wearing a golden cross on a golden chain around her neck.

"Maria dear, how are you, darling?"

Oh this kind, kind voice! Not only stones, but big rocks fell from my heart when I heard that tone. How could I ever have worried? No, Reverend Mother was not like *that*—making a fuss about little things like whistling—and so a faint hope rose in my heart that she might perhaps talk to me now about the definite date of my reception.

"Sit down, my child. No, right here near me."

After a minute's pause she took both my hands in hers, looked inquiringly into my eyes, and said: "Tell me, Maria, which is the most important lesson our old Nonnberg has taught you?"

Without a moment's hesitation I answered, looking fully into the beautiful, dark eyes: "The only important thing on earth for us is to find out what is the Will of God and to do it."

"Even if it is not pleasant, or if it is hard, perhaps very hard?" The hands tightened on mine.

Well now, she means leaving the world and giving up everything and all that, I thought to myself.

"Yes, Reverend Mother, even then, and wholeheartedly, too."

Releasing my hands, Reverend Mother sat back in her chair.

"All right then, Maria, it seems to be the Will of God that you leave us—for a while only," she continued hastily when she saw my speechless horror.

"L-l-leave Nonnberg," I stuttered, and tears welled up in my eyes. I couldn't help it. The motherly woman was very near now, her arms around my shoulders, which were shaking with sobs.

"Your headaches, you know, growing worse from week to week. The doctor feels that you have made too quick a change from mountain climbing to our cloistered life, and he suggests we send you away, for less than one short year, to some place where you can have normal exercise. Then it will all settle down, and next June you will come back, never to leave again."

Next June—my goodness, now it was only October!

"It just so happened that a certain Baron von Trapp, retired Captain in the Austrian Navy, called on us today. He needs a teacher for his little daughter, who is of delicate health. You will go to his house this afternoon. And now kneel down; I want to give you my blessing."

I knelt down. The fine, delicately small hand made the sign of the Cross on my forehead. I kissed the ring and, as through a veil, I had a last glance into those unforgettable eyes, which seemed to know all about woe and sorrow, grief and suffering, but also victory and peace. I couldn't utter a single word without bursting out loudly, but no words were needed, anyway.

"Now then, go and do it, and wholeheartedly, too."

That was all.

A few hours later I was seated on one of the green benches under the old chestnut trees at the Residenzplatz in Salzburg, waiting for the bus that was to take me to Aigen. One hand was clasped tightly around a piece of paper which said: "Captain Georg von Trapp, Villa Trapp, Aigen bei Salzburg"; the other one held the handle of an old-fashioned leather satchel, which stood next to me on the bench, and which contained all my earthly possessions, mostly books. Under my arm was pressed the neck of an almost inseparable part of myself, my guitar. Years back, when I had started to work my way through college, I had bought it with my first self-earned money. It had accompanied me everywhere, on all the many trips and hikes through the Alps, up to the holy hill of Nonnberg. And now it went with me into exile.

I was still bewildered, everything had happened so fast. I tried to review the last few hours, which had passed like a bad dream. After I had come back from Reverend Mother Abbess, my Mistress of Novices, Frau Rafaela, was already waiting for me in the candidates' room, her arms full of clothing. When I had entered the convent a year before, I had exchanged my Austrian costume for the black dress and black mantilla of the candidates. My own clothes had been given away during the year to some needy persons after the Chapter meeting had decided I was to be admitted for reception. I could see that Frau Rafaela felt quite badly about the whole situation, too. She looked a little helplessly at the clothes on her arm, which had belonged to another novice who was a little shorter and wider than I. She chose one dress and, obediently, I put on an old-fashioned blue serge gown with funny latticework around the neck and sleeves. I put it on three times, because I could not make out which was front and which was back. Next came a leather hat, which looked exactly like a fireman's helmet. It went right down to my brow, and I had to give it a little push when I wanted to see Frau Rafaela, who just said:

"Now let me look at you."

As she stepped back a little, her eyes wandered from the hat down to the blue dress, on to the black stockings and heavy, black shoes. She nodded approvingly.

"Very nice—very elegant."

Frau Rafaela was a saintly, elderly nun; the days of her farewell to the world dated back at least thirty years. I feel pretty sure now that I must have reminded her vividly of the young ladies of her own day.

Then came a few instructions: On my day off I should always come back to the convent; I should remember the doctor's advice to get enough sleep and exercise—but moderate, moderate; and finally,

I should always bear in mind that my home and place was Nonn-berg, and although I had to deal with the people of the world, I was *just loaned* to them.

My heart ached when I had to bid farewell to the other three young candidates with whom I had shared the big, lofty room over-looking the green valley of the Salzach River. While Frau Rafaela bent over a little scrap of paper to write down the name of the place where I was to go, I took in with one last glance the picture of the large, oblong room with the six windows, the white-curtained cells along the wall, where we slept, the large table in the middle, and the huge, old-fashioned *Kachelofen,* the European tile stove which can radiate so much comfort and warmth in the severe Salzburg winters. How happy I had been there, and how long it would be until I should be back; but "Thy Will Be Done" was painted in faded, old-fashioned letters over the door on the whitewashed wall.

A few more words, a final blessing, and for the last time my fin-gers dipped into the pewter holy water font. For a few moments I knelt at the choir grate, looking down to the main altar, asking Our Lord for strength. Then the old oaken door opened with a cranky squeak, unwilling, it seemed to me, to let the youngest child of Nonnberg go back into a world from which it would much rather have protected her.

When I stepped from the cool archway into the centuries-old graveyard, my eyes, half blinded by tears and the bright sunshine, fell upon the inscription of a weathered gravestone, crooked with age: "God's Will Hath No Why."

Under the arched doorway which was cut into the big outer wall of the cemetery I turned for a last loving look at the cherished walls and whispered: "I will be back—soon."

Then I was on the road that led down the hill on which Saint Erentrudis had built her castle of God in the eighth century. And a castle it was, built on solid rock, with its huge walls nine feet thick at the foundation. Where this foundation seemed to grow out of the rock a little terrace had been cut into the stone. Here I paused for a few moments, looking over the railing into the deep valley from which the rock rose steeply for almost three hundred feet, down where the houses of Salzburg nestled to the green mountain side. I was still higher than the steeples of the churches. I looked over the quaint old Grabendächer ("ditch roofs," a roof construction frequently used on old houses in Salzburg), followed with my eyes the silver ribbon of the Salzach River, way over to the mountains from which it came. Over there must be Aigen, where I was to go.

Where I was to go—for heaven's sake—I had to reach the bus; and down I went the hundred and forty-four steps, two at a time, forgetting already the very recent admonitions. On the Residenzplatz I learned that the next bus was due in half an hour and so, a little breathless from running, there I was now sitting on one of the green benches.

I felt quite uprooted and a little empty in my head. What was to come next? My eyes fell on the crumpled piece of paper in my hand, and I read again, "Captain von Trapp." That made me wonder. I had never been at the seashore, nor had I ever met a sea captain in my life. I knew them only from story books and pictures.

"I guess he is an elderly man with a bushy, gray beard, red cheeks, and sharp, blue eyes," I thought to myself. "Most probably he chews tobacco and spits quite a bit. If he is a captain, he must have been around the world many times. Surely all his walls must be plastered with trophies, lion and tiger hides, weapons, pottery, and whatnot. It will be awfully interesting."

At the same time I felt a certain awe creeping into my heart, because surely he would shout a lot, as sea captains are supposed to be very gruff. At this very moment I remembered the story of the mutiny on the Bounty, a silent picture which I had seen just before I entered the convent, and which had haunted my nights for quite some time. There was one scene of sea wolves who not only boxed the ears of their sailors, but beat them half to death and imprisoned them with bread and water—oh, shouldn't I rather—

A terrific noise interrupted my anxious thoughts. Wrapped in a cloud of dust and blue gasoline fumes, a big vehicle roared across the Residenzplatz and with a sharp and daring curve, stopped right in front of me. A man dismounted from the bus. I wanted to see if he was the driver, but my leather helmet fell over my eyes, and I could see only as far as his mouth, from which protruded a huge toothpick. Pushing the hat back a little, I saw a driver's cap.

"Is this the bus for Aigen?" I asked. The toothpick man nodded.

"When are you leaving?"

"At once."

For a moment he looked searchingly around to see whether there were any more passengers. I stepped in and sat down on the right front seat, my precious belongings close beside me. My satchel looked exactly like the bag of a horse-and-buggy doctor. The driver stepped back in, closed the door, and said: *"Zwanzig Groschen,"* (twenty cents). After a gentle push on the helmet I looked up at him and, while he was getting the change, I watched the toothpick. He could wave it up and down and sideways, move it from one corner of his mouth to the other, even while speaking or spitting, but he never lost it.

The driver sat down at the wheel, pushed a button, and, squeaking and groaning, we started down the Residenzplatz, across the Mozartplatz, down towards the Salzach River, in such sharp and masterful curves that twice I landed on the other side of the bus. After only a few minutes we crossed the bridge over the Salzach River, the Karolinenbrücke, and almost immediately we were in the open country, passing by a few estates with large gardens and then meadows and fields. Several times we stopped abruptly to take farm people aboard. They all seemed to know each other, shouted greetings, yelled answers, because with all that roaring and rattling you had to raise your voice quite a bit even to say a word. Mr. Müller, as I heard the people greet our driver, had to answer many questions, give many explanations, laugh at jokes. Between cigarettes he spit artistically through a little hole in the left front window, but he never dropped the toothpick.

After about twenty minutes' drive, the bus stopped suddenly and, pointing the toothpick straight at me, Mr. Müller said, "Aigen."

I got out and was immediately clad in a smoke screen. After the bus had disappeared and I had pushed back my helmet, I could see only one house, which said "Inn."

"Do you know the Villa Trapp?" I asked a man who was smoking in the doorway of the inn. He didn't say whether he did or not, but he came out on the dusty country road and, pointing with his pipe across the meadow to a group of large trees, he said: "There."

On the right side of the railroad tracks across the way the road was lined by a high iron fence, which seemed to encircle the park of an estate. On the other side, wide meadows stretched towards the foot of a pretty high mountain, which I knew was the Gaisberg.

The narrow road seemed to lead straight to the foot of it. No, there was a turn. It had already been quite a long walk, and I had changed my things from one hand to the other several times. I tried to peep into the park, but the trees and bushes made a solid green wall. Perhaps these were the trees which I had seen from the bus stop. Then there must be a house, *the* house. And there it was. Suddenly the iron bars opened into a wide driveway, and beyond a large, green, oblong patch of lawn, through the yellow leaves of old horse-chestnut trees I could catch glimpses of a building. I stopped for a moment, pushed back that nuisance of a hat impatiently, and looked. Here now was the place! I was torn by conflicting feelings: there was still the sad note of the hurried farewell from the beloved sanctuary, there was a strong curiosity about the exotic home of a real navy captain, mixed with some awe of that captain himself, and a general uneasiness.

"But you can't stand here forever," I told myself.

As I stepped out from under the trees to the gravel driveway, I had a full view of the big gray mansion with a little tower on the right corner. Ivy covered this side of the house. My attention was immediately attracted by the windows on the first floor. They were exceptionally tall. I could see something red and white hanging from a wall inside. Two steps led up to a heavy, two-winged, arched, oaken door. The way it opened with a little squeak after I had rung the doorbell made me feel homey.

"Is this the Villa Trapp?" I asked the good-looking man who stood in the doorway, dressed in a gray Austrian costume, only there were silver buttons instead of the familiar staghorn.

"Yes, M'm."

"I am the new teacher. Are you the Captain?"

Not a muscle moved in the tanned face.

"No, M'm, I am Hans, the butler."

"How do you do, Hans," and I stretched out my hand to greet him.

He shook it a bit hastily, I thought, and didn't seem quite at ease. He took my satchel and ushered me through a double glass door into a sumptuous hall, which extended the full height of the house, bade me sit down, and disappeared quietly before I could say another word. I was somewhat disappointed. In the small mountain village of Tirol where I came from and where everybody knew everybody else, we were never in such haste. I should have liked to talk a little while to the friendly-looking man and ask a good many questions before I had to face the first sea captain of my life. But perhaps this was the way butlers had to be. I had never met one before in my life. There weren't any in our mountains, nor in the boarding school in Vienna, nor at Nonnberg, either. They only occurred in novels and movies, like sea captains.

There I sat on a richly-carved, dark chair, which reminded me somewhat of the choir stalls in the Abbey. Curiously I looked around for the lion and tiger skins and the strange weapons, but only a few ancient pieces of furniture stood in the large hall, and two dark oil paintings hung on the wall. Through the large windows I had admired from the outside, the full sun shone on an exquisite staircase, which wound upwards in an elegant curve. The red and white hanging from the wall turned out to be the largest flag I had ever seen in my life. It was at least thirty feet long, red—white—red, with a huge crest in the middle.

Suddenly I heard quick footsteps behind me, and a full, resonant voice exclaimed: "I see you are looking at my flag."

There he was—the Captain!

The tall, impeccably-groomed gentleman standing before me was certainly a far cry from the old sea wolf of my imagination. The air of complete self-assurance and somewhat lordly bearing would have frightened me, had it not been for his warm and hearty handshake.

"I am glad you have come, Fräulein. . . ."

I filled in, "Maria."

He took me in from top to toe with a quick glance. All of a sudden I became very conscious of my funny dress, and sure enough, there I was diving under my helmet again. But the Captain's eyes rested on my shoes.

We were still standing in the hall when he said: "I want you to meet the children first of all."

Out of his pocket he took an odd-shaped, ornamented brass whistle, on which he piped a series of complicated trills.

I must have looked highly amazed, because he said, a little apologetically: "You see, it takes so long to call so many children by name, that I've given them each a different whistle."

Of course, I now expected to hear a loud banging of doors and a chorus of giggles and shouts, the scampering of feet of youngsters jumping down the steps and sliding down the banister. Instead, led by a sober-faced young girl in her early teens, an almost solemn little procession descended step by step in well-mannered silence— four girls and two boys, all dressed in blue sailor suits. For an instant we stared at each other in utter amazement. I had never seen such perfect little ladies and gentlemen, and they had never seen such a helmet.

"Here is our new teacher, Fräulein Maria."

"*Grüss Gott,* Fräulein Maria," six voices echoed in unison. Six perfect bows followed.

That wasn't real. That couldn't be true. I had to shove back that ridiculous hat again. This push, however, was the last. Down came the ugly brown thing, rolled on the shiny parquet floor, and landed at the tiny feet of a very pretty, plump little girl of about five. A delighted giggle cut through the severe silence. The ice was broken. We all laughed.

"This is Johanna," her father introduced the little giggler, "and here is our baby, Martina."

What a delicate child, I thought. Reservedly she held both hands behind her back and glanced at me silently and critically.

"Hedwig is already a big school girl," and the father pointed to the third of the younger ones. All three had their hair cut in low bangs, whereas the fourth girl, whom the Captain introduced as, "My oldest daughter, Agathe," wore a large white hair ribbon atop her shoulder-length curls. I felt a strong liking for that young child with the unusually grave countenance and the shy little smile. I wished with all my heart we might become good friends.

There was no time, however, at this moment to try, as their father was continuing: "And here are the boys, Rupert, the oldest of them all, and Werner."

Rupert seemed to have his father's somewhat aloof bearing. Werner was a little fellow with eyes like dark velvet, whom I wanted to take into my arms and hug right there and then.

"Which one is my pupil?" I asked the Captain.

A shadow came into his smiling eyes when he answered: "You haven't met your pupil. I will show you up."

With a nod he dismissed the children.

While I followed him up the staircase, he explained.

"This child has been a problem to us for years on account of her poor health. Ever since she had scarlet fever, her heart has remained weak. Now she has had grippe, and doesn't seem able to recover. Poor little one."

At the second floor landing the Captain opened a door, and we climbed another flight of stairs, this time narrow and winding, to the third floor and our destination, a large, sunny room opening out on a balcony. Propped up on a mountain of pillows in an ancient, oversized, carved-wood bed, sat a little girl.

"This is Maria, Fräulein," the Captain said and, bending over the yellowish little face with the dark rings under the large black eyes, continued in a tender undertone, "I am sure you two will get on really well together, little one. You even have the same name."

A faint smile lit the small face, and a little voice answered, "Yes, Father," and, "I am very glad to meet you, Fräulein Maria."

"Now Fräulein must go to her room," the Captain explained, "but she will be back to see you soon."

As we descended the staircase together, he turned suddenly and asked: "Well, how do you like the children?"

The question took me unawares.

"They have the most beautiful eyes I have ever seen," I stammered, "but they all look so pale and serious."

I hated myself for saying this, which their father could very well take for unduly quick criticism, so I hastened to add: "But they are all very well behaved."

"Not always," said the Captain with a little twinkle.

Then suddenly serious—he had evidently heard more than I had intended to say—he added in a lower voice while we were continuing down the stairs:

"You see, you are the twenty-sixth in a long line of nurses, governesses, and teachers we have had to look after them since their poor mother died four years ago. That will explain many things to you. The last teacher stayed with us only two months, but I have the feeling it will be different this time."

"Yes," I smiled, "nine months."

Then he opened the tall, white door for me, and with the words, "The bell will ring for dinner soon," and a slight bow, he took his leave.

It was a large, sunny room with a big bay window. An oriental rug covered most of the floor. Heavy antique furniture and costly wallpaper gave it an aristocratic air. The white bed in the niche was covered with pale blue silk; the table in the middle, under the carved chandelier, with heavy brocade. In Nonnberg we had no rugs, no silk, no brocade; but on the walls hung centuries-old paintings and wood carvings of Our Lord and Our Lady and all the dear Saints. At every door one found a holy water font made of pewter or silver or ceramic by artistic hands. Nothing of this kind could I find in my new room. At the foot of the bed stood a simple stool on which lay my shabby, worn satchel and the unfortunate little hat; the guitar leaned against the bed. They felt like strangers here, and so did I. I sat down on the stool, took them into my lap, and for a moment I was quite forlorn and lonely when a rich, strange sound made me jump up: the dinner bell.

A little later we all met again in the elegant dining room. At the head of the table was the Captain. The children sat along both sides. The other lower end was taken by a middle-aged lady. I sat at her left, the baby at her right. I learned that she was Baroness Matilda, the *Hausdame,* a lady of noble background who presided over the whole household. She had a kind, friendly way about her. Her whole bearing breathed refinement and reminded me of lavender.

This hour in the dining room just added a few more questions to the many that already crowded my mind: Those many different silver and crystal dishes—what were they for? Why did Hans, the butler, wear gloves—indoors—all of a sudden? What was the matter with his left hand that he held it so tightly to his back? (Perhaps there was a hole in the other glove.) Why did the Baroness ring that little bell? Why didn't she call him when he was only standing right behind the door? And so on, and so on.

Right after dinner I was told that I was free for the evening to do my unpacking and get settled.

Well, the unpacking didn't take more than five minutes. The toothbrush and the few pieces of underwear, the brown velvet dress, looking hopelessly like a sack, and the dozen books were quickly disposed of. The satchel and the little hat wandered into the darkest corner of the huge wardrobe. The New Testament and the Rule of Saint Benedict, together with a little Cross, were placed on my night table.

Then I went over to the window. In the red light of the setting sun there stretched a large park with meadows and groups of big trees and meadows again. And a little farther I saw, sharply drawn against the pale evening sky, the profile of my beloved mountain, the Untersberg, the same way we had seen it every day from Nonnberg. And there were all the others, too: Tennengebirge, Hagengebirge, Staufen, Watzmann.

I felt a little better already. When you are a child of the mountains yourself, you really belong to them. You need them. They become the faithful guardians of your life. If you cannot dwell on their lofty heights all your life, if you are in trouble, you want at least to look at them. The man who wrote three thousand years ago: "I will lift up mine eyes unto the hills, from whence cometh my help," * knew this, too. And even Our Lord, when He was weary and tired out and wanted to be alone with His Father, ascended a mountain.

Happily, like a little school girl, I made myself a calendar which showed two hundred and fifty days, the exact number I should have to endure in this house. The first day was crossed out, and the last thought which went through my mind at the end of this important day was: After all—I don't belong here; I am just loaned.

* All quotations from the Bible are translated from the German.

Glories of the Past

THE next few days I lived in a continual state of bewilderment. Nothing—nothing at all—was familiar to me in this house. First, I had to get used to the different people. There was the Baron and there were his seven children. There was Baroness Matilda, and then came the staff of servants, headed by Hans, the butler. In the kitchen reigned Resi, the round, good-natured chief cook. Once in her early years she had cooked on an English steamer. She had been in Australia and India, and sometimes in the evening she would tell the little kitchen maid, Mariandl, gruesome stories about pirates and cannibals. It happened usually on such occasions that the two housemaids, Poldi and Lisi, and Pepi, the gardener, gathered in the kitchen, too. And even Hans preferred to clean the silver in the kitchen because "there was better light." Resi's stories were just too good to be missed.

Only Franz never showed up in the kitchen. He didn't need to listen to Resi's wild stories. He had been the Captain's orderly while on active duty in the Navy, and he could have told stories himself about submarines and torpedoes, but he thought his stories too good for the kitchen. He lived with his family in the big house, too. As the Captain did not need an orderly any more, Franz was in charge of the farm. Being a farmer's boy, he had adjusted himself better to the change of his way of living than his master. Every now and then, however, one could see the Captain and his former orderly smoking a pipe together in the evening after the chores were done, talking about the glorious times in the Navy.

Besides the large family and the servants, which amounted already to twenty persons, there was the spacious old house to get used to. So many rooms, hallways, corridors, bay windows, balconies— and in the rooms, so many quaint things I had never met before.

On the third day after my arrival the Baron left for a hunting trip to Hungary. The same evening Baroness Matilda said to me during supper: "When all the children are in bed, wouldn't you like to come over to my room?"

I accepted gladly, and started immediately to list in my mind the most important questions about the children, the house, and last, but not least, the Captain himself.

"Come in and make yourself at home," Baroness Matilda's high-pitched, soft voice called in answer to my knock on her door. I went in, but I could not make myself at home right away. There was too much of something in this room; what was it? An instant later I knew it was ruffles. The white lace curtains at the windows fell in wide, ruffled curves. The bed had what seemed to be a petticoat of long muslin ruffles all around. The dressing table with the large silver mirror and the many tiny bottles and flasks was also clad in white muslin with big ruffles. The chaise longue, which reached diagonally into the big room, had a rich display of silken ruffles. And even the silken cushion on which the Baroness had been resting displayed a yellowish halo of ruffles around her head. My rather masculine mountain-climber's heart shrank back from so much femininity. I must have stopped involuntarily in the doorway, for, "Won't you sit down, dear?" said the friendly lady with the wide black velvet ribbon about her throat.

Next to the chaise longue, on the little ebony table, stood a silver tray. Baroness Matilda took from it a crystal carafe, removed the silver stopper, and poured golden wine into two crystal glasses. Then she put an odd-shaped ceramic dish on my lap, filled with the Austrian pastries, *Mozart Kugeln* and *Vanilla Kipferln,* and said: "Help yourself."

Then, raising her glass, she continued with a warm undertone in her voice: "Welcome, welcome, and may you never have a successor!"

It took me a moment to realize that this meant she wished me to stay until the children were grown up and would not need a teacher any more. Now, wasn't that nice, and I started to warm up—ruffles or no ruffles.

I had never been spoiled with cookies or candies in my life; and those delicacies on my lap simply loosened my tongue, and I poured out questions to my heart's delight. Patiently and smilingly the Baroness answered the hundred and one whys and wherefores, until

I said, finally: "There is one thing that I understand least of all. Why does the Captain not look happy with those precious children, this wonderful home of his, and everything that money can buy?"

The smile vanished from the face of my companion, and she repeated: "Everything money can buy—that is very little. Oh, the poor man has lost so much!"

Baroness Matilda looked forlornly into the golden glow of the lamp. I felt rather embarrassed now; perhaps I should not have asked questions about the master. Perhaps now I should take my leave and go to bed, and I fidgeted uneasily in my chair. Baroness Matilda seemed to awaken from deep thought. She turned to me again and said in a friendly manner:

"No, you don't have to go yet, my dear child. I may just as well tell you the whole story. The Captain is not always easy to understand, and this may prove a key for you in future happenings."

And then I listened to a very odd story. Captain von Trapp had been born and brought up on the seashore, as his father had also been in the Navy. At the age of eighteen he had earned his first decoration fighting in the Boxer Rebellion in China. He was one of the first to sense the importance of the submarine in warfare. He applied for transfer to Fiume, where the newly invented torpedoes were being built for all Europe. This transfer decided his whole life. He was given command of one of the first submarines the Austrian Navy put into service.

The young lady who christened this submarine was the granddaughter of the inventor of the torpedo and owner of the torpedo plant, Robert Whitehead. When the submarine was christened, the heart of its commander was captured. Hers was the fairy-tale combination of rare beauty, charm of character, and fabulous wealth. Before long they were married. In Pola, the Austrian Navy Yard, they built a costly villa overlooking the blue sea, and they were very happy.

The outbreak of World War I brought a sudden end to this fairy tale. All civilians had to leave Pola. The young wife went with their two little babies to stay at her mother's estate in the Austrian Alps, and the Captain's interesting hobby turned suddenly into a bloody profession.

He soon found out that those first submarines had not yet passed the stage of experimentation. Exhaust gases swept through the boat causing the crew to be poisoned. The periscope could not be raised or lowered, but the whole boat had to be moved with the periscope. However, Captain von Trapp truly did miracles with the poor material he had. He haunted the shores of the Adriatic Sea, he crippled convoys and very soon he had cleared the home waters of enemy ships. Soon his breast was covered with medals, headed by the rarest decoration Austria can give, the cross of Empress Maria Theresia; and I learned that this highest award an Austrian officer could receive in time of war had been founded by the Empress as an award for an act of personal bravery performed on one's own initiative at one's own risk, sometimes even against orders. That meant if the act were successful, one was given the Maria Theresien Cross and automatically raised to the baronetcy. But if it should happen to fail, one was faced with a court-martial.

He became a legendary figure among the gallant heroes of the Army and Navy as the war went on. His family had grown to five children now. His friends prophesied that at the end of the war he would certainly be made Lord Admiral. His whole nation was proud of him. He was not only popular, but really beloved.—But then it all turned out so differently. Austria was defeated and stripped of her entire seacoast. The proud Imperial Navy was no more. In the prime of life near the peak of his fame the Captain was brushed aside in the whirlwind. Now he was a captain without a ship, which in his special case meant almost a body without a heart.

Only his wife, the queen of his heart and his faithful companion made life still endurable for him. Two more babies arrived after the war. Then an epidemic of scarlet fever took his young wife. Half of his life had died with the Navy. Of the remaining half, most seemed to be buried with her.

"The shining hero of Austria's youth became a silent man with an empty look in his eyes," the Baroness went on. "He moved his seven children from the familiar scenes of his happiness to this newly purchased estate, which is not haunted with memories. He became restless. He tried to go back to sea again. He started the Vega Shipping Company. After that he went into the lumber business, which he soon gave up to try to do something with ships on the Danube. He traveled, he went on long hunting trips. He again tried different businesses, but nothing thrives if done with an aching heart."

"But how about the children?" I could not help asking.

"That is really the saddest part of the story," the Baroness answered in a depressed voice. "He loves the children more than anything else in the world. He provides everything for them that he can get for money. He supplied a whole staff of servants, a governess for the older one, another governess for the little girls, a nursemaid for the baby, a private teacher for Maria. That is what we had before you came. It was a pity! The governesses fought each other and had to be changed frequently. All these people were brought in to take the place of the one. Somehow, he is a little shy with the children. They seem to remind him too much of their mother. He never stays long at home. He drops in unexpectedly, showers them with presents and surprises, becomes restless very soon again, and leaves for another trip. His relatives have persuaded him now to think about one person to replace this whole staff—a new mother for his seven little ones."

And with these words the Baroness rose:

"We expect his engagement to Princess Yvonne to be announced at any time."

From the bottom of a heart which was stirred up by pity and sympathy I added to my night prayers shortly afterward:

"Dear Lord, send him a good wife who will be a good mother to his dear children, and let him be happy from now on."

"The Baron Doesn't Want It . . . ."

AS THE weeks passed by, I grew more accustomed to my work. There was a certain routine to be followed every day. The Baroness liked to rest in the mornings. I was in charge of all the children, had to wake them up, take care of their breakfast, and see the older ones off to school. That was quite a chore because there was so much to think of. The children had to wear leather hats, leggings, and leather gloves. On rainy days rubbers and umbrellas were added. I had managed in an incredibly short time to mix up things. One morning I could find only left gloves and right leggings, and it always took a long time to get hold of the respective mates.

Desperate, I looked for help.

"Couldn't we get some sturdy hobnailed boots," I approached Baroness Matilda, quite exhausted from hunting for some rubbers.

"Two left leather gloves got lost," I had to admit. "Wouldn't woolen mittens be less costly and more practical for the children? And you know, Baroness, a *Wetterfleck* for each one would really be a bargain."

"A what?"

"But, Baroness, everybody wears a *Wetterfleck* nowadays," I laughed at her blank look. "You know, those woolen capes with a hood. Then we would be rid of those dreadful umbrellas."

The Baroness listened politely.

"I always thought an umbrella a great comfort," she said finally. "Maybe it would be handier for the children the other way— But you know," and she sighed resignedly, "the Captain just wants it this way."

When the older children had left for school, I began classes with Maria and Johanna. The latter had started out bravely to walk the two miles to school with the others. There were no school buses in Austria. Little Johanna was quite exhausted from her long walk every day, and so it was decided that I could teach her at home for the first grade.

It was sheer joy to teach the children, different though they were. Maria was very delicate. On account of her heart condition she had to be kept completely quiet. She was not supposed to run or climb, nor play any wild games.

How hard it is for a child always to stand aside when other children play and have lots of fun! But Maria was an exception. She never showed any disappointment. She was always friendly. Only once in a while I saw an expression on her face which showed extreme longing, almost hunger, in the beautiful dark eyes, while she watched her sisters and brothers at noisy play. The first time I saw that look in her eyes I resolved to do everything in my power to make up somehow for the many sacrifices which were asked of the child.

First, I tried to make school as fascinating as possible. She was intelligent and grasped everything immediately. There were twelve main subjects of study: religion, grammar, composition, literature, history, geography, physics, botany, French, geometry, algebra, and Latin. Besides these we had drawing, needlework, and music theory. She was especially gifted in mathematics, science, and music theory, but we simply flew through all the other books as well. In six weeks we had completed all the work for the first regular school semester. I was almost troubled about so much enthusiasm and thoroughness. Often I came to her room and wanted to interrupt her in school work, saying: "That is plenty now for today, Maria. Let's play a game of backgammon."

Then she usually lifted a hot little face up to me, and, with eager eyes, said: "Oh, this is so much more fun, Fräulein Maria," pointing to an algebra problem or some intricate design in geometry.

As long as she was happy, I thought, I simply didn't have the heart to add any more don'ts.

Maria was definitely not a communicative child. She kept everything to herself, but one day she confided: "I don't really mind so much if I cannot run around with the others, but what I *do* mind is that I have had to give up my piano lessons."

I remembered that I had found in the music room two mahogany violin cases.

"Oh, how nice! Who plays the violin?" I had exclaimed to the Baroness.

"Nobody now."

I had understood.

But with Maria now in mind I went to the Baroness and asked: "Could I take one of the violins up to Maria? She could have it in her room and practice only a little every day."

I was not refused. I was even allowed to look for a teacher who was to come twice a week for lessons. The quiet child beamed with happiness, and the frail little fingers proved to be very clever on the violin.

Johanna was different. I never had to stop her in school work. Oh, no, quite the contrary! The little lady had a good mind for studying, but she just loved a comfortable life. After the first half hour of sitting up straight, she usually tried to climb on my lap, "because I can hear you better." She was incredibly inventive in distracting my attention. Her weapons were tiny, almost invisible wounds on face and fingers, which hurt so terribly that we simply could not go on writing big *m*'s and *n*'s or counting by twos. Once in a while I really had to be strict and frown. For nothing in the world did she want to hurt anybody, though. Big tears rolled down her cheeks immediately, and climbing up into my lap, she pressed her arms tightly around my neck and sobbed heartbrokenly: "I will be go-o-o-od!"

She was *so* affectionate! After the first lesson I had given her, she came over to my chair and said, standing on tiptoe: "I want to tell you something."

When I bent down, she whispered in my ear: "I like you an awful lot," and then kissed me loudly on the mouth.

The plump little girl with the white skin, pink cheeks, and black hair was so very pretty that people used to turn around in the street and stare. She had the most expressive large, dark eyes, and dimples in both cheeks when she smiled; and she smiled always. This little "Snow White" was a real sun ray.

Baby Martina, however, was entirely different from both my pupils. She did not seem affectionate at all. She didn't want to be kissed or hugged. When I wanted to take her on my lap, she stiffened. She rarely smiled. I wondered about that serious little youngster. She was fascinated by the lessons, though. For hours she would stand next to Johanna, with her hands behind her back, watching with her large, dark eyes everything I said or did. The minute I turned to her, however, and addressed her, she dove under the table and stayed there quiet as a mouse for the rest of the lesson. At the same time, she was not shy or bashful, as I had thought at first. If she wanted something, she was outspoken. She seemed to me cool and rather matter-of-fact, until I saw her tenderly hugging a Teddy bear which was her inseparable companion. I knew quite clearly, though, that a child's confidence is like a walled castle for which one must have the key. It wouldn't do any good to try to break the lock and force entrance. As I had not been invited yet, I knew I had to wait patiently outside. Maybe the key would be handed to me some day.

School in town started at eight o'clock and lasted until twelve. Of course, there were no school cafeterias, and the children were sent home for their noonday meal. Four times a week they were expected back at two o'clock for some more lessons until four or five. Wednesday and Saturday afternoons were free.

The manor was surrounded by a large garden, beautifully designed. Close to the house were borders of dahlias, chrysanthemums, asters, and many flowers and shrubs I had never seen before. Gravel paths divided the well-kept lawn into large patches leading over to meadows, shaded by small groups of singularly beautiful, large trees—elm, maple, and pine. On one side the estate was enclosed by a patch of woodland. On the other, hidden behind a tall screen of arbor vitae, were the garage, the cow barn, and the greenhouse with the vegetable garden, from which a path lined with currant and gooseberry bushes led up to a large orchard.

Baroness Matilda and all the children showed me over the whole estate on their first free afternoon. When we passed by a large bed of tall yellow flowers, Rupert said proudly: "This is *echte amerikanische Goldrute* (genuine American goldenrod). Papa says it is quite expensive, and we are not supposed to pick it. Pepi, our gardener, takes special care of it with a special kind of manure mixture."

I admired wholeheartedly this noble guest from America, whose golden blossoms attracted all the bees of the neighborhood.

When we came back from our round trip, Werner took my hand and said: "Let me show you my favorite."

We went over to the north side of the house. There stood a group of trees, evergreens, which looked neither like fir nor spruce. The needles were softer and smoother. The branches swayed gracefully in the wind.

"Papa says these are foreigners, too—Canadian hemlock," the proud boy announced. "They are very rare, but I will let you have a little piece."

And the little cavalier presented me with a tiny twig about an inch long.

I was quite overwhelmed by it all, and could not help exclaiming: "What a paradise for children!"

Agathe, who was walking right in front of me, turned around and asked, quite astonished, "Why?"

"Well," I said, "just think of the many wonderful things one could do in such a wide garden, the many games one could play, and . . ."

"Oh, that's what *you* think," interrupted Agathe, and her young voice sounded very wise. "But you see, if you want to play ball, for instance, the ball always runs off the gravel path into the meadow. If you have to get it out of the damp grass, you get wet feet and catch cold. Or if you try to play in the woods over there, there is so much underbrush, your hair gets caught, your dress gets torn, and you get scolded. So you really can't play in the garden much. We usually take walks."

More than amazed, I stopped right in front of the house, and was just about to explain that I was not of the same opinion, when Baroness Matilda interrupted hastily: "Agathe is quite right," and gently pushed me to the door.

To my heartbreak I learned during the next weeks that it was true: you can't play in the most beautiful garden if you have always to take care of sailor suits and nice shoes on weekdays, silken dresses and white socks on Sundays. You couldn't expect a white sailor blouse to look the same after you had climbed that spruce over there in the corner. But do you *have* to wear a white sailor blouse when you want to climb trees? I thought to myself. And now I had it!

Quite excitedly I stormed over to the Baroness' room, not even waiting for the *Herein* after my knocking, to pour out my newest idea.

"Oh, Baroness Matilda, couldn't we buy play suits and sandals for all the girls? They wouldn't have to watch their dresses in the garden and would have a really good time. Before supper, of course, we would change into sailor suits again. And couldn't we please have a volley ball and a net for the girls, and a bat for the boys, and a spear and a disc, too?" So far, I had looked around the house in vain for these items, which were inseparable from my memories of gay pastimes during college years. Baroness Matilda must have attended another school, though, as her face did not light up at the mere sound of these words. She said politely:

"It all sounds very interesting, indeed, Fräulein Maria; but you see, I would not *dare* to order any of those—'play suits,' you said? —without asking the children's father first. You know, the Baron wants the children always to look clean and tidy; and those games you mention—I have never even heard their names. When I was a young girl, we used to amuse ourselves by playing croquet. The children could play that on the big lawn when the weather is dry; otherwise, we stick to our healthful walks through the gardens."

After the last good-night to the children, I went straight to my room. For a long time I sat on my bed in the dark, brooding about the Captain. That man was funny! He had a big house, a wonderful garden, and lots of money. Couldn't he find a way to let his lovely children enjoy all this instead of jamming them into silly clothes which spoiled all good fun! The poor Baroness must have an awful job to watch out for all his orders.

The great sympathy I had felt for the Captain after having heard his life story faded somewhat, and I changed the end of my night prayer into: "—and let the children be happy from now on."

Now it was November, and the trees had shed their last golden tear; the weather was often rough. Long periods of rain set in, the famous "Salzburger Schnurlregen," which put an end to our walks.

It was a rainy Saturday afternoon. Everyone had finished his homework. The older children came over to us in the big nursery, hanging around, wondering what to do. Werner's eyes fell on the guitar, which was hanging on the wall near my bed.

"Can you play that, Fräulein?" he asked.

"Yes, I can," and I went over to fetch the instrument. "Let's sing something."

After a few chords I started a well-known folk tune. The children listened very attentively, but silently. I stopped.

"Why don't you sing with me?"

"We don't know that song."

"All right, let's sing another one."

But they didn't know that one, either, nor the third, nor the fourth.

"What songs *do* you know, children?" I finally asked.

" 'Silent Night,' " little Johanna stated truthfully.

The others giggled, but I had started already: "Silent night, holy night." A little shyly, a little thinly, we sang the first verse in unison.

"Let's do it again. This time you sing the first voice, and I shall sing the second."

So we did.

"Who dares to sing the second voice now, so that I can sing the third?" I asked.

Maria and Werner wanted to try. I was quite astonished how well it sounded. No one was bashful any more. With full voice we sang now all three verses of "Silent Night," and it did sound lovely.

Then I put my guitar down and said: "Now let's think hard what other songs you remember."

After quite some time we had worked out a small list: a few Navy songs, some of them in Italian, which they had learned from their father, one hunting song, two funny songs in our native dialect, two or three church hymns, the first verses of the "Linden Tree," *"Heiden Roslein," "Die Lorelei,"* two more Christmas carols, and the national anthem. That was a rather meager collection, indeed. They didn't know a single one of our wonderful, old folk songs.

When I said: "Do you know this one?" and started a few chords of an old ballad, they all cried: "No, but please sing it." And so I sang my favorite songs, one after the other. The little ones were huddled at my knees. The older ones had settled themselves on the table in order to watch me playing the guitar, when suddenly the door opened.

"Did nobody hear the dinner bell ring? Oh, children, how awful, sitting on the table! What would Father say!"

The next day was Sunday, and it was still raining outside. It had been arranged that the Baroness and I should take turns having Sundays off. This was my Sunday on. Baroness Matilda had left to visit some friends. The children were enthusiastic about learning new songs. They all seemed to be quite musical. It didn't take long at all to teach them the old songs in simple settings. After supper the boys begged: "Let's make a fire in the fireplace in the library. That's so cozy."

That again was something new to me. With interest I watched the boys light the logs, which had been prepared by Hans. Very soon we all sat on the thick, soft carpet, looking into the flames, I in the middle with the guitar—and we sang our whole repertoire: eight old songs and six new ones.

"But girls, *girls!* Ladies never do that. I told you your father does not want you to sit on the floor. Take those low stools."

The Baroness had obviously returned from her visit. There it was again: the restraining hand of their father.

Bang! went the E string.

"We have to stop now," I said; "a string has broken."

An Austrian Christmas

CHRISTMAS came nearer and nearer. Around the large table in the nursery we had long conferences about what to make for Father and Baroness Matilda, and for Grandmother, who lived in a castle near Vienna. I even suggested it would be nice if every child had a surprise for every sister and brother. That kept us very busy. The big, round table was covered with paper and paints, knitting wool, needles and thread. The boys' room soon looked like a workshop, with the smell of glue fighting the smell of Werner's white mice.

While the hands were busy, the mouths didn't keep still, either. We were learning Christmas carols, each evening a new one, out of the treasury I had acquired when, with a group of boys and girls from the Austrian Catholic Youth Movement, I had wandered through the Alps. We had stopped in hidden valleys or at lone mountain farms, listening to the people's songs, which had been handed down for generations. There we had found the most beautiful Christmas songs. I knew dozens of them.

One evening Baroness Matilda had left for home to stay overnight with her sick sister. The children and I decided to have a general rehearsal of all our new songs. Maria, who already played simple tunes on her violin, would try to play with us.

We went down and obediently arranged ourselves on the big sofa which stood opposite the fireplace, and on a few comfortable chairs. But that way we were very far apart from each other and could not hear very well, so somehow or other it happened that we all landed again on the thick carpet. Agathe held my guitar. I had shown her how to accompany simple songs. With cheeks red from excitement, Maria played a descant, while we sang in three parts, "*In Dulci Jubilo.*" Suddenly somebody opened the door.

"Papa, Papa," cried the children and stormed towards the tall figure standing in the doorway. Now there! and we were sitting on the floor. I rose slowly, picked up the guitar from the floor and put it on the sofa. Meanwhile the Baron had kissed all the children and, with Martina on his arm, he came over to me to say hello.

"I am sorry, Captain," I said.

"What are you sorry for?" and then, with a knowing undertone, "Oh, I understand, this should have been a surprise for Christmas. But don't you worry, a surprise it is—children, I can't believe it. It sounded simply wonderful! Let's have some more. No, don't turn on the light. Let's sit right down here. Come on."

And he settled himself comfortably on the floor, pressing his back against one of the heavy seats, pulling the little girls down to his knee.

"You have learned a new song. What is it? Do it again."

"*A* new song?" the children echoed. "Just one?"

"What do you mean?" said the father. And then, astonished, "Fräulein, are you looking for something?"

I was still standing. I couldn't believe my eyes.

"N-no," and I sat down on the sofa.

"Oh, no, come over here to us, right down on the carpet. Don't you think this is more *gemütlich?*"

I had never doubted that. So I joined the group and we continued singing, and it turned out to be a very nice evening.

Time and again the Captain interrupted: "But children, children, isn't that wonderful!"

His enthusiasm was so genuine it was contagious. He praised Maria and Agathe highly for their playing, and all of a sudden, he reached out for the violin himself, and began to play a soft descant to one of our old ballads. Then we sang all twenty-two verses. The guitar played two more chords after the voices had ended, but the violin kept on playing very softly. Nobody moved. Suddenly the Captain stopped and, as if awakening, put the instrument down.

"I didn't think I would ever play again!" he said with a deep sigh. Then he put new logs on the fire, which had burned low, and asked: "Now, children, tell me what is the news? How is school? How are you, little one?" And tenderly he pulled Maria's head towards his shoulder. A noisy chatter started now. After the children had told about school, they wanted to know all about the hunting trip. The little girls discovered that Father's pockets were full of rabbit tails, out of which one could make a fur coat for a Teddy bear! Too, too bad that it was eight o'clock and high time to go to bed!

It was the Saturday before the first Sunday in Advent. During lunch I said to Maria: "Where do you usually put up the Advent wreath?"

"Put up what?"

I was aghast. "Don't you have an Advent wreath every year?"

"No, we never did. What is it?"

"It is a large wreath made of fir greens, holding four candles, one for each of the four Sundays of Advent. People put it up in their living rooms. It reminds them of the coming of Christmas. They light the candles and sing Advent songs."

"Oh, how nice! Couldn't we have one this year? Papa, please buy a large Advent wreath for us."

"Oh, you don't *buy* Advent wreaths. We could easily make one ourselves," I interrupted, and then explained to the Captain that we would need about two basketsful of fir twigs and perhaps one of those wagon wheels from an old buggy I had seen in the tool shed.

"What else?"

"A spool of thread, four wax candles, and eight yards of silk ribbon." The Captain offered to fetch those from town. Everybody was excited getting the Advent wreath ready in time. The gardener was ordered to bring the fir twigs and the boys ran out to fetch the wagon wheel and clean it before it was brought into the nursery.

Then we went to work. The children picked the fir twigs out of the basket and passed them on to me, and I wound them around the wheel, fastening them with thread. It took quite some time because it was to be a large wreath. Four long spikes had to be put through the wheel at equal distances to be used as candle holders. When we had just finished and were starting to clean up the mess we had made on the floor, the Captain came back from town. Now the candles were put on the spikes, the ribbon was cut into four equal parts, which were fastened to the wreath so that it could be suspended from the ceiling. Our first Advent wreath was finished.

"What can I do for you now?" the Captain said. I was a little uncertain.

"It should be hung from the ceiling in the middle of the living room, but as this house doesn't have a living room, couldn't we have it here in the nursery right above the big round table?"

Armed with hammer and nails, the Captain climbed up on the table. We all held the wreath, and he fastened it to the ceiling. Suddenly he stopped between two hammer strokes and, looking down on me, he frowned.

"What do you mean, this house has no living room?"

"No," I said, "it doesn't."

"How about the big drawing room, the little drawing room, the library, and the music room?"

"No," I insisted, "that is not the same. Father, Mother, and children really have to live in the same room—work, read, play, and write in it. Then it is a living room."

The Captain finished and came down. We all stepped back and admired the beautiful big wreath with the four candles. It gave the whole room a festive look and a festive smell, too.

"What are we going to do with it next?" asked Agathe.

"Well, tonight the family will gather under the Advent wreath, your father will read the Gospel of the first Sunday in Advent. Then he will light one candle, and the whole family will sing Advent songs and Christmas carols. Next week he will light two candles, the next, three, and then all four."

"How do you know about it?"

"Oh, that is just an old folk custom—one of the many."

"One of the many—do you have more in store for us?"

I had to laugh. "Maybe a few."

"All right then," and the Captain grasped the remaining nails and the hammer. "Let's meet tonight after supper under the Advent wreath in our *new living room.*"

That was meant for me, I knew. Whether it was only teasing or whether he took my remark about the living room for criticism, I could not make out. This very thing had troubled me all these weeks: that the family as such met only at mealtimes. Otherwise, the children were not even supposed to be together. The boys were supposed to keep to their room, the older girls to theirs, and they were told by Baroness Matilda time and again that they had no business in the nursery with their little sisters. When the older children had begun to visit us recently, knocking politely on the nursery door and asking a little shyly, "May we come in?" I had been tempted to say, "Now stop that nonsense. Aren't you all one family?"

But that was none of my business. It was just one more of many unwritten laws. I simply didn't understand how it could possibly be good to keep the children of one family divided into three parties which, of course, fought each other. I had tried to find out from Baroness Matilda. She wasn't really able to explain it, either. I only learned that this was the custom in most of the aristocratic houses, to have a governess for the older children, a nursemaid for the younger ones, and maybe a tutor for the boys. Unfortunately, it happened many times that those governesses were jealous of each other. They even taught their respective pupils to play tricks on the others.

Personally, I was depressed about the whole business. I had been told that my field was the nursery, that I had nothing to do with Rupert, Werner, Agathe, and Maria, except for Maria's school lessons. If I had behaved correctly, I should have sent the older children away instead of starting to teach them to sing together. Now, again, had I *had* to say that about the living room? I felt rather ill at ease when I thought of Baroness Matilda. For nothing in the world did I want to hurt her. How would she feel about this new living room idea, about the children being together? But I consoled myself; she was the one who always referred to the Captain, saying that things must be done the way he wished. After all, *he* had pronounced the nursery our new living room, not I. But this would be the last time I ever attended to something which was not my own business, I resolved strongly and solemnly.

After supper that night we and the Baroness Matilda, who had returned from her sister's, gathered together in the new living room. The Captain read the Gospel and lit the candle. We were all sitting around the table on which a tall, thick, red candle was burning. This was a surprise from me to the children. I had brought it from Nonnberg on my last visit there.

"It is the Advent candle," I had explained to them. "It is a symbol of Christ, Whom we call the Light of the World. That should burn every evening until Christmas—just another folk custom," I said in the direction of the Captain. When I heard even Baroness Matilda's soft voice joining our little choir, all the tension left me, and I started to enjoy fully the beautiful wreath, the sound of the children's clear voices, and the Captain's violin playing.

Santa Claus does not come to the children of Austria. Nobody comes down the chimney to fill your stocking; it isn't so easy as that. All the small and big children of Austria have to write a letter addressed to the Christ Child on the first Sunday in Advent. He is believed to come down from heaven, Himself personally, on Christmas Eve, accompanied by angels and bring the Christmas tree and the wonderful things under it. This letter is a very important one, for in it you make known all your most secret wishes, and at the end you have to make a personal promise. Then you put it on the window sill before going to bed, and next morning your first look will be to see whether your letter has gone. Good children's letters always disappear during the first night. Some children, however, have to wait two or three days, and if this should be the case with you, you really get quite anxious. It does help a lot in making you eat your spinach and put your clothes tidily over a chair at night.

After the last carol, still sitting around the table, we started to write our Christmas letters. After a short thought I wrote down:

"Dear Christ Child: It would make my life so much easier if You would bring each child here in the house a pair of nailed boots, a *Wetterfleck,* and a pair of wool mittens. I myself do not need anything, as I shall go back to Nonnberg soon anyway."

The excitement of the first Sunday in Advent had hardly died down when the sixth of December came around, one of the most momentous days for all houses where little children lived. On the vigil of this day Saint Nikolaus comes down to earth to visit all the little ones.

Saint Nikolaus was a saintly bishop of the fourth century, and being always very kind and helpful to children and young people, God granted that every year on his feastday he might come down to the children. He comes dressed in his Bishop's vestments, with a mitre on his head and his Bishop's staff in his hand. He is followed, however, by the Krampus, an ugly, black little devil with a long, red tongue, a pair of horns, and a long tail. When Saint Nikolaus enters a house, he finds the whole family assembled, waiting for him, and the parents greet him devoutly. Then he asks the children questions from their catechism. He has them repeat a prayer or sing a song. He seems to know everything, all the dark spots of the past year, as you can see from his admonishing words. All the good children are given a sack with apples and nuts, prunes and figs, and the most delicious, heavenly sweets. Bad children, however, must promise very hard to change their life. Otherwise, the Krampus will take them along, and he is grunting already and rattling his heavy chain. But the Holy Bishop won't ever let him touch a child. He believes the tearful eyes and stammered promises, but it may happen that, instead of a sweet bag, you get a switch. That will be put up in a conspicuous place and will look very symbolic of a child's behavior.

The excitement was great on the fifth. Soon after dark we assembled in the hall, looking out through the large window into the driveway. Martina's hand was clasped tightly in mine, her little figure half hidden behind my skirt. You could almost hear Johanna's heart beating, and Hedwig's obvious superiority was very poorly played.

Suddenly one could see the little flicker of candlelight through the bare bushes. A tall figure bearing a lantern and high staff turned into our driveway, followed at some distance by a little black fellow. The heavy double door opened wide, and in came the Holy Bishop, reverently greeted by young and old. The white beard which cascaded down below his waist showed his old age. Nobody could see that half an hour before, it had been plastered on Hans' patient face with the help of the white of a raw egg. Saint Nikolaus wore his glasses, as elderly people sometimes do, far down on his nose. He had to, because his eyesight was so good that Resi's spectacles almost blinded him. After he had sat down, he gave the Captain his lantern to hold, and then he produced from under his white cloak a large package with a big golden Cross. Through the white paper cover one could read faintly *Encyclopedia, H. to HZ.* In this magic book were written down all the many crimes, big and little, which had been committed by the children of this house. It was quite incredible how well informed Saint Nikolaus was: how Werner had played hooky three times instead of going to Greek class; Hedwig had pinched Martina; Rupert had smoked in secret; and Maria had practiced the violin much longer than the doctor allowed; Resi, the cook, had burned the Sunday cake once and then thrown it into the garbage can without telling; Pepi, the gardener, was sometimes slow in getting up in the morning. And Saint Nikolaus shook his finger and frowned at the sinners as they were called to his feet. They all felt very uncomfortable, and promised fervently to reform. The Holy Bishop rose and waved his hand towards the door; a big sack was pushed in, which Saint Nikolaus opened. There was a bag with fruit and candies for everybody except Resi, who got a large switch; and she even had to kiss the Bishop's hand when he gave it to her. With a final admonition and his blessing, the holy man left the house.

"How many days still until Christmas?" was the excited question every morning. One morning, when the answer was "only seven," we came down the stairs as usual, and found the double door leading into the big drawing room, which was usually wide open, closed. New excitement; that meant that the Holy Child with His angel assistants was working inside, preparing the room for Christmas. From then on, the children only tiptoed in the vicinity of those closed doors, and every conversation downstairs died down to a reverent whisper.

The whispering continued deep into the night, when the children were long asleep and the Captain, Baroness Matilda, and I were busy behind the secret door with the still-empty Christmas tree, opening parcels, writing Christmas cards, adjusting small wax candles to small candle-holders which could be clamped onto the green branches. Slowly but surely, the big room began to look like the toy department of a large store. Out of the many-shaped parcels emerged all the blessings of our modern toy industry: a dollhouse and doll kitchen, a small perambulator with a beautiful baby and, of course, the whole outfit—diapers, bottle, bathtub, etc.; picture books and games, an electric railroad, a BB gun, a Victrola with records, more books and more games, a new guitar, skates, skis—never in my life had I seen so many beautiful things in one spot. The trouble was that I could hardly keep my mind on my duty, which was to unpack and distribute, because it was so tempting to try out the new games, change the baby's diapers, and investigate the many books. Anything the loving heart of a father could get for money was assembled around the tall, beautiful tree. I felt as though I were in fairyland myself. I was drunk with Christmas, counting the hours until I could slip again into the realm of the Christ Child and angels.

It was the twenty-third, and the little ones had sung all day long the traditional song, *"Morgen Kinder Wird's Was Geben."* They were unusually helpful, quiet and good, knowing that the house, and especially the nursery, was under constant observation by the angels coming and going to the Christmas room. Only Rupert and Agathe seemed to know a little more; from Maria down, the belief in the holy doings behind the wide doors was unshaken. Why—didn't you find a silver hair on the staircase and a cookie with a red thread near the door?

This last evening was devoted to the decoration of the tree. It was at least fifteen feet tall. The Captain, standing on a ladder, took care of the top, while Baroness Matilda and I busied ourselves with the lower branches. There were cookies made of different doughs, *Lebkuchen,* and *Spanischer Wind.* Hard candies and chocolates had been wrapped in frilled tissue paper, figures and symbols made of Marzipan, gilded nuts and small apples and tangerines, all these were hung on red threads all over the tree. Then came a hundred and twenty wax candles, loads of tinsel dropping from the branches, and tinsel chains swinging loosely all around the tree. As a finishing touch the Captain fastened a large silver star to the very top. Then we all stepped back and admired the most beautiful Christmas tree I have ever seen in my life. The tables around the walls were so laden with presents that the white linen covers were completely hidden.

The next day was the big day, Holy Eve, as it is called in Austria. Snow had fallen overnight. We went to church with the older children. The church was filled as on Sunday. Everybody goes to confession on Holy Eve, so one had to wait in line. It was quite early and pitch-dark outside. There were no electric lights in the church, and, of course, it was not heated. The people had brought candles with them, fastened them to the pews, and, holding their hymn books with heavily-mittened hands close to the little flame, they could read the words of the ancient Advent song, which was softly accompanied by the organ and sung by the whole community: *"Tauet Himmel den Gerechten."* In the flicker of candlelight one could see a neat little frosty cloud in front of every mouth. From under the choir loft, where the confessional stood, one could hear the shuffling of hobnailed boots and also, eventually, the rubbing of hands, the feeble attempts to keep warm when it was below zero outside with yard-long icicles growing from the church roof. But cold belonged to Christmas as heat to the haying days. This was as it should be, and nobody gave it a thought.

When Holy Mass was over, we went with the children to the side altar. There, in a little wood of spruce trees, was the whole town of Bethlehem spread out before our eyes. The shepherds were already out in the field with their flock. Mary and Joseph had arrived at the cave. They were kneeling beside the manger, which was still empty. Ox and ass, the sheep in the pasture, and the angels in the air seemed to hold their breath, waiting in holy expectation of the little Child to come. Mankind had waited patiently thousands of years for this moment. It couldn't wait any longer; and this is the very feeling you bring home from church yourself in your own heart after a glance into the still-empty manger: you think you can't wait any longer. That is the theme song for Holy Eve wherever children still believe in the coming of the Christ Child.

As everything comes to an end in life, so also the long hours of the afternoon passed. Holy Eve is a fast day, and so lunch was over quickly with only one dish, a thick soup. The children spent the day putting their rooms, wardrobes, and drawers in perfect order. In the afternoon we all dressed in our best and, for the last time, we all met under the Advent wreath, all four candles lit. The servants were called in, and once again we sang the old Advent hymn. Before the third verse was over, the silvery sound of a little bell was heard. This was it! The Holy Child had come. Led by the father of the house, the two youngest girls clinging to his hands, we all went down the curved stairway. After a few steps through the wide-open door, we all stopped in a semi-circle, gazing in speechless wonder at the Christmas tree, whose solemn beauty commanded the room. The Captain started, "Silent Night." After we had sung all three verses, there was a moment of complete silence. A fine scent of fir, wax, and *Lebkuchen* lingered in the air. One could almost hear the flicker of the many little flames, and the large star on the top of the tree, moving in the warm candlelight, looked so real. The room was bathed in that mild, golden light which only one source can give—wax candles; but wax candles on Christmas, for on no other day of the year do they radiate such penetrating happiness and peace. It must be that through all the centuries the light on Christmas Eve borrows its shine from the Star of Bethlehem, which witnessed the first Christmas message of peace to men of good will.

Then the Captain turned around, and going from one person to the other, he wished everybody a blessed Christmas. The spell was broken. Soon the house resounded with "Blessed Christmas," everybody wishing it to everybody. Then everyone was led to his place by the Captain. For a while one heard only the rustling of wrapping paper, and little more or less suppressed cries and exclamations. I was very busy helping Martina attend to the baby when the Captain came and wanted to show me to my own place. There were several parcels wrapped in white tissue paper, and one very large box with the inscription: "For Fräulein Maria for Distribution." Surrounded by the children, I unpacked it, and out came eight pairs of woolen mittens, eight beautiful, soft, gray *Wetterflecks,* and eight pairs of heavy boots. This was a great surprise, and with a guilty heart, I hardly dared look at Baroness Matilda. But tonight was Christmas, and, shaking a finger at me, she only laughed. That wasn't the end of my surprises, though. When all my parcels were unpacked, there lay on my table two beautiful new dresses and a nice-looking little hat. What a grateful sigh of relief went up to the Holy Child for so much consideration.

After dinner, which had been very early, the Captain asked for some Christmas music. I had been waiting for just that. My Christmas present to the family was a Crêche, put up under the Christmas tree. Now I got the big, red candle, and we all grouped around it on the floor. After we had sung our songs, I took Agathe's new guitar and, for the first time, I sang my own favorite Christmas song, "The Virgin's Lullaby."

A few hours later I knelt in my place in the old church at Nonnberg; I had come home for Midnight Mass. But it was curiously different from my other homecomings. It was very difficult to keep my thoughts collected. Pictures of huge Christmas trees and happy children's faces continued to busy my mind. There was one picture, especially, which I could not shake off, try as I would:

When I was about to leave the house for Midnight Mass, the Captain had come out of his room and, taking my hand in both of his, had said: "I always feared Christmas more than any other day. But this year you have made it very beautiful for us. Thank you." There was a warm light in the beautiful, dark eyes which, for the first time since I had known him, did not look pained and restless. That had made me very happy, but now the picture kept coming back and disturbing me in my prayer.

Turning to the Holy Child, I said fervently: "I thank You so much for sending me there. Please help me to draw them all closer to You."

At this moment the community rose and, with a jubilant voice, the young priest down at the altar intoned the age-old Christmas message: *"Gloria in excelsis Deo et in terra pax hominibus bonae voluntatis."*

"God's Will Hath No Why"

THE following weeks were very happy ones. Real winter had set in, and the hobnailed boots, mittens, and ski pants were in daily use. We didn't understand how we ever could have gotten along without them.

To the great joy of the children, their father canceled a number of invitations and stayed home with them, taking to skiing again and obviously enjoying it.

With the beginning of March the snow turned more watery, and that was exactly the right kind of material you needed to erect a large fortress with turrets and towers, big enough for five persons to huddle inside, and even light a fire.

Then on a beautiful sunny day in March their father announced during lunch while glancing through his mail: "Well, children, Aunt Yvonne is coming."

A moment of complete silence followed. Then Maria said: "Why, Father, do we still need her?"

Quite astonished, the Captain said: "What do you mean?"

"You said you want to marry her because we have no one to look after us; but that has changed now, hasn't it?"

After a short, warm smile in my direction the child looked eagerly at the father. At this moment Baroness Matilda, who apparently had felt rather ill at ease during the last minutes, ventured the question: "When exactly can we expect the Princess?"

"Tomorrow on the noon train, and let's put her in the big room with the balcony."

Princess Yvonne—how exciting! Now I should see the future mother of my darling children. In my young romantic imagination I saw a figure out of Grimm's *Fairy Tales;* young and slender, blue-eyed, blonde-haired—well, I didn't really expect her to wear a crown, but something near a halo I certainly did expect. Oh,

I could picture her already, how she would glide into the room with soft, fairy steps, a dreamy look in her deep blue eyes—hands like the petals of a lily, oceans of affection and love emanating from her towards the poor, motherless little ones and their lonely father—Princess Yvonne. The mere name put me in a festive mood, and on the knees of my heart I was worshipping her already.

How slowly the time dragged during the lessons of the next morning! Finally, the gong sounded for lunch, and in solemn expectation I entered the big drawing room, where the exalted guest must be. Oh, had she missed the train? Because the lady who entered now together with the Captain from the library couldn't possibly—but lo and behold, the girls were curtseying, and "Hello, Aunt Yvonne," and "How do you do, Aunt Yvonne?"

Then I heard the Captain's voice: "Yvonne, may I introduce—" and I looked down into cool, but not unfriendly eyes.

"Well, well—the wonder girl of whom I have heard so much," and we shook hands. And this was my first meeting with a real princess in the flesh.

During lunch the children chatted about the happenings of the last weeks. Finally, Hedwig broke out: "And you know, Auntie, what I like most of all my Christmas presents, that's my ski pants. Now I can do anything outdoors the boys do," and the little face glowed with pure enthusiasm.

With lifted eyebrows the Princess answered, genuinely surprised: "But, my dear, a decent young lady doesn't wear pants."

Seven young heads turned to me, looking for support; but when I realized that what I was about to say might not fit into the picture of a decent young lady, either, my open mouth closed soundlessly and, deeply blushing, I busied myself with my food.

There were no lessons this afternoon, everybody being busy with the regal guest. Sitting at my desk, I tried to keep my thoughts on tomorrow's school work, telling myself over and over again, "This is none of your business—none of your business at all," when someone knocked at my door, and—look, it was the Princess! A little bewildered, I bade her come in and sit down. She looked at me for a moment, not at all unkindly.

"My dear child, I have to talk to you." Expectant silence, and then the blow fell: "Do you realize that the Captain is in love with you?"

As if bitten by a rattlesnake, I started up. "But— Princess—!"

Quietly and quite unemotionally she retorted: "But he told me so himself."

With weak knees I sank down on my chair. So far, no one had been in love with me, nor had I ever been in love. This extraordinary happening I had met only in books, in the pages of Goethe, Schiller, and Shakespeare, where being in love usually ended in murder and blood; and now that that terrific thing should happen to me, and—and—but if he himself had told her so, there was nothing to argue about.

I tried to compose myself and say, as matter-of-factly as possible, the only thing I could think of: "Then I am leaving this afternoon for my convent. Will you kindly look for another teacher for Maria?"

Now it was her turn to look startled.

"But why, for heaven's sake? That's no reason to run away. It's all straightened out with the Captain. Of course, he isn't really in love, not much, I mean. He just likes you because you have been so congenial with the children—maybe a little bit too much on the wild side, but this I will easily straighten out later."

But nothing she said impressed me any more. I was scared stiff.

"But how does everything go on from now on?" I wanted to know.

"Why—exactly as before. In a few weeks the Captain and I will be engaged, and you will stay with the children until after our marriage. On our wedding day you must give a nice little party for them here."

I swallowed dryly. "Won't they be at the wedding?"

"Oh, certainly not," she laughed lightly. "Just think, what a commotion!" and she shook her head, amused. Then she went on. "The wedding will be in the summer, and when we return from our honeymoon, it will be time for school again. I have noticed that although the children have improved physically, they look quite rustic now—their manners have suffered badly. The Baron agrees with me that the best place for the girls will be the Sacré Coeur, and for the boys, the Jesuit College in Kalksburg. There they will be among youth of their own standing, and soon they will stop being little roughnecks."

"But why in the world do you marry, then, if you send the children away from home?" I asked in utter consternation.

Up went the eyebrows again.

"My goodness, did you think I was marrying the children? What a queer little youngster you are!"

What I had just heard was much worse than the recognition of the fact that fairy-tale books are not like mail-order catalogues for princesses. I knew instinctively that I couldn't stay; I wouldn't fit any more. So I repeated stiffly: "I have made up my mind. I shall pack and leave immediately."

Now the Princess was really worried, and after another unsuccessful attempt to make me change my mind, left me rather hurriedly. With trembling fingers, I started to empty my drawers.

Late in the afternoon I was called down to the library. From the garden I could hear the happy laughter of the children throwing snowballs with their father. It cut my heart, and quite helplessly I thought to myself: "No, I can't say good-bye to any of them. I will simply leave."

Then I opened the door of the library. There was the Princess and a strange priest in a brown habit with a long, gray beard. I hesitated at the door.

"This is Father Gregory," the Princess said, "my confessor. I have turned to him to help us out, and he will tell you now what he thinks you should do."

The elderly Father came over to me and, taking my hand, led me over towards the table, and very kindly started to explain.

"You must understand, my dear child, that there is nothing to the kind affection the Captain feels towards you, as you are quite popular with his children; but you must also understand that there is a great danger of kindling this emotion into more than merely a fatherly affection if you should leave now, abruptly, and therefore, I counsel you to do as the Princess wants you, and . . ."

"Father, this I cannot do," I interrupted, and looked at him imploringly.

"But my dear child, this is the Will of God," the kind old voice stated.

Now I was cornered. It had become second nature through my

training at the convent to look for and to carry out to the best of my ability—the Will of God. I was silent.

Happily the Princess said: "You see, Father, I told you, she is quite a sensible girl."

The old priest took my hand again and said: "Now promise me that you will stay here until the Baron and the Princess have been wed."

Tonelessly I repeated: "I promise I shall stay, but only until the thirtieth of June, on which day I shall be received into the Benedictine Abbey of Nonnberg."

With a kind, "All right, my child, go in peace," I was released.

My hands were shaking still as I put all my things back into the drawers again. I was utterly and thoroughly bewildered. Wasn't it already like Schiller and Shakespeare? But, my God, how could it go on now? What was coming next?

The Princess had left, and we resumed our daily routine again. But life wasn't the same, because I had become self-conscious. The heavy burden of my new knowledge followed me through the day. I avoided the Captain whenever I could, and when he wanted to join our games or singing evenings in the nursery, I felt how I stiffened and, at the first possible moment, broke up whatever was going on. I wasn't supposed to mention anything to him of what had passed between me and the Princess, so he absolutely could not make out why I had suddenly changed. Good-naturedly he blamed the spring at first for what he called "moodiness," but after a while I noticed how hurt he looked when, for instance, I declined politely to have him accompany us on a hike or when he wanted to join a game of volley ball. If, however, he jokingly insisted on taking part, it wouldn't be long until, after one excuse or another, I would slip out. One day we happened to meet in the house doorway. When he stretched out his hand to open the door for me, I stopped him, saying: "Thank you very much, I can open it myself."

This was just a little too much. He walked away brusquely, leaving me very miserable and bewildered. How I hated myself for acting so, and still, I couldn't help it.

Baroness Matilda had gone to the wedding of her brother when, on a beautiful morning in May, I was asked to see the Captain in the library.

"Think what happened," he greeted me. "Baroness Matilda has broken her leg, and it is such an ugly fracture that she won't be with us any more for the rest of the year. What are we going to do? Could you take over the household affairs until I find another lady?"

I laughed right out: "Oh, Captain, I understand nothing at all about keeping house. You see, in boarding school and then in the novitiate I learned many other things, but not that. I hardly know how to hold a broom."

"But couldn't you learn it out of a book?" he asked after a little hard thinking. "The other day I saw in the window of Hoell-riegel's Bookstore a book on housekeeping."

In my heart of hearts I had the greatest doubts as to whether this science could be learned out of books, but he looked so eager and expectant that I said: "Well, there's nothing like trying," earning a sigh of relief and a grateful look from his fine eyes. For a moment it was like old times. There was the air of confidence again between us, and I ventured to speak.

"Captain, now I have done something for you; may I ask you to do me a favor?"

"Certainly, go ahead."

"Will you please get engaged to the Princess right away?"

With a sharp swing he turned around and, facing me eye to eye, asked slowly: "Am I doing you a favor by that?"

I was already retiring towards the door, mumbling something about the approaching end of the school year—motherless children —reception at the convent . . .

The same evening the Captain gathered the eight servants in the library and introduced me as their temporary housekeeper, from whom they would have to expect, for the time being, all orders.

He left the next day.

When he said good-bye, he asked: "Would it be too much for you to send me a daily report on how things are going?"

With these words he handed me a book. Glancing down, I read: *The Golden Book for Housewives: A Guide Through the Year, Together with Five Hundred Recipes and One Thousand Advices.*

I had never in my life thought about how a household is run. In the boarding school where I had spent most of my young years, the food was always ready on the table at mealtimes, the rooms were always tidy and clean, the windows washed, the laundry taken care of; but it all happened somehow backstage, quite noiselessly. You never saw anybody doing it; you only saw the result and took it for granted. In the convent there were those lovely, humble, quiet lay sisters with a white veil, who did the cooking, washing, and cleaning. But we of the novitiate were not supposed to talk to them, so again I heard no details of how it all was done.

When the Captain introduced me as temporary housekeeper, I had noticed an exchange of glances between the cook and the gardener, the first and second chambermaids; glances half amused, half knowing. There was also some good-natured mockery in the somewhat super-submissive air with which mighty Donna Resi asked on my first evening in office: "Is Fräulein Maria coming downstairs after supper to give orders for tomorrow?"

"What orders?" I asked, and wanted to bite my tongue immediately after. Oh, what a neophyte I was! But if she knew, the cook didn't show it, but continued almost respectfully:

"Well, whatever you want us to do tomorrow; me and the two girls in the kitchen, the two chambermaids and the gardener, the chauffeur, and the laundress."

I almost said: "Oh, please, do what you want, all of you," but, fortunately, remembered in time that Baroness Matilda had spent a considerable time every evening in the servants' quarters. "Yes, I'll come"; and with this I ran upstairs and consulted *The Book*.

But nowhere in the eight hundred pages could I find any indication of what to say to the servants in the form of today's orders for tomorrow.

When I was confronted later with the eight expectant faces, I tried to solve the problem diplomatically, and asked: "What did you intend to do tomorrow?" or "What do you suggest comes next?" That worked fine, and I almost patted myself on the back for this good idea; that gave me time to devour *The Book,* and in a few days I would not have to ask anybody for suggestions any more.

I started on page 1, and spent many hours every day in serious study on how to become a good housekeeper.

Every evening a little note went out, saying: "Dear Captain: We are all well, and everything in house, garden, and farm is going all right. Sincerely yours."

Three weeks had passed, and we had heard little from the Captain. The children and I received postal cards with greetings; that was all. Time was getting short. Only a little over a month lay between me and the convent. So I ventured in one of my notes to add after the "all well": "And when will you get engaged?"

By return mail a letter came back which said: ". . . I wish I could see your eyes when you read the announcement of my engagement."

The moment I read that, something flared up within me. I sat down immediately and, without any salutation, I put my one strong feeling down on paper: "My eyes are none of your business. I thought you were a man and kept your word. I am sorry, I was mistaken."

No "sincerely yours" softened this very essence of my wrath. After all, what did he think? Still hot with anger, I ran out and mailed this document, registered.

On a beautiful May morning the Captain and the Princess had seated themselves on an old stone bench in the dense woods which led into the famous and ancient park of Castle G——. In many long talks the Captain had tried to convince the Princess that it was time to forget the various obstacles to the engagement, for instance: she had to wait until she had assisted her sister in childbirth, or until she had purchased an entirely new outfit, or she had to carry out a promise she had given her roommate in boarding school way back and visit her in her castle somewhere in the Balkans—well, all these obstacles had now been overcome: the dresses were bought, the child was born, and she was back from the Balkans. This very morning he had made up his mind not to come back from the walk unengaged.

"Yvonne . . ." he started; and then they heard footsteps.

Charles, the old butler who had faithfully served three generations, came down the path hurriedly. On a silver platter he carried a letter.

He said apologetically: "Baron, I thought it might be important. It's a registered letter."

Looking at the letter, the Captain said: "Excuse me, Yvonne, but this comes from home. I hope none of the children is sick," and broke open the letter. He stared at the three lines with no heading and no greeting; after quite some time he put the letter into his vest pocket. He got up from the bench and seemed deeply moved.

"Well, what's the matter?" the Princess asked. "Anybody sick?"

"No, nobody is sick," he answered slowly; and then, taking both her hands, he added: "but I know now I cannot marry you, Yvonne; I love somebody else. I am sorry, but you let me wait too long. You should have taken me when I asked you three years ago."

In deep silence the couple went back to the castle, and the Captain departed immediately for home.

The very same evening the telephone wires carried the message from one castle and *palais* to another that Maria, the young teacher of the Trapp children, was expecting a baby and the Baron, in his loyalty and knightliness, had resolved to marry her. That was why he had had to break off his near-engagement to Princess Yvonne. Because this *must* have been the content of that letter which had made the Captain change his mind, mustn't it?

Who starts such a story? Nobody. It doesn't start as a story; it starts as an inflection of the voice, a question asked in a certain tone and not answered with "no"; a prolonged little silence, a twinkle in the eye, a long-drawn "w-e-e-ell—I don't know." These are the fine roots of the tree whose poisonous fruits are gossip and slander.

The Captain had come home and had almost immediately vanished into his private quarters. The family saw very little of him; even for meals he stayed in his study now. All we knew was that he was writing his memoirs and didn't want to be disturbed. Ever since I had cooled off after mailing that poisonous little note, I had had an awful feeling in my stomach. What was worse, I couldn't make out what had happened. He didn't look engaged, to me, at least, not according to my conception of a happily engaged man. But there was something unusual in his bearing in the rare moments when he was visible, and I did not dare ask any questions.

One night I tenderly consulted my private calendar, "time eaters" we had called them at school, and it showed only thirteen more days in exile. The next morning I started spring cleaning. Under my direction the maids were taking down the curtains and proceeding to brush the walls, when I saw the three youngest children knock on the door of the study. It didn't take long and out they came again.

Running over to me as I stood on a ladder washing a big crystal chandelier, they yelled from afar: "Father says he doesn't know whether you like him at all!"

"Why, of course I like him," I answered, somewhat absent-mindedly, because I had never washed a chandelier before. I noticed only vaguely that the children disappeared behind the study door again.

That same night I was arranging flowers in several big, beautiful oriental vases. This was the last touch, and then the spring cleaning was over, and it had been really successful. When I had arrived at the last vase, the Captain came in. Stepping over to me, he stood and silently watched what I was doing with the peonies.

Suddenly he said: "That was really awfully nice of you."

An altogether new tone in his voice, like the deep, rich quality of a low bell, made me look up, and I met his eyes, looking at me with such warmth that I lowered mine immediately again, bewildered. Automatically I asked what was so nice of me, as I only remembered that awful letter.

"Why," he said, astonished, "didn't you send word to me through the children that you accepted the offer, I mean, that you want to marry me?"

Scissors and peonies fell to the floor.

"That I want to—marry—you?"

"Well, yes. The children came to me this morning and said they had had a council among themselves, and the only way to keep you with us would be that I marry you. I said to them that I would love to, but I didn't think you liked me. They ran over to you and came back in a flash, crying that you had said, 'yes I do.' Aren't we engaged now?"

Now I was out of gear. I absolutely did not know what to say or what to do; not at all. The air was full of an expectant silence, and all I knew was that in a few days I would be received into my convent, and there stood a real, live man who wanted to marry me.

"But Captain," I started out, "you know that in a very short while I shall go back to my convent; and one cannot enter a convent and marry at the same time."

The beautiful eyes saddened.

"Is this your very last word? Is there absolutely no hope?"

"Well"—I had an idea—"you know," I said eagerly, "I have something that you don't have. I have a Mistress of Novices. Whatever she says I'd consider as coming from God. It *is* the Will of God. Let me go and ask her."

And in my eagerness to leave, I did not wait for an answer, but started right away, heading for Nonnberg. It was a short hour's walk, and I was happy to have found an excuse to visit this beloved place in the middle of the week.

"Now I know," I mused to myself while speeding along the bank of the Salzach, "that he isn't engaged. What could have happened?" I felt sorry for the poor man, but quite relieved for the children. Whenever I thought of that motherless little flock, a pang went through my heart. But all I could do was pray even harder now that God might send them a good second mother; and why not start right away? So I began to say the rosary.

With a sigh of relief I dropped on one of the old oaken chairs in the community room where the postulants lived.

"Oh, it's so good to be home," I sighed, and took a deep breath of that incomparable smell of herbs, incense, and simply old age, within the old walls.

At this the door opened, and Frau Rafaela, my Mistress of Novices, entered the room.

"Maria, what are you doing here in the middle of the week?"

That made me remember, and I repeated to her the whole "incident."

"And you see, if you tell me now that I cannot marry him because I shall enter here, then the Will of God is made clear, and that must help him, too." Frau Rafaela's old, motherly eyes rested on me, but she didn't say a word. Suddenly she got up and went out of the room. In an hour she returned to tell me that Reverend Mother was expecting me.

I felt quite honored, and lightheartedly I walked through the open galleries, through the cloisters, and up the stone stairs, but this time with no bad conscience at all. The same old oaken door, the same squeak when it opened—oh, here I was surrounded by good old friends, and very soon I should be with them forever. With these thoughts I was already kneeling at Reverend Mother's feet and kissing her ring. She took both my hands in hers and looked at me lovingly and long without saying a word, until I felt rather uncomfortable. Finally she spoke.

"Frau Rafaela has told me your story. As you came home to find out the Will of God in this most important moment of your life, I assembled the community in the Chapter Room. We prayed to the Holy Ghost, and we held council, and it became clear to us"—here her hands pressed tighter—"that it is the Will of God that you marry the Captain and be a good mother to his children."

Minutes had passed, and I was still kneeling, trying to understand. I knew this was final, and no argument was possible. Yes, it was true, I had wanted to know the Will of God; but now when I met it, I refused to accept it. All my happiness was shattered, and my heart, which had so longed to give itself entirely to God, felt rejected. Heavy waves of disappointment and bitterness swept over it. With dry eyes I stared down at the large ring on the Abbess' hand, and mechanically I read over and over again the engraved words around the big amethyst: "God's Will Hath No Why." Reverend Mother's silence showed that she had learned from long experience that words are of no help when will meets will in a world beyond words. When, still dazed, I looked up, I saw her lips move soundlessly in prayer, and the beloved eyes were filled with tears of compassion. That broke the dam and melted the stubborn resistance. In true sincerity of heart I asked:

"What does God want of me now, Reverend Mother?"

"He wants you to serve Him well where He needs you most, and serve Him wholeheartedly and cheerfully."

Slowly I wound my way home. It was a moonless night, and when I walked along the river, which I could not see, but only hear, the words of the psalm came to my mind: "The dark waters of the bitterness of exile threatened to drown me."

The children must be in bed by now, I thought, when I opened the big house door as quietly as possible to slip in unnoticed. But there stood the Captain.

"Well, and . . ." was all he said.

Timidly I went over; and all of a sudden there came all the tears I hadn't found before.

"Th-they s-s-said I have to m-m-m-marry you-u!"

Without a word he opened his arms wide. And, what else could I do—with a wrenching sob I buried my face on his shoulder. . . .

The next day after breakfast their father told his children that they had been right; only if he married me I should have to stay forever. And for that reason he was going to marry me. It was touching and heartwarming to feel behind all the kissing and squeezing that followed, the genuine joy and relief of the children —my children.

Soon afterward the Captain left for a long journey which would keep him away until fall. He explained to me that he had to do this; otherwise, people would talk.

"Talk? About what?" I said.

"Well, about us."

"But why don't they talk now?" I wanted to know.

But the Captain was somewhat mysterious, and insisted that it was for the best. If he and I had only known how terribly busy many tongues had already been all these days.

"I shall come back two weeks before the wedding. Then you will go to Nonnberg, where we shall meet again on our wedding day; and then I shall never leave again," he added almost passionately.

And he was right. Everything worked out fine. Through the summer months the children and I grew closer together every day. And the figure of their father grew more and more distinctly into my life with every letter I received from him. It was a happy and peaceful time.

The leaves turned yellow and red, and the first heavy autumn storms shook them from the trees. The Captain came back, and I learned to call him Georg. Then I went for the last time into my beloved convent for a ten-day retreat to get prepared for matrimony, which is a great sacrament indeed.

It was the Saturday before the first Sunday in Advent, November 26, 1927. When the great day finally dawned, I greeted it with a heart full of happiness and readiness to "serve God where He needed me most—wholeheartedly and cheerfully." I was dressed in my bridal gown in the same vaulted room where I had spent the happiest years of my life so far. My three former roommates, now in the white veil of the novices, helped me dress. Frau Rafaela put the wreath of Edelweiss on the white bridal veil, and then the wonderful bells of Nonnberg began to call. It was time to go down into the church. The whole community accompanied me, and for the last time I walked down the age-worn stairs, over the cobble-stoned yard, passing by the old statues, through the cloisters where the Sisters were lined up for a last farewell. On Reverend Mother's hand I approached the heavy portal. As it opened, I knelt on the threshold for the last time, for the last blessing. Outside the procession had formed. Through swimming eyes I saw a packed church. Oh, and here were the children. The two oldest girls were leading their father, who was in his Navy uniform. The two boys waited for me, and the three little ones busied themselves with my long train. At this moment the big organ began with a jubilant chord. Slowly and solemnly the procession marched up the aisle and up the many steps into the sanctuary, where Father Abbot stood waiting for us, adorned with his golden Ornate. Then the voice of the organ died out, and in the great silence which hovered over the big church, surrounded by the seven children, we promised each other loudly and solemnly to "take each other for better or for worse . . . till death do us part."

THE TRAPP FAMILY SINGERS

BACK ROW: Werner, Rupert, Father Wasner, Georg Trapp. SECOND ROW: Agathe, Hedwig, Rosmarie, Maria, Eleonore. FRONT ROW: Johanna, Martina, Maria Augusta Trapp, Johannes.

VILLA TRAPP, AIGEN, AUSTRIA

"We sang them to our hearts' delight outside in our park . . . We were intoxicated with music, drunk with the wonder of song."

Feasts in a Family

AFTER the Christmas vacation life settled down to its normal routine; that is, for the children. But for me everything was new. It was queer—there was the same house and the same people, and still it wasn't the same. Now they were my children, and I was their mother. There was a world of difference. We all loved each other in a new way, and it was very beautiful. If I had to take the same step now—oh, I am sure I wouldn't dare. I would see all the dangers and difficulties in taking over the place of a second wife and second mother. I would be very doubtful whether all seven children would ever take to me. I wouldn't feel adequate to take over so much responsibility—I simply wouldn't *dare*. But at twenty you are beautifully unconscious of possible complications.

Everybody went to school, even Maria, who was well again—except little Martina, who was too young. Quietly she followed me around the house until I settled down to some letter-writing or mending or embroidering. Then, contentedly, she would nestle at my feet. Quite undemonstrative with her affections and emotions otherwise, she poured all the love of her young heart into a family of little dwarfs she owned. There was a mother dwarf, a father dwarf, and a little child dwarf, from ten inches down. They looked ancient and sorrowful, and Martina was inseparable from them.

"Hedwig's and Johanna's dolls," she insisted, "are silly. But my dwarfies know everything."

Everyone was anxious to have all his homework done before supper, because then came the most beautiful time of the day, the evenings spent together. A fire was lit in the fireplace. The older girls brought their knitting, the younger ones, their dolls or dwarfies; the boys and their father usually worked on wood, carving or whittling; and I, settling in a most comfortable chair, started to read aloud. It is most amazing how much literature you can cover during the long winter evenings. We read fairy tales and legends, historical novels and biographies, and the works of the great masters of prose and poetry.

After having read a couple of hours, I would say: "That's enough for today. Let's sing now; all right?"

That was the signal for everyone to drop whatever he was doing. We sat closer together and started out. First we sang rounds. You can do that for hours on end, and it is a wonderful schooling for the ear. It leads quite naturally to polyphonic music. The rounds teach you to "mind your own business"; sing your part, never to mind what your neighbor sings.

After the First World War the Catholic Youth Movement sweeping all over Austria and Germany had done a wonderful job for music. These young people were fed up with glee club stuff, with all that coy, sweetish, unnatural material which was sung everywhere. They wanted genuine music again. They went up and down the countryside, collecting real folk songs and folk tunes, delved into archives and libraries and copied unpublished music of the old masters, the great unknown ones. In mimeographed and hand-copied sheets this music went from town to town and brought about a radical change in musical life within a few short years.

I was lucky enough, in my student years, to belong to one such group of young ones. Boys and girls didn't "go steady" at that time. We met in large groups of thirty or forty and had the most wonderful time doing things together. A large portion of our free time was spent with music. Out of the enthusiasm of those hours blossomed beautiful settings of the melodies we brought home from our hikes through the mountains, for two, three, four, and five parts, *a cappella* and with the accompaniment of instruments. There were violins and cellos, French horns, and clarinets, and there was the newest and oldest of them all, the revived recorder, the ancient flute. There we sat together by the hour, singing and playing and enjoying ourselves thoroughly.

How grateful I was now for those experiences! Sitting around the table, we worked on at least one new number every evening. If we had more than three parts, I had to take the tenor part, while my husband took care of the bass. How I wished in the depths of my heart that one of the boys would kindly turn into a tenor later; lo and behold—one of them did!

There came a time when we hardly got around to reading or singing together because we were so busy, and that was the birthday season. In a large household there are a number of family holidays which occur yearly; the birthdays and feastdays. In our particular family we have two distinct seasons: from the end of January to the beginning of May, and then again from the end of September to the first of November. My people had only celebrated the birthdays, whereas we on Nonnberg disregarded those and only celebrated the feastdays. These are celebrated on the feast of the Saint in whose honor you are named. Now we put both customs together and, since there were nine of us, there were eighteen holidays right away. It was a matter of course that the lucky one whose holiday came around could expect a present from everyone in the house; and of course, one didn't just go to a store and buy with cold money something turned out by a factory with no relationship at all to the young sister or brother. How could you possibly get for any money that particular dwelling Martina's dwarfies needed, a cross between a foxhole and a little cave, interwoven with roots, with a carpet of moss, with furniture made of spruce twigs!

A loving heart and gifted fingers can produce a wonderland of little miracles, especially after the room next to the library has been turned into a workshop with work benches, a band saw, a lathe, and a circular saw.

All great feasts of the Church have a Vigil; they start, so to speak, the evening before. So our family feasts were celebrated on the evening before, too. The birthday cake with the candles was put in the center of a table, which was also covered with all the different presents. While I was going to fetch the lucky hero of the day, the others lined up in a semi-circle, each one holding a flower. The moment we entered the room they started singing *"Hoch soll er leben!"* the Austrian equivalent of "Happy Birthday to You."

The Birthday Child went now from one to the other and was kissed, wished a happy birthday, and presented with a flower. It may come from the flicker of the little candles which mirror themselves in the eyes of a happy child—but there is always something like a faint flavor of Christmas around such a birthday celebration. There is an old belief that if you think hard of a wish and then blow out all the candles on your cake with one breath, the wish will come true. Now the presents are discovered and admired and each giver is found out, which means renewed kissing and hugging. Then he or she is made master of ceremonies for the next twenty-four hours. That means the menu for three meals and the plans for "what to do tomorrow after school is over."

The feastdays were a little less elaborate. There was no cake with candles, the presents were arranged around one's plate at lunch; but the kissing and hugging and having a good time were the same, because the root and source of all happiness, that warm love, was the same.

Besides the family feasts which recur every year, there are others which come only once in everybody's life. There are the "firsts": your first school day, the First Holy Communion—in a few years it will be the "lasts": graduation from grade school, from high school, from college. But whatever the day may be, it is turned into a feast only by that genuine affection of which a large family is a real powerhouse. If people would only understand that you cannot buy feasts with money. They must come out of your heart, out of that love which makes one inventive. I don't want to say that money must necessarily spoil a feast. If used rightly, it can enhance it and add a good deal to it; but only—and this is very important—if it comes on top of the other, never as a substitute. The foundation has always to be this mutual fondness without which there can be no festive spirit. A birthday table can be laden with flowers from the fields and presents made with the clever fingers of your children, the monetary value of which are only cents, but which to you are priceless.

Weeks passed and turned into months. The time between Epiphany and Ash Wednesday is celebrated in Austria, as in all other Catholic countries, as a carnival. Festivities of all kinds and sorts are going on until *Fasching Dienstag* (Mardi Gras), when the last ball is stopped sharp at midnight and the season of Lent begins. At least, so it was before the war.

We didn't feel much of *Fasching* that year. My husband had never been a friend of official entertainments; big parties with all that goes with them had always scared him. He also didn't want to be told by any Emily Post what he had to do and when and where. In spite of the rule book which required a newly married couple to make the rounds in society after so and so many weeks, we hadn't paid a single visit to society; and as society was strictly prohibited by that same book from paying us the first call, there simply were no calls; no five o'clock teas, no formal dinner parties. Surrounded by an ocean of social activities, we lived on an island all by ourselves.

On *Fasching Dienstag,* however, we had our own party. At lunch it was announced that there would be a costume ball in the big living room, beginning at six. The festive dinner would be at seven-thirty. Of course, the afternoon was free, and all over the house one could hear the tapping of busy feet, bumping of doors, and, as the afternoon progressed further, gales of laughter.

When I came down at seven o'clock, trying to look as Chinese as possible in that beautiful costume which my husband had brought from Hongkong some years ago, complete with shoes and ornaments for the hair, I was almost run down by an ill-mannered sailor, who should not have been admitted in the first place, I thought sharply. Tattooed all over, hands, arms, neck, chest—and you saw a good portion of it, too, through the net shirt—his hat on one ear, smelling of tobacco, he tried to whisper lovely things into my ear. I was a little bit annoyed. Georg should not have invited strangers to this home party. And it took me a long time to discover my dearly beloved husband behind the dirty sailor boy.

The party was such a huge success that we laughed ourselves almost sick. There were the three little bears with paws and snoots and all, uncannily well reproduced with camel's hair blankets and cleverly worked papier-maché. They could eat out of your hands, they could dance, they were very cute and very fresh if you didn't give them a penny each time they begged.

We danced the Walzer, Polka, Sir Roger, Ländler, and other folk dances.

When the clock struck twelve, the gramophone was stopped in the middle of a waltz. We said one "Our Father" aloud together and wished each other a blessed season of Lent.

Lent, the six weeks' preparation for Easter, is very rigorously observed among the country people in the Catholic countries. On purpose I don't say simply "in the Catholic countries," because the big cities have shed all these peculiarities in order to be admitted into the big-city corporation around the world. The national costumes they exchanged for street clothes worn the same in Paris, London, New York, or Shanghai on their respective Fifth Avenues; folk dances were replaced by international ballroom dances; and instead of folk customs—the century-old voice of your own people informing you what your forefathers did at certain times and what you should imitate—they have books now, the Emily Posts of the respective countries, giving minute instructions on what to wear if you want to be called "smart," how to behave if you want to be "socially acceptable."

The people living in the country still celebrate Lent as it was understood by the many generations since the beginning of Christianity: by voluntary penance and mortification we should participate in the sufferings of Christ in order to be able to celebrate also the day of Resurrection together with Him. We should die to our old sinful self and rise as a new man. To this end fasting is one of the oldest precepts. In Poland, Italy, some valleys of Austria, and especially the Balkan countries, the fast is most conscientiously observed. One meal a day only, and no animal products: no meat, no fish, no eggs, butter, cheese, or milk.

Of course, when Easter comes and these goods are back on the table again, the stomachs feast and celebrate together with the souls, sometimes so much so that a doctor is needed. The money which is saved by fasting goes to the poor, and the time which is saved is invested in prayer. Ancient devotions like the Stations of the Cross are much practiced. Pilgrimages are undertaken, and the soul, sobered and helped by the bodily chastisement, finds easier the access to heavenly things.

Some time before Ash Wednesday my husband and I were figuring out what we should do together with the children during the Season of Lent.

"You know what I really miss?" he said to me. "Catholics don't read the Bible as much as Protestants do. I wish that my children would get thoroughly acquainted with Holy Scriptures." (My husband had joined the Church only a year before I had come into the family.) "Let's start them with the New Testament and let's read it together every evening until Easter. And I guess I'll give up smoking," he continued, and this grave announcement was followed by a sigh which seemed to come up from the depths of the earth, because he was a heavy smoker.

Generosity calls for generosity.

"Then I won't even look at candy or any pastry," said I, and my sigh wasn't a bit different, because mine is a sweet tooth.

"We shall leave it to the children to choose their own mortifications," said Georg; and it was interesting to see what followed. One saw the whole character in the making from the way each one reacted.

There was the practical-minded little one: "I shan't pinch Johanna and I won't spit at Werner—until Easter," and it was very hard to convince her that this was by no means a superman's generosity, but merely her duty.

One of her older sisters, the warm-hearted, enthusiastic type, said: "I shall carry the little ones' school bags, I shall eat no dessert at all, I shall say three rosaries a day, and . . ." she also was hard to convince that the more resolutions you make, the less chance there is that you keep any.

It turned out to be a beautiful six weeks. The reading of the Gospels together proved to be wonderful. It proved to be the Book of Books, the only one in the whole world to which a four-year-old girl would listen with enraptured interest, while all the philosophers are not yet able to get to the bottom of its divine wisdom.

Then Holy Week was close at hand, with Palm Sunday ushering it in; we made little excursions into the woods and came home with armloads of pussy willows. With the help of small branches of boxwood and fir twigs they were arranged into nice, round bouquets, fastened to a stick about three feet long. From the workshop we got nice, curly wood shavings, which were dyed blue, red, and yellow with Easter-egg dye, and hung all over the bouquets. They looked lovely and cheerful, and on Palm Sunday the church was a sight. Hundreds of children, each one with his *Palmbuschn,* jealously rivaling his neighbor's in beauty. They were blessed in a special solemn way by the priest in remembrance of the palm branches which were used to make Christ's entrance into Jerusalem such a triumphant one.

In the afternoon of Palm Sunday they were taken out into the fields. Each meadow or field or wood patch got its own; on each stick was fastened a small bottle with holy water, and the family went around distributing them while they said the rosary together. Thus the blessing of the Church was brought to the meadows, where the cattle would graze; to the fields, where the grain for the daily bread would ripen; to the woods, where the beams for the house and the boards for table and bed were growing, to protect them against "the snares of the Enemy": flood, hail, and fire.

Most of these ceremonies and customs as old as Christianity were new to Georg and mostly also to the children. How wonderful it was to travel into that land of wonder with them. At no other time does the Church display the whole splendor of her liturgy as she does around Easter, and who can appreciate any pageant so without restraint and inhibitions as a child?

Every morning we walked to the Cathedral a little ahead of time to get a seat in the front pews.

Then comes Holy Thursday. How happily it starts. The huge organ gives all it has, and so do the choir and so do the musicians: violins, trumpets, horns, as if they all tried to praise and thank Our Lord for the institution of the Blessed Eucharist, because this is its anniversary. But suddenly a shadow falls upon the festive mood: the Church remembers that on that same Holy Thursday Our Lord started His bitter Passion. He was betrayed by one of His disciples and abandoned by the rest of them, and when He was sweating blood in Gethsemane because His anxiety and fear had become so unbearable, there was nobody to wipe His face because even His three best friends had fallen asleep. In remembrance of this the Church becomes sad. She silences the organ and the musicians, and the choir goes on singing alone, bewailing compassionately the fate of the Master. At the end of Holy Mass the Blessed Sacrament is carried in solemn procession to a side altar. There it is locked into a tabernacle as Jesus was locked up in a cold and dirty dungeon for the rest of this terrible night. But now the people want to make up for all the horror and lonely suffering. This altar is flooded in candlelight and covered with flowers, and people come day and night to keep Him company in love and compassion.

The Gospel of Holy Thursday having told, after the institution of the Blessed Sacrament, the touching incident of Jesus washing the feet of His disciples, finishes with these words: "If then I, being your Lord and Master, have washed your feet, you also ought to wash one another's feet."

Therefore, the venerable old Archbishop, acting as Christ's representative, taking off his gilded vestments, and dressed only in the alb, a long linen garment, kneels down humbly before twelve poor old men, washing their feet, drying and kissing them. "For I have given you an example that as I have done to you, so you do also."

Of course, there is no school. The week of Easter holidays has begun on Wednesday, and in all the homes a feverish activity starts: spring cleaning. Only in one corner the artist of the family has closed his workshop, and violently refuses to let any broom or duster come near him: he is making Easter eggs. First, they are boiled in their colors: red, blue, yellow, green, and purple. After they have dried, magic things happen to them. You can erase patterns from the foundation color with certain acids. You can paint with oil paint flowers and birds and words, even little bits of music, on them. The words may even give slight indications as to whom this egg is going to belong. You can fasten little flowers, leaves, or herbs on the egg before you throw it into the hot color bath. When you take it out and remove the string, the shape of the flower or herb is clearly outlined. There is no limit to your imagination, and the master of this craft is an important person in the house during these days.

The evening meal is a solemn one. Before the place of the father stand filled wine glasses and a plate with small buns. He breaks the bun, makes the sign of the Cross over it, and taking with it a cup of wine, he hands it to each member of his household, and they eat and drink in His memory, standing, while the father reads the Gospel of the day. After that the family sits down and eats a roasted lamb, and it is all solemn and a little sad and still festive, like the morning in church.

When you come to church on Good Friday, you feel right away you are entering a house of mourning. The face and voice of your pastor tell you, bringing home in a half-hour sermon the tragic happenings of the first Good Friday: how the people had killed their Best Friend and Benefactor, their Lord and God; and why? Some out of jealousy; others, for hatred, or envy, or for fear of

losing out in business, or even for mere ignorance and misunderstanding.

And you may bow your head and take a deep look into your
innermost heart, feeling miserable and guilty and oh, so sorry.
When the holy service is over on Good Friday, the Church wants
to show outwardly: Christ is dead, buried in the tomb. Thus the
altars are stripped of their linen, the candle holders are overturned,
the doors of the empty tabernacle are wide open, the vigil light is
extinguished. No flowers, no candles, no sound, only a large crucifix lying on the altar steps, and the people come in and kneel in
silent adoration, and then bend to kiss the wounds of the Lord.

But in Austria and in other Catholic countries there is still a
side chapel of the church where there is seemingly great activity.
This is the Holy Tomb. More or less elaborately an oriental tomb
has been constructed according to the imagination of the local
artist, and there one sees the figure of Christ resting in death. It
is the ambition of the whole parish to make this resting-place a
thoroughly beautiful one. Hundreds of potted plants are brought
by the people, and hundreds of candles and blue and red vigil
lights, giving testimony of the burning faith and love of the donors.
A guard of honor is there always: two soldiers on each side pre-
senting arms, two firemen in their best uniforms with shiny hel-
mets and a stern look, two little boys, two little girls, two men,
and two women, representing the civil and military elements of
the community, paying a double homage, keeping a watch at the
tomb of their most beloved Friend, and adoring, at the same time,
the One Who said: "I will be with you till the end of time"; because high above the tomb on a little throne stands the Blessed
Sacrament in a monstrance, covered with a transparent white veil.

As a child you live through these days in an exalted state of
mind. They are not like any other ordinary Thursday, Friday,
Saturday; and young as you may be, your little heart is shattered
by these tremendous mysteries you help to celebrate. When you
come back from your visit at the Holy Tomb, you don't feel as
if you were coming from your parish church. You have just been
in Jerusalem and Calvary and in that garden where they laid Him
into the sepulchre. You can't put it into words, but there is no
need for the grownups to tell you; you don't feel like yelling
around anyhow.

Then comes Holy Saturday. Right away you feel a different atmosphere when you come near the church. In front of it is a pile of wood and people standing around with lanterns in their hands. These are the same peasants who walk for hours during the weeks of Advent to the frozen little church. The door of the church opens, and the priest comes out with the two altar boys and the sacristan. Under the breathless gaze of the bystanders, the sacristan succeeds finally in getting a spark out of a stone and thus lighting the woodpile. This morning it has to be a God-made fire which the priest is going to bless, not an artificial one which people have caught and captured in the form of a match.

From this blessed holy fire, the Easter Fire, the priest lights the three candles on the triangle, the symbol of the Holy Trinity, and carries it into the church, singing jubilantly: *"Lumen Christi!"* ("Light of Christ!") while everyone answers: *"Deo Gratias!"* ("Thanks be to God!")

Now the church is not dark any more. She has her light back, Christ the Lord. Today the church seems to try hard to restrain her joy and happiness, remembering all the time, it is only Saturday. The choir starts *a cappella* and in minor chords, but finally her anticipation of the great Easter glory is overpowering, and she bursts forth into the cry of triumph which goes back through the millenniums: "Alleluia, Alleluia!" Now there is no holding the music back any longer. There is the organ with all its might and power, there are the trumpets and horns, and the high voices of the violins, and all the bells in the steeple and all the little bells in the church join the human voices in one big, victorious "Alleluia!"

Little children who still believe in the Easter rabbit and the mystery of the Christmas tree being brought from heaven have been told that on Holy Thursday all the bells fly to Rome, where the Holy Father the Pope blesses them, and on Holy Saturday they travel back to the places where they belong, freshly blessed.

You would have to be unconscious, should your heart not feel at least some of the happiness of the victory of light over darkness —life over death. Whatever troubles and sorrows may overshadow your own path, they have become lighter today—thus you have been a witness to the ultimate victory: Christ is risen—also in your own life. "Alleluia, Alleluia, Alleluia!" In solemn procession the Blessed Sacrament is carried from the Holy Tomb out of the church through the streets and adjoining valleys to make known to all mankind the message of the great "Alleluia!" This procession turns into a real and veritable pageant: everybody is wearing his new spring clothes. This is the moment where the wintry felt is exchanged for the straw hat. The soldiers, firemen, the war veterans, the little children, everybody wearing his best, help thus to congratulate their Lord. The youngest and the oldest heart is filled on that day with that wonderful confidence: if He was victorious, we shall be so one day, too, because He said so.

Christianity nowadays is like a big household where many cousins live under the same roof. They all belong to the same clan, but at times they have very different ideas about how to run their family affairs.

Some of them, for instance, have no use for any outside devotion. God is a spirit, and He wants to be worshipped in spirit *only,* they say. Consequently, they have dispensed with all liturgy. They don't want any distracting ceremonies, no incense, no vestments, no music, no pictures and images, not even sacraments—only the service of the spirit.

The trouble is, however, that as long as we live here on earth, we simply *are* not pure spirits, but we have also a body, and in that body, a very human heart; and this heart needs outward signs of its inward affections. That is why we embrace and kiss the one we love; and the more we love, the more ardently we press him to this very heart—somehow it seems as if these cousins had overlooked that fact. But you can't cheat the heart; it knows what it wants, and it knows how to get it. Therefore, we see how, beside the liturgy of the Church, another liturgy developed, consisting of the same elements. The vestments withdrew from the Church into the glee club performances with their wide-sleeved velvet gowns and quaint-looking birettas; the processions grew into the costly and gaudy pageants; even the ceremonies around the Pontifical High Mass found a substitute. On the throne, however, was not a bishop, but a pretty young girl, the May Queen, or Corn Queen, Orange Blossom Queen, or Potato Queen, who was crowned and honored.

Well, times change and so may ideas; but the human heart and human nature remain the same. It is very wise for us to remember that we are made of flesh and blood, and to know just *when* our bodies should fast and *when* our hearts should feast. And Easter is such a time!

When Sunday arrives, the biggest of all Sundays of the year, the hearts and the homes are ready for the great Easter joy; both have been cleansed from all dirt and dust in a spring cleaning, inward and outward. Long lines have filed before the confessionals in the church, and contrite hearts have sought forgiveness of their sins. Even the ones who are too busy during the year to come to confession, or too favorably impressed with themselves and can't usually find anything to confess, even these obey that old call of the Church: "All the faithful shall confess their sins at least once a year, receiving reverently at Easter the sacrament of the Eucharist."

We, too, had stood in line in front of the confessional, waiting our turn. Many times during the year had we been there under the choir loft in the dark, waiting to hear the consoling words: "Thy sins are forgiven thee." But this was a different night. While we still stood in the dark, we could see how loving hands were busy transforming the House of God into a beautiful garden with shrubs and young trees, and flowers—flowers—flowers—wherein He could worthily celebrate the anniversary of His Resurrection this coming morning. It filled your heart with happy anticipation of the great Easter message: "My peace be with you."

This morning, when the families walk to church, you see them carrying bundles large and small. On the Sunday of Sundays even the food which will be on the table later for a sumptuous Easter breakfast is blessed. The father carries the big ham, the mother, the artistically baked Easter bread with raisins popping out all over, and the children are entrusted with the basketsful of Easter eggs and little dishes of salt. Before the solemn service of Easter Sunday begins, the priest pronounces a special benediction over the food. Thus provided with blessings for soul and body, the family returns from the Solemn High Mass. The grownups, who have observed the fasting, are full of anticipation of a good feastday meal, and the little ones want to know when the Easter rabbit is going to come.

"In the afternoon," says the mother, and smiles. And sure enough, in the afternoon when they go out with little baskets through the garden, behind the barn, under the trees, hidden by a bush, there are the most beautifully adorned Easter eggs: painted ones, chocolate ones, some made of sugar or dough. Father and Mother have to come along on the Easter egg hunt. The mother, torn this way and that by impatient little hands, has to admire, and finally help out with her big apron when the baskets are already full. The father strolls leisurely behind them in his white shirtsleeves, the Sunday coat around his shoulders; while he listens to the outbursts of joy of his little ones.

His sharp eye catches sight of a little red spot at the edge of the wood over there. Oh, yes, that's the blessed palm he put there himself a week ago; his glance goes slowly all over his little kingdom: the woodland, the meadows, the pastures, the fields, the barns, and the house, his wife, and his children—blessings wherever his eye reaches. And although he couldn't put it into words like city people, so easily and gracefully chatting along wherever they go and stand, deep down in his soul he feels *"that* peace which the world cannot give."

A Festival Summer and a Baby

SOON we started talking about the summer, what to do and where to go.

"I should love to take the older children to some of these exquisite concerts and operas," I said. "After all, the whole world assembles here in Salzburg for the Festivals. Why don't we take advantage of it, too?"

Georg was a little doubtful as to the true pleasure this plan would provide, but when he saw that I *really* wanted to attend the Festivals, he gave in with a somewhat mysterious smile, as if to say: "You'll see. . . ."

Salzburg was at that time a city of about thirty-five thousand people, nestled along the river between the mountains which crowded from all sides. The origin of this ancient place—Iuvavum—goes back to Roman times. It was Christianized as early as the fifth century. It had its catacombs and its martyrs. Later Saint Rupertus built the Benedictine Abbey, Saint Peter, and bade the monks do the same good job they had done all over France and parts of Germany in clearing the woods into tillable land, and likewise in clearing the hearts of the natives into fertile soil for the seed of the Gospel of Christ. Soon afterwards he called his niece, Saint Erentrudis, a Benedictine nun, and built an abbey for her on the hill above Saint Peter: Nonnberg. Around these two venerable places the city of Salzburg began to grow. The old part of the town hasn't changed much as century after century left its mark. That's why you meet Romanesque and Gothic churches, Renaissance palaces and Baroque chapels standing in harmony side by side. During the year it was a rather quiet town with everybody going about his own business but during the summer it changed all of a sudden into a metropolis of music. Elegant cars with license plates from all parts of the world passed slowly

77

through narrow streets, and you could hear as much English spoken when crossing the Staatsbrücke as Salzburg dialect. All the big people of the world of music assembled here: Toscanini and Richard Strauss, Lotte Lehman and Bruno Walter, and the whole place buzzed with activity. If you didn't make reservations months ahead, it was next to impossible to get a room anywhere. The town put on its best dress: flags could be seen from all the official buildings, standards all along the bridges and all around the Festspielhaus, the festival auditorium, and the people on the street seemed to be in a holiday mood, too.

One morning at breakfast my husband said, looking through his mail: "A distant cousin of mine writes to ask whether we can put him and his family up for the Festivals. He hasn't seen me for a long time, and he says he is longing to renew the old relationship. I didn't know that he was so attached to me. That's how easily you misjudge people," he added regretfully.

The next day again, at breakfast, he whistled through his teeth.

"Now—not for your life could I tell you who he is, but here he writes black on white that he is the son of my college roommate's oldest sister, and I never even heard of him. Isn't it funny! He would like to come for the Festivals, too. Well, we have room all right."

When, a couple of days later, an old uncle telegraphed that he also wanted to attend the Salzburg Festivals, and a week after that a cousin from Germany with wife and seven children was wondering whether . . . my husband looked at me and said: "See what I mean?"

They all arrived, aunts and uncles, cousins and friends, who hadn't seen *dear* Georg, of whom they had *always* been so very fond, for *such* a long time . . . and who were *so* happy to meet his lovely wife, and oh, *how* the children had grown . . .! The big house became almost small, so crowded it was.

Cousin Hermann wanted to see the town.

"Rupert, will you go with him and show him . . .?"

"I know," Rupert replied, "The Fortress, Mozart's birthplace, the house of *The Magic Flute,* the Mönchsberg, the Kapuzinerberg, the Cathedral, the Franciscan Church, Saint Peter, Nonnberg, and the Festspielhaus."

Cousin Elvira, who had seen the town yesterday under Rupert's able guidance, was entrusted to Agathe, who would show her the lovely little castle Hellbrunn and the water works. Uncle Edmund, who didn't care, as he said for old stones and old iron, wanted to visit some of the famous brewery gardens around Salzburg with Werner as his guide. Maria conducted a small flock of children to the world-famous puppet theatre downtown, while Georg drove some transient Navy friends up the beautiful mountain road to the summit of the Gaisberg, where you have a lovely view.

And so it went now for the next thirty days. In the evenings, tired from sightseeing, we would go to one of the masterfully produced operas or to one of those unforgettable concerts; but you were never enough at ease to enjoy it really, because just before you stepped into the car to leave for the opera, another telegram had announced a newcomer "who hadn't seen dear Georg . . . who was wondering whether. . . ." And while Leporello surpassed himself in the "Register Aria," you were counting beds in your mind and blaming yourself bitterly for not having changed the order at the butcher's. Now there wouldn't be enough steaks tomorrow, and it was so hard to get anything at the last minute during this time. As the weeks passed, I avoided my husband's eyes. There was a certain glitter, a certain twinkle which annoyed me.

Finally everything has an end. When the last guest had been waved good-bye, we sat around the dining room table, alone once more. It was so quiet. Rupert seemed to mumble something to himself, and Maria was deeply concentrated, counting on her fingers.

Finally they burst forth: "I visited Mozart's birthplace nineteen times. I went all over the fortress twenty-one times, the churches fifteen times, Hellbrunn and the water works eighteen times, and . . ."

Georg put down fork and knife. His whole being seemed to sizzle with glee.

But before he could even open his mouth, I put my hand upon his and said, and every word was underlined: "Yes, I know what you mean. If we want to enjoy music, we shall go and visit a festival somewhere else. But the summer months we shall not spend in Salzburg again."

One day after the guests had left, and the children were playing on the lawn, Hedwig said quite indignantly: "Now, Mother, this is the third time that you haven't played volley ball with us. That's no fun. Come on; here's the ball."

I took them all along with me, and sitting in front of the log cabin in the park, I told them that some time after Christmas God would send them a little sister or brother.

"Oh, Mother, let it be a boy," sighed Werner. "We have five girls already!"

And Martina said: "If it is only coming after Christmas, how do you know now?"

So I told them.

This was one of those rare hours where heaven seems to touch earth, where a firm bond is woven between hearts.

Advent had come again, the most beautiful Advent of all; that life of real expectation. When the long evenings set in and we met around the fireplace, there was the same atmosphere, which can only be characterized by that untranslatable word, *gemütlich*. There was something new, which one could feel but not put into words. That mood of cheerful anticipation had taken hold of the whole family. The knitting needles in busy young hands did not bring forth lengthy men's socks any more, but the cutest little sweaters and caps and playsuits and panties, all in blue, of course, because "we already had five girls." Georg and the boys were working noisily on a beautiful cradle; and when I read aloud the passage of a fairy tale where it says: "And after a year the young queen gave birth to a little son, and they lived happily ever after," Martina looked at her toy dwarfs and nodded gravely.

The Christmas story about the Holy Mother with her Holy Child blooms all anew in your heart when you are living through the great mystery of becoming a mother yourself, a bearer of life.

After Christmas I called on Frau Vogl to make arrangements. She was the youngish widow of a doctor, and had been recommended to me as the best midwife in town. Together we did some figuring, and then it was decided that the baby was due by the middle of February.

"Do you have everything ready for the baby?" Frau Vogl asked me.

"I don't know," I said, rather nervously. "I'll tell you what I have: ten dozen diapers; three dozen shirts, size one; and three dozen, size two; six dozen diaper-panties, sixteen jackets, a cradle, a crib, a basket, and a carriage."

"For heaven's sake, stop!" cried Frau Vogl. "You don't expect triplets, do you?"

Very few of these things had been newly acquired. Most of them were still there from the older children. I only had to get them down from the attic, have them washed, ironed, and pleated, because these cute little things were full of ruffles and tiny pleats.

By the middle of February Frau Vogl came to stay, and two days later it was obvious: this was the day.

As it hadn't occurred to anyone to bring a doctor into the picture during those past nine months, so it also didn't occur to anybody that I should take even so much as an aspirin. Frau Vogl's presence radiated confidence. Everything was just fine, the pain simply belonged to it; thus it was ordained by God Almighty ever since Eve ate the apple.

Georg was sitting at my bedside, and that was very necessary. He knew so much more about it all than I; he had gone through it seven times. He assured me that I was not going to die, and the less I moaned now, the more strength I would have later, and this was only the beginning. He said it so casually that it took the edge off my anxiety. I went through the entirely new sensation that this was not a pain like a toothache, which at times seems to screw itself into your very bones. These pains seemed to come in regular intervals like breakers at the seashore. The moment they stopped, you felt perfectly wonderful and ready to dance, only to change your mind rather quickly when the next breaker came.

"Will it take longer than half an hour?" I whispered to Frau Vogl, who didn't seem to understand, because she only said: "Breathe deeply."

That was early in the afternoon. When Frau Vogl came back after supper, the uninterested expression on her face changed suddenly. She became all concentration.

Through the open door I could hear the children. They were saying the rosary now. After every decade they sang a song—softly and only in two parts, as the tenor and the bass were missing. It sounded to me like angels. What a wonderful prayer the rosary is! For eight hundred years it has carried the sorrows and troubles, the joys and happiness through the hands of the Heavenly Mother to the Throne of God. When we repeat over and over: "Holy Mary, Mother of God, pray for us . . ." it is like the begging of little children who want something with all their heart: "Please, Mother, please! Oh, Mother, please, please!"

With all my heart I joined the chorus silently. Georg hadn't left the room during those long hours. His strong hand was like an anchor to which I clung when the hurricane of pain tossed about the little boat of a frail human body.

During the first weeks of the nine months, we had been rather choosy. It should be a boy—blond-haired, blue-eyed, tall and thin. Georg wanted him to look like his mother, whereas I definitely wanted him to be the image of my hero. The closer the time came, the less fussy we were. If he is only healthy with straight arms and legs, even the color of eyes and hair wouldn't matter any more. And right now it was just the same whether it was a boy or a girl. All the strength of the whole being was concentrated on the one thing necessary:

"Oh God, help, help that this Thy child be born healthy in body and soul."

When a piercing little shriek cut through the solemn silence, I heard the children downstairs jump from their seats and jubilantly break into the hymn of thanksgiving by the old master Bach: "Now Thank We All Our God," while Georg was bending over me, kissing me on the forehead. In these precious moments the human being feels itself lifted up into the heights of God, partaking of His power, a co-worker of God, the Father, Creator of heaven and earth.

Then Georg stepped over to Frau Vogl and looked at his sixth daughter.

"Looks like every other newborn baby," he said in the tone of one who knows what he is talking about—"like a little monkey." The spell was broken. Under my feeble protest he left the room "to tell the children."

Had he seen a tear welling up in the hurt young mother's eye? He was right back and with a warm glow in his fine eyes, he whispered earnestly:

"But little monkeys are the loveliest, sweetest creatures, and I wouldn't want her to look any other way!"

What could I do but laugh through tears? Then he left me to

Frau Vogl's professional hands. Later, after the children had tip-toed in to admire the baby and to kiss me good-night, I suddenly felt very tired. It had been a full day. Right in the beginning of my evening prayer: "I thank Thee, oh God, for these and all Thy gifts," I fell asleep. My last thought was:

"It—was—wonderful!"

That was in the winter of 1929, when Europe had a cold wave such as the oldest people couldn't remember having lived through. The temperature went down to forty-five and fifty degrees below. Since our churches didn't have heating systems, we asked the good friend of my Nonnberg days, Father Bruno, to come out to the house and baptize the baby there. Rupert and Agathe were God-father and Godmother, as they had wished so fervently to be, and the child was given the name: Rosmarie Erentrudis.

Uncle Peter and His Handbook

A DISTANT cousin of my husband's, Peter, had also visited the
Festivals in Salzburg the previous summer. With his wife and
six children he had stayed in the friendly little inn half-way up the
Gaisberg, and it was only towards the end of the season that we
had made his acquaintance. The two families liked each other
right away. Their children were the same ages as ours, and we
discovered many common interests in music and art.

Peter had been a Major in the Imperial Prussian Army. He was
a lovely person with a heart as big as himself, which made it easy
to get along with him. When it came to duty, however, Peter was
made of iron and steel, and as everything in his daily life was classi-
fied either as a duty towards God, or his fellow men, or himself,
there was a lot of duty around.

Peter also loved handbooks.

When Peter was newly married and they were expecting their
first baby, he immediately got the proper handbook, which would
guide him safely through the next nine months. In the seventh
month the handbook said: "Carpets and curtains should be removed from the bedroom, and the walls and floor washed with
antiseptic." Peter who, as a Major, had two orderlies at his command, was standing in the middle of the bedroom, book in hand,
supervising these activities. At the same time Laura, his wife,
slipped on the kitchen floor and, feeling a strange pain, went upstairs, heading for bed, saying to Peter:

"Please, dear, call Mrs. X."—her Frau Vogl—"at once."

Peter merely glanced at her, amazed. Then, looking over the
rim of his spectacles, he uttered in a helpless tone of voice:

"Laura—impossible! I am only in the seventh month!"

In order to escape another Festival summer, we had made plans

with Peter and his family to go down south and camp on an island
in the Adriatic Sea during July and August.

We hadn't given it another thought when, at the end of February, Georg received a letter from Peter, saying:

"MY DEAR GEORG:

"I am very sorry to inform you that your idea of camping out-
of-doors is not a good one, as I can prove now by experience. I
have spent several nights by an open window on the floor of my
bedroom, wrapped in a blanket, and I am sorry to admit that
thereby I have contracted the worst cold of my life. My duty to
my family obliges me to cancel our previous summer plans.

"Your loving cousin,

"PETER."

Georg answered:

"DEAR PETER:

"Sorry about your cold. Stay in bed, drink plenty of hot grog
and sweat it out; that's the best way. As far as the summer goes,
don't worry. The difference between the temperature of your home
in northern Germany at the end of February and the island in
July is at least eighty degrees. We'll have a wonderful time.

Love,

"GEORG."

And a wonderful time we had. First, many more pleats had to
be ironed out of Peter's troubled conscience, but finally they arrived at our house about the beginning of July. Looking satisfiedly
over his eighteen pieces of luggage, Peter assured us that the big
luggage he had sent by freight to Pola. Pola, situated on the south-
ernmost point of the Istrian peninsula, was the former Austrian
Naval Base, which is now Italian, and the island was a few miles
offshore.

The main feature of last Christmas had been a bicycle for everyone except little Martina, who got a scooter. Since Peter's older
children had brought their bicycles, too, the plan was this: they
should join our older ones and me; we wanted to start ahead and
tour over the Alps on our bikes. Georg, with Laura and all the
smaller ones, were to follow in a few days by car; and Peter wanted

to go ahead by train to take care of the luggage. There were not many cars on the highways at that time, and the country through which we cycled was so unearthly beautiful—we had a wonderful, wonderful time. In five days we were in Pola, where we met the rest of our families and, eating the most delicious fried fish and drinking the dark native wine, we sat together until deep into the night, telling of our adventures.

The children were all excited, and surpassed one another in happy reminiscences—topped by Hedwig who, almost choked with giggling, said:

"And you know, Papa, what happened? Every day when we had our big rest at noon, Rupert disappeared. On the fourth day we followed him, wanting to know what he did. And you know where we found him? Sitting in the middle of a clearing in the woods with a mirror on his knees—sha-a-a-a-aving!"

Poor Rupert! He blushed to the roots of his hair, and you could easily see how he would have loved to strangle his dear little sister, who had given away the deep secret of his sixteen years.

"Never mind, Rupert," came Georg to his rescue. "That's one thing for sure in which Hedwig cannot imitate the boys!"

And then it was really time to go to bed. The next day we hired a big boat to take us over to Veruda, our destination. When we came to the pier, several men were already loading huge boxes.

"Heavens! The big luggage!" escaped my lips.

That's what it was. Peter, in the thorough fulfillment of his duty towards his family and himself, had followed the guidance of the *Handbook of Camping* word by word, which tells you what is the minimum you need per person (a) for eight people, (b) for six weeks, (c) for sunshine, (d) for rain, etc. It was all in the boxes. Georg and I exchanged a glance. We *knew* we would have a good time.

The island had no pier; one had to wade ashore. Our luggage consisted of six tents; and a hammock, plus sleeping bag, plus two blankets, and a rucksack with personal belongings, per person. We had camped before.

It had been very hot in the morning, and now black clouds were gathering. A critical look at the sky and Georg said to us:

"Make camp—hurry!"

In no time the six tents were put up in a circle, and the rest of the luggage stored in the big tent, which would serve as living and dining room on rainy days. We had been silently busy, everyone knowing exactly what to do next. Only now I remembered Peter. Where was he?

"Peter, Peter!" I called, and followed hurriedly the muffled "Here!" of his answer.

Behind a bushy pine I found what is left to be seen if the whole upper part of a man is plunged headfirst into a deep box. At this moment he emerged, purple of face, triumph in his look.

"Here it is!" he shouted victoriously.

And what was it? The *Handbook of Camping,* which by mistake had been buried in the very bottom of the biggest box. Nervously he searched for his glasses, which he never, never found, for they were usually pushed up on his forehead. Then opening the book on page one, he said: "Now, cousin, let us commence." And then he read to my unbelieving ears:

"'The first step to be taken upon reaching the prospective site of the camp is to investigate whether the site is: (a) sandy, (b) rocky, (c) swampy, (d) hilly, (e) flat.'"

Up went the glasses, and with the voice and air of Julius Caesar, Peter shouted:

"Children, 'ten-*shun!* Let's investigate."

Georg, appearing on the scene and not having witnessed what I had, interrupted the strategic manoeuvre with a suggestion:

"Peter, I think you'd better get your boxes into one of the tents. It will pour within the next five minutes."

I felt sorry for "Caesar," so I said: "The site is flat and sandy—come on!" The first drops, big as cherries, began to fall.

The highlight, when the storm was over, was the unpacking of the big boxes. Looking back on it, I can only compare it with the Boy Scout Department at Macy's. Brand-new tents with a rubber floor attached to them; acetylene lamps for each tent; two folding boats with three sails each; and the most fancy sleeping bags and fluffy pajamas; shiny kitchen equipment; a gramophone and records; one box full of books, and one box full of wine, another one filled with silk-hemmed blankets in lavender and pea-green, and dainty cushions; still another one filled with canned *delicatessen* foods; and in the middle of this *"Handbook-of-Camping-Come-Alive"* stood Peter, beaming, opening his arms wide and saying:

"Help yourselves, help yourselves! We have much more than we need!"

Veruda is one of the many small islands off the shore of Istria and Dalmatia, which on one side emerges gently out of the sea, rises gradually up to about 150 or 200 feet, and ends abruptly on the other side in a steep cliff. In an hour one could walk around it. The sea had eaten deep into its shoreline, forming many little bays as big as a large room. One part of the island, about fifty acres, was covered with dense pine groves. The rest was fields and pastures. Franciscan Fathers had once owned this beautiful spot. On the highest point of the island the ruins of the church and the convent were still standing. The monks had planted a garden with medicinal herbs. Long after the Fathers had been driven away by Napoleon, the herbs had spread all over the land, and during the hot summer days and nights they exhaled the most wonderful fragrance, which one could smell for miles and miles out at sea: thyme and lavender, dill and sage, mint and sweet geranium and rosemary, and many more which we couldn't name. The old walls were overgrown with honeysuckle, wild roses, oleander, and laurel. A walk through this little paradise in the full moonlight was unearthly beautiful.

Georg had known Veruda since his boyhood days. He had been born in Zara, half-way down the Dalmatian coast, into the family of an Austrian Navy officer. They had lived a while in Trieste and, until 1918, in Pola. He also knew Signor Pauletta, who had owned a hardware store in Pola before the war. Afterwards he had acquired Veruda and retired there. He had fixed himself a couple of rooms in the old monastery, and there he lived now, as his island's only inhabitant, very contentedly on fish he caught and vegetables and fruit he planted, needing next to no money. Very rarely he went "downtown," which meant Pola. He had invited us to come and camp on Veruda, and now—here we were.

Right at this moment our host came down from his stony hermitage to greet his guests. His eyes grew bigger and bigger when he saw that fancy display of what modern people, according to the book, need when they want to go "back to nature" and lead a "simple life" in the country, feeling, of course, like aborigines. Signor

Pauletta, who owned a couple of pots and pans, a Sunday suit, and fishing tackle, was deeply impressed.

"*Varra, varra!*" he repeated many times clucking his tongue. (This means "What do you know about that!")

Our little tent city was erected on the east side of the island, where it slopes gently down to the water, but every day we went up to the cliffs, watching the surf or the big ships out at sea, heading for the Mediterranean, or watching Signor Pauletta fishing. We slept in naval hammocks under the pine trees, and after the first couple of unquiet nights, when you had to pick yourself up from under your hammock several times, it became a most restful way of sleeping. The strong scent of the pines, the quiet murmur of the waves, the moonlight coming down through the branches, the gentle swinging of the hammocks—oh, it was heavenly!

At first, everybody was radiantly happy. Georg, who was the supreme commander, assigned the duties, such as cooking, getting the fresh water from the cistern up yonder, watching the baby, washing dishes. There was a bi-weekly exchange, the two families taking turns. The first thing every morning was a quick swim. Then we met for morning prayer and breakfast. After that little groups formed for fishing or swimming, paddling, sailing, or just strolling around. After a few days we noticed that our children were scattered all over the place, having a wonderful time with the boats, while Peter's children were mostly ashore. Upon investigation I learned that the *Handbook* advised not leaving land if: (a) the wind comes from the land, (b) cumulo-nimbus clouds are forming on the horizon, (c) during the past three days there has been a storm, (d) sure signs indicate a storm to come within the next twenty-four hours, (e) the temperature is higher than eighty degrees, (f) you feel the slightest indigestion, (g) or headache, (h) or general tiredness. Cousin Peter, therefore, could be seen every morning after breakfast, licking his right forefinger, according to the book, holding it up, and finding sadly that the wind was coming from the land, which it did every morning, changing every night to wind from the sea, all during the summer on this coast, book or no book. To the passionate pleading of his children he only shook his head sadly.

Georg and I had a council of war. It was finally agreed that I was to take care of Peter every morning after breakfast until Georg had successfully sent off all the children. When the last one was cleared off the island, I would be informed by a signal on his boatswain's whistle.

The next morning I watched Peter to see what he was going to do after breakfast, and soon discovered that he was going to have his morning shave in peace and quiet. Laden with two sizeable leather cases, several towels and smaller boxes, he descended into one of those little bays, of which there were eight or ten next to each other. I changed into my bathing suit and made myself at home in the cove next to him, watching him from behind a stone. It was awful, but what could I do? It was my order of the day to prevent Peter from licking his finger before the whistle had blown. I didn't even know yet, myself, how I would do it. For the time being, I was perfectly enraptured by what I saw: Lovingly Peter spread the different towels over flat stones. Then he opened the first leather case and took out a brush, a piece of soap, several little flasks, a razor strop, and many other little items, the identity of which was unclear to me but which, of that I was sure, were in the book. Then he opened the second leather case, which obviously contained washing and bathing utensils, soap for salt water, talcum powder, etc. All this was arranged in rectangular lines, like soldiers on a drill field. Then Peter stepped back and, after an approving glance, nodded. It was good. But it became more breath-taking than that. Sitting down on a low stone, Peter took that leather strop and a razor and, sticking his big toe through the middle ring of the strop, holding the other end in his left hand, sharpened the razor, counting aloud: ". . . twelve, thirteen, fourteen . . ." Merely by listening I was informed that the book suggested, at least on Wednesdays, twenty strokes. I was spellbound, and almost forgot my duty to *my* fellow men. When he started to produce lather in a lovely pink bowl, my conscience awoke.

For heaven's sake, I must not let him shave, and, "Peter!" I wailed, rising behind my stone, "Peter!" not knowing yet what else to say.

He gave me the clue. "What bothers you, Cousin Maria?"

"You know, I don't like this cove. Would you mind, Peter, changing with me?"

And now, shameful me, I sat down on a stone, watching him completely pack and unpack for the next ten minutes, going through all the procedure patiently once more, considering cold-heartedly that I *would* have to chase him into still another cove if I didn't hear . . . But there it was, the "all clear" signal, and Peter had his uninterrupted shave and I, a good swim.

This had to be repeated for the next few days until Peter was convinced that none of Cousin Georg's arrangements for the children had proved fatal.

It was a wonderful summer, full of adventure and the healthiest out-of-door living we could wish. The two families were closely knit together; friendships formed among the children which were to last a life-time.

The last evening came. We had stretched the vacation, and it was high time to go home if the children were to be in time for school. This was now definitely the last evening. With the kind of tender sadness that always comes before a farewell, we sat around the campfire. A waning moon shed a greenish light, which only stressed the doleful atmosphere. In the evening the children had asked me to tell ghost stories—"true ones." So I had invented "true ghost stories" of monks wandering around the island not finding rest for their souls because . . . Of a hollow voice which could be heard on moonless nights, moaning and groaning, which belonged to the Emperor Napoleon, who had persecuted this monastery, and would have to groan until somebody rebuilt it and gave it back to the Franciscans . . . Of . . . and soon I had to accompany my young audience to their respective hammocks. Now we grown-ups were sitting around the fire alone. After we had talked about the rich beauty of these summer months, Peter, once more filling the glasses from the last bottle, said all of a sudden:

"You know, it just comes to me that after the first few days I didn't even open a book again. By the way, Laura, have you seen that old *Handbook of Camping* anywhere? I mislaid it right at the beginning."

And this was perhaps the greatest praise which was ever pronounced upon Veruda, that hidden pearl of the sea.

An Operation, A Turtle, and a Long Distance Call

IT WAS a beautiful day in May. Rosmarie was two years old. It was Ascension Day, a holiday, and the whole family was in church. Rosmarie had stayed home with me, and I had called Frau Vogl that it was time for her to come again, perhaps one of the next days. And then it happened, and it happened so fast that I hardly had time to inform Frau Vogl she had better hurry. While the church bells were ringing, little Eleonore hastened into this world. That somehow stuck with her. She still seems to be in a hurry.

On the evening of her baptism—she was named after her God-mother, Tante Lorlein—Georg said to me thoughtfully:

"I don't know whether this has anything to do with our getting girls all the time, but ever since the first child, I wanted to name one Barbara. You know, for some mysterious reason Saint Barbara is the patron Saint of the Navy. The first child, however, was a boy, Rupert. The next one had to be named after her mother, the third after her Godmother, and so on; and Saint Barbara seems to send girl after girl until I keep my promise."

"And why didn't you tell me that in the first place?" I asked reproachfully.

When Eleonore was a little over a year old, we were making summer plans again, and went back to Veruda. That joyous living in bathing suits, which made you feel so amphibious, came this time to a sudden end for me.

On one of our hikes, when I was newly married, we had stayed overnight with a farmer whose children were sick in bed with scarlet fever, which, unfortunately, he told us only the next morning, when it was too late. Sure enough, a few weeks later, when the incubation period was not quite over, Martina and Johanna woke up one morning with high fever, sore throats and red tongues. I withdrew with the little ones into the guest wing, and there we lived in seclusion. When they were out of danger and up and around for the first time, it got me. It wasn't a bad case, though, and everything was under control. Weeks after I had returned to human society and still couldn't get rid of a rather annoying back-ache, I asked a doctor about it, and the result of this consultation was the discovery that the scarlet fever had infected my kidneys. "But don't worry; just keep on a strict diet: no meat, no salt, no eggs, no milk, no fat."

Little did I know that this was to be my program for the next twenty years. Off and on I tried "not to worry; just keep on a strict diet: no meat, etc." But if one doesn't have a character like Abraham Lincoln or Joan of Arc, a diet simply disintegrates into eating exactly what you want to eat, but with a bad conscience.

During our weeks in Veruda I felt the pain most disagreeably on our boat rides, especially in rough weather when we got drenching wet. So one day I again went to a doctor. He grew quite serious and talked about kidney stones and a necessary operation. Upon my return home I went to Vienna.

Maria came with me. Since the very earliest times when she had been a convalescent and I her teacher, we had grown especially fond of each other.

That first week in Vienna was lots of fun. During the day I was in a private clinic for the necessary tests to be made in order to find out definitely what was wrong with the kidney. In the evening we went to the opera or the theatre. We enjoyed ourselves thoroughly, and I almost forgot what I was in Vienna for, until the doctor informed me that the tests showed it *was* kidney stones, and an operation was unavoidable. That put an end to our gay visits at the Staatsoper and the Burgtheater. Maria sent a telegram to her father, and he flew up on the day of the operation. The operation proved worth while: nineteen stones were removed, and so much gravel and sand that the wound had to be kept open in order to drain during several weeks.

I had never had much talent for being sick or keeping quiet, and after the first few miserable days, I found it extremely difficult to lie on my back motionless.

"Could you think of some kind of animal which I could have right here in bed with me?" I asked Georg.

He rushed off and came back with three tiny little baby chicks. I was simply thrilled, called them Caspar, Melchior, and Balthazar in honor of the Three Holy Kings, and during the long hours when no visitors were allowed, I had the nicest company. Contentedly they rested on my chest, were perfectly tame, and made those little squeaks baby chicks make all over the world. Unfortunately, they did not remain little yellow cotton balls, but grew, and after a week the diaper situation of my baby chicks became extremely difficult. I could see it by the expression on the face of patient Sister Agrosia, my nurse. Sister Agrosia was a saintly nun with only one fault: In her childlike innocence she believed every word I said, however silly my stories might be. She had stirred up in me the urge to find out to what depths her trustfulness would go, which made my stories sillier each day, and still I hadn't reached the limit of her credulity.

When it was evident that Caspar, Melchior, and Balthazar had to be taken to greener pastures, Georg went to a pet shop and came back radiant.

"Look what I got you!" and he put a little turtle on my bed. At this very moment Sister Agrosia came into the room.

"Oh," she said, "what is that?" looking curiously at something she had never seen before in her life.

Truthfully I answered: "That is a turtle, Sister."

"A turtle, what is a turtle?" she wanted to know.

That was bad. All my evil instincts were at work.

"A turtle is an animal which feeds on the toes of newborn babies," I said, looking straight into her eyes.

This she *can't* believe, I thought to myself. But I was mistaken.

"Oh, oh!" Sister said, and looked with horror at that little brown lump on my blanket. "But we'll have to be very careful and keep the door shut."

I had been given the only vacant room in the whole house, which happened to be next to the maternity ward, babies being born constantly all around me.

Cruelly I answered: "That won't help any, Sister, because a turtle can make itself flat like a sheet of paper, crawl under the door and blow itself up outside again."

COR UNUM, STOWE, VERMONT

"From September through April we were traveling constantly with only a short stop around Christmas."

Sadly I must confess that I was not a bit ashamed of myself at that moment, nor was I next morning when I heard from eye-witnesses that Sister Agrosia had been seen sitting on a chair outside my door with a stick in her hand while the little turtle slept peacefully on my chest.

During the next days I did my best to break the spell. I assured Sister Agrosia that I had been mistaken. This was not the wild type of turtle, but a tame one, living on turtle feed. She wanted to know whether it was a "he" or a "she." Now Georg had forgotten to ask this important question when he bought it. We didn't know and couldn't imagine. So I called it Glöckerl, which means "Little Bell," a neuter name, and soon we were good friends all around. I asked Sister Agrosia for a spool of thread, and with a piece of adhesive tape I pasted the end of the thread on Little Bell's shell. Then it was allowed to go grazing all over the room. When I wanted it back, all I had to do was start winding up the spool, and reluctantly it came gliding along the parquet backwards and was hoisted up on the bed, looking mournful as only turtles can. When I finally left the hospital, Little Bell stayed behind with Sister Agrosia.

At Pentecost I was still fast in bed.

"Sister, I would like to go to confession tomorrow," I said.

Kind Sister Agrosia went out to find a priest at the next parish church. Soon she was back, excited, jubilant, triumphant:

"They have a new priest in the parish, and the pastor said he will send him. I haven't talked to him, but I know you will like him very much. Oh, he is so beautiful! He has a face like an angel!"

And the dear old sister, her cheeks flushed, her eyes turned to heaven, looked a little like a holy card herself. I must admit with grief that the great expectation of the next morning was divided between the receiving of the sacraments and the curiosity to see "Father Angel-Face," which grew stronger every minute.

At seven o'clock the door opened, and at one glance I could verify it: Sister had been right. Father looked like the statue of Saint Aloysius come to life. But now it was time for me to concentrate on my sins. Father got a chair and sat down at my bedside; and after he had pronounced the Latin blessing, I confessed my sins, including all the mischief with poor Sister Agrosia. When I was all through, Father looked up and said only two words:

"Nem értem," which means, "I don't understand."

Father was Hungarian!

For a split second we looked at each other in desperation, and then we had a hard time not to laugh. Father commenced questioning me in Latin: *"Have* you done this or *have* you done that?" and I, wanting to answer, "I *have,"* or "I *have* not," just said: *"Habeo—Non habeo";* which was definitely not correct Latin, but accepted by God in His representative.

Soon afterwards my husband came to get me out of this swanky private clinic. The summer months we again spent in Veruda, and in September we came back to Salzburg, glad to be home again.

We had hardly walked into the house when my husband was called to the telephone, long distance from Zell am See. The distance is only about sixty miles, but it was long distance, and we were in Austria, where a long distance call or a telegram are used only in utter emergencies, usually death. And so you hurry to the 'phone with shaking knees, take the receiver with trembling hands, and reach for the nearest chair. Still now, after ten years in America, it fills me with awe to see how differently long distance calls are handled here. Back home such a call was the great event of a day. If, once or twice a year, you had to make one, you announced it solemnly to the operator the first thing in the morning, lived in exalted expectation from then until late in the afternoon, when your call would be announced. Here, sitting in New York, people casually pick up the receiver, and as casually, say: "Toronto," or "Hollywood," and before one can catch one's breath, the other party is on the line. It takes less than a minute. The greatest thrill, however, is yet to come. The person talking to Toronto or Hollywood does not, as I had expected, talk at the rate of three hundred words a minute, all in one breath, looking concentratedly at one point on the wall—oh no! In the most comfortable, easy-chair manner he leans back and starts chatting about the weather in New York. "And what are you having in Toronto or Hollywood? Rain? Oh, isn't that too bad. It's a gorgeous day here. By the way, what I wanted to say is . . ." Then, only, comes the business; I am exhausted. This is still for me the symbol of the higher standard of living, so much so that I am sinfully addicted to long distance calls myself.

But back to the historic telephone call: the voice on the other end announced:

"The banking house Lammer and Company is bankrupt."

It was our bank.

Aren't We Lucky!

IT HAS happened many times that rich people have, in one moment, lost a fortune. When you read about such losses in novels or see them acted on the stage, they always seem dramatic. It is most interesting to go through it once yourself. That voice announcing the bankruptcy of our bank had put a definite period to the end of a very comfortable chapter in our life: the chapter "Rich."

The bank where our money was deposited at that time was owned by a lady, Mrs. Lammer. About this time Hitler and his Nazis across the border began to make things difficult for little Austria. In order to force Austria to her knees, all tourist trade with Austria had been forbidden overnight, thus cutting her lifeline. This caused serious repercussions in the world of finance. Mrs. Lammer was not the only banker who looked with much worry into the near future. My husband knew and esteemed her as a brave and smart woman. When he heard that she was in serious difficulties with her bank, he took all his funds, safely deposited in a big bank in England, and came to her rescue. That sounds like a fairy tale. But in fairy tales it sometimes happens that the rich prince with the good heart, through some witchery, wakes up one day a poor man, and has to undergo terrible adventures before his final reward.

And so it happened. In spite of the—for Austria—very big sum of money, the bank couldn't be saved; the money was lost.

My poor husband! He tortured himself with reproaches.

"I should never have taken the money out of England," he moaned. "Never! Oh, the poor, poor children!"

"Now, listen," I said finally, "you didn't do that to give yourself a good time. You wanted to help somebody in a desperate situation, didn't you? What do we read the Gospel for? Don't you remember that it says, whatever we do for love of Him, He will reward us a hundredfold in this life, and on top of it we get life everlasting?"

After all, we were not exactly starving yet. But we had to face realities. Most of the money was gone. There was just enough left to pay the most necessary bills if one lived less stylishly. But there was a great deal of real estate, representing a nice sum. This, however, would not be touched; it was set aside to secure the future of the children. We had to reduce our standard of living, give up the car, send away six of the eight servants, keeping *only* the butler and the cook, close the big rooms downstairs and on the second floor, and live cozily together on the third floor, where it would be easy to get along without a maid. My poor husband felt like a beggar. He was so depressed, and I felt terribly sorry for him as I watched him walking up and down, back and forth through the room by the hour, chewing the edge of his moustache and looking hopelessly sad.

On top of all his worries, I was getting on his nerves, too. Somehow or other, I just couldn't share his utter despair. Ever since the moment when we had learned the money was lost, I had experienced a strange expectancy. I felt elated, and not for my life could I look discouraged, try as I would. Did I perhaps feel faintly —remotely—that we were just at the beginning of the great crescendo in the song of our life, which would from now on continue uninterruptedly?

The "hundredfold reward" set in almost immediately with the reaction of the children: their complete unconcern as to whether we had a car or not, their unrestrained willingness to take over new duties, new responsibilities, and this not in an attitude of suffering and resignation, but with rolled-up shirtsleeves.

Rupert, the oldest, was the only one not at home. He was in Innsbruck in pre-medical school, and I went to see him to break the bad news, not only that his liberal allowance had to be stopped right away, but he would have to work his way through the university. I came home glowing with enthusiasm.

"Aren't we lucky, Georg, that we lost that money! How would we ever have found out what fine fellows the children are?"

And I told him how Rupert had taken it with a smile. And that cheerful smile of the boy went a long way—it lit up the troubled face of his father. When I saw Georg's reaction after so many worried days and nights, my joy had no end. Too much joy can't be taken alone; it hurts. And so I hugged and squeezed my poor husband until he freed himself laughingly, catching his breath.

"What's the matter with you? You act as if you had made a million dollars."

"Oh, much more," I said. "I have just found out that we were not really rich, we just happened to have a lot of money. That's why we can never be poor. I am so happy to know that we don't belong to those for whom it is so hard to enter the Kingdom of God."

But in spite of all my enthusiasm, something had to be done. We had to earn our living. But how?

In those days we reaped the first harvest of that blessed custom we had started long ago of reading the Gospel together with the children. At every crossroad, in every tribulation one word or the other would pop up, which seemed made for the occasion. "Whatsoever you shall ask," said Our Lord, "you shall receive."

"Whatsoever." So we started asking together for the right light, for the right guidance, and the answer was just around the corner in Nonnberg. I went there to ask them to help us pray in this tight situation.

"Why don't you ask the Archbishop for permission to have a chapel, as so many other castles and estates do," said Frau Rafaela. "I am sure he would send a priest to stay with you, and you could rent the extra rooms of your house to students of the Catholic University."

As simple as that! The good old Archbishop Ignatius, personification of kindness and love, gave his permission most readily. One of the big rooms downstairs, not in use now, seemed just made for a chapel, with a bay window in the corner for the altar; the pews were on the side facing each other as in a quaint old convent chapel. The pastor from the parish church most kindly helped us out with the most necessary vestments and vessels, and one of the professors of the Theological Faculty was just looking for a quiet place where he could write a scholarly book. He was our first boarder, and besides, he said Mass in the morning and gave Benediction in the evening. Whenever my husband met me alone these days, he said hastily: "Yes, we are lucky, and I wouldn't want it any other way."

But really—weren't we lucky? Never before had we been so close to each other in the family as now, or had seen, with such gratitude to God, the good qualities in the children's characters; not a murmur, not a reproach. After all, it would be thinkable that one or the other of the older ones might have mumbled something about lack of foresight or carelessness. Such accusations didn't even dawn on them. Never before had we had a priest in our midst, a chapel and the Holy Eucharist in the house. This was not just being lucky any more; this was a blessing!

I don't know which word to use now; was it funny, comical, or pathetic to watch the reaction of our rich neighbors? One of the worst things that can happen to a rich man seems to be the suspicion that you might want to borrow some of his money. Anticipating this grave danger, they have to prevent it by all means. So whenever they met my husband, they started talking about the bad times and how they didn't know how to make ends meet. Once Georg came home good and angry.

"Just think what happened."

"Here we go!" I thought as he walked to and fro in big striding steps, chewing his moustache.

"First I met Maxi." (One of the richest men in the countryside.) "Out of a blue sky he started to explain to me that even if his own brother were to ask him for a loan, he would have to refuse. 'In these times, you know,'" and he imitated Maxi's mournful tone of voice. "And a few minutes later," he continued, "I met Baroness K., and she said, almost disappointedly: 'I met your children the other day and I was astonished how well they look and how cheerful, and still so neatly dressed.' *Still*— I love that! Say—" and he stopped short in front of me. "Are those people crazy? And don't tell me again I'm lucky!"

"Yes, I do," and I kissed him in the middle of his angry mouth, "because you are. Very lucky, indeed. For all the money in the world you couldn't have found out who your real friends are, and now you know."

At this he had to laugh, and after you have once laughed, you aren't really angry any more.

A year later the house was full of people, young professors and students from the Faculty. Never before had we had so much fun and such interesting evenings. We didn't make much money from the boarders, but enough to meet the bills and to keep the big house going.

Seldom before had there been so much laughter, so many spirited discussions, so many worth-while people to meet. Professor D., our first boarder, had quickly become a very dear and wonderful friend. When his book was nearly finished, his publisher came to visit him, and stayed afterwards for a cup of tea in the library, where the fire in the fireplace was roaring. It was a miserably cold day in November. This was only the first visit of many, many to come. Otto Müller, the young publisher, was counted among our closest friends, and shortly all the writers, scientists, professors who came to visit him, landed finally in our house. What richness that brought into our lives, especially to the growing children. On such evenings I couldn't quite suppress a triumphant look at my husband who, to avoid hearing the dreaded word "lucky," put his hand soothingly on mine. "I see what you mean."

During all that time we had never stopped singing and making music together, much to the enjoyment of our house guests. The new chapel was a strong incentive to sing more seriously than ever before.

At Easter, 1935, Professor D. had to make a journey, and asked a priest friend to come and say Holy Mass in his stead. Afterwards at breakfast the young priest, whose name was Father Wasner, said: "You really sang quite well this morning, but . . ." and he explained in a few words several important things to us, and right then and there at the breakfast table, made us repeat a motet, conducting it from where he was sitting. None of us knew then just how lucky we were:

This was the birth of the

TRAPP FAMILY SINGERS.

"Never Again"

IT WILL be very interesting one day to follow the pattern of our life as it is spread out like a beautiful tapestry. As long as we live here we see only the reverse side of the weaving, and very often the pattern, with its threads running wildly, doesn't seem to make sense. Some day, however, we shall understand.

In looking back over the years we can discover how a red thread goes through the pattern of our life: the Will of God.

After the first Lent when my family had started to read the Gospel together and had since kept up this practice until it had turned into a habit, it became clearer all the time that this was the message Christ came upon earth to teach us. It is the heartpiece of our religion—of all religion—to do the Will of God.

And here we had found our guiding star which should lead us faithfully through all tempests into the final haven.

When Father Wasner found out that we were seriously interested in our home music, he came more and more often to join us. He proved to be an outstanding musician. A master on the organ, he also played the piano beautifully. But his most enticing charm was his way of making music simple and uncomplicated. What a joy it was to listen to his mellow voice when he sang the Lieder of Schubert, Brahms, and Hugo Wolf. And up to this very day we have never stopped admiring his vast knowledge of musical history and theory. He has never behaved like one of the great, who dwell in unapproachable light. He simply was full of music, and wherever you touched him, it came out.

What a wonderful summer! Father Wasner came every day, and singing turned serious now. With burning enthusiasm we plunged into deep waters. Motets and Masses by Palestrina, Lasso, Vittoria for the chapel, which we could never have tackled alone, we studied now under the magic guidance of a true musician. How that old music came alive, how we reveled in those ancient tunes!

These months still belong to our most precious memories. It was a time of first love, with all the flavor of being in love. This music welled up out of our hearts simply for pure love of music. At that time we sang because we had to, and nobody and nothing could stop us. We didn't need an audience. We didn't even want one. It would only have disturbed us. In the morning we sang for God alone, for His greater honor and glory during the divine service. In the evening we worked on madrigals, ballads, and wonderful ancient folk songs in settings by old masters, and we sang them to our hearts' delight outside in our park or in one of those mountain meadows overlooking the valley. Six hours spent like this was nothing at that time. We were intoxicated with music, drunk with the wonder of song.

On a memorable day in August, 1936, we were sitting together once more behind the screen of pines in our park. It was late in the afternoon, a Saturday. Everybody had stopped working and changed into Sunday clothes. Together we had said the rosary, a ritual which began our Sunday. During the week we had been working on the motet, *"Jesu Meine Freude"* by Bach. Now we sang the movements already memorized, the different verses of the chorale and that wonderful fugue. And then we sang over and over again our newest favorite of which we were especially proud because it was in English: "The Silver Swan" by Orlando Gibbons.

All of a sudden we were interrupted by a strange clapping of hands. A little bewildered, a little embarrassed, we went around the pine screen and met—who could describe our amazement?— the one whom we had so far admired from afar as Marschallin in *Der Rosenkavalier,* or as Fidelio—none other than the great Lotte Lehmann.

She had heard that we had let our house in previous summers and wanted to inquire about renting it; and now, just by chance, she had heard us sing, hidden behind the pines. Right there and then she proved how really great she was, for only the great ones can appreciate the achievements of others. With what enthusiasm, her beautiful eyes glowing with warmth, she talked about our "art," which made us blush and want to kiss her.

"Oh, children, children," she exclaimed over and over again; "you must not keep that for yourselves, that precious gift. You must give concerts. You have to share this with the people. You have to go out into the world; you have to go to America!"

Her genuine enthusiasm swept us off our feet. Not that we believed it. Even the poor boy in the fairy tale must have a hard time to believe it when he is suddenly told he is a prince.

"Don't forget," our illustrious guest continued, "you simply have gold in your throats!"

But the mere thought of having to step on a stage was so frightening that the gold—hidden in the depths of our throats anyhow —was no temptation at all.

"Tomorrow is the festival for group singing. You have to take part in that contest. You simply have to!" She coaxed earnestly and fervently.

Pale with anticipated stage fright, we insisted:

"N-n-n-n-no . . . n-n-n-n-never!"

My husband was aghast. He loved our music, he adored our singing; but to see his family on a stage—that was simply beyond the comprehension of an Imperial Austrian Navy officer and Baron.

"Madam that is absolutely out of the question," he said, and meant it.

"Oh, not at all," Lotte Lehmann said with a twinkle in her eyes. Finally, believe it or not, she had us all convinced. She herself placed a telephone call which, at this late hour, entered us in the contest.

After Lotte Lehmann had left with renewed expressions of her enthusiasm and best wishes for good luck for tomorrow, we woke up. What had we done? What had we gotten into? We were desperate, frantic, beside ourselves, miserable, disconsolate, depressed, broken-hearted—(these are all the words I can find in the *Thesaurus,* but they by no means exhaust what I want to describe as the state of our minds on that evening).

When our name was called the next afternoon and our turn had arrived, we stumbled onto the stage, stepping on our own and everybody else's feet, alternately blushing and growing pale, with a lump in our throats and a wild fear in our hearts. Why had we ever said "yes"? In a daze we sang our three numbers, and none of us can remember today which ones they were. A gentleman down in the audience tried hard to look mildly interested but perfectly detached. Poor Georg! Our only wish, when we were off-stage again, was to evaporate immediately, but we had to stick it out and wait for the awarding of prizes. As if in a fog, we saw the judges return from their conference. Silence settled over the vast crowd, and from afar we could hear the announcement:

"The first prize is awarded to the Trapp Family from Salzburg."

I remember that I didn't understand the meaning of these words, because I applauded wildly with the other people, looking blank. Upon instruction we had to go on the stage once more and receive our prize, a diploma signed by the Governor of Salzburg. More applause, more shaking of hands, smiles all around—but when my eyes searched around for my husband, his seat was empty. He had left in despair. Success or no success—the whole thing was a nightmare to him. It pained him bitterly to see his family on a stage, and only the solemn family resolution never, never to do such a thing again put his troubled mind at ease.

From Hobby to Profession

THE SUMMER with all its excitements had passed, and the family had settled down again to routine life.

It was a great day when I walked up the hill to Nonnberg with my little daughter Rosmarie holding onto my hand, entrusting the child to those sacred walls for schooling. Years before, I had torn myself away from this beloved spot with so much heartache, but in a way I had never altogether left. While carrying out the doctrine of the Will of God, I and my family with me, while living in the world, never became wholly a part of the world; and here I came back now with my dear little child. It was with tears and laughter that I stood in the parlor and handed the little one over to Frau Gertrudis, who had shared the times of waiting for the novitiate with me.

A few days later a telephone call came from the Salzburg radio station. It worked like a stone thrown into a quiet lake. The manager had heard us at that historic contest, and ever since, he had wanted us on the air.

"Please be up at the Mönchsberg next Saturday at four o'clock. Thank you." And he hung up. It didn't even occur to him that somebody might perhaps decline such an offer. Of course, we wouldn't go. We had said we'd never sing in public. During lunch I casually mentioned the call at the table.

"You said no, didn't you?" asked Georg rather anxiously.

"He didn't give me any time. He just told me and hung up. But I'll call right after lunch."

"But, Mother, perhaps it is the Will of God that we sing on the radio," said Hedwig. She meant to tease her father. But was it a joke? How did we know? The fact that we resented it so fiercely ourselves, that we didn't *want* to appear in public, that we loved our privacy more than anything—did that mean that we could act accordingly? We had to admit that there was absolutely nothing wrong about singing over the air; the opportunity had been brought to us from the outside; our music might bring joy to many people all over Austria—and what could be said against it? —simply that we didn't want to do it. That didn't seem enough reason, even Georg said with a deep sigh; and to our own great astonishment, we found ourselves on Saturday at four o'clock at the studio on the Mönchsberg.

Kurt von Schuschnigg, Chancellor of the Austrian Republic, was a very busy man. He rarely had time to spend with his radio. Once in a great while he turned it on. This time, I am told, he listened, fascinated: a small choir sang from Salzburg. He had never heard any of their selections before, but ardent music lover that he was, he was entranced by this beautiful music. A thought flashed through his mind. There was a great solemn reception to be given by the Chancellor for all national and foreign dignitaries, the diplomatic corps and military authorities—his first public appearance since the recent death of his wife. For the entertainment he had engaged the Vienna Philharmonic Orchestra, and ever since, had looked for another artist, something out of the ordinary. Now here it was, and the Chancellor pushed a button and wanted to know the whereabouts of that singing group, whose voices were still coming to him over the air in Bach's "Hymn of Thanksgiving." And out of the enthusiasm of the moment, he sat down and wrote to that Trapp Family in Salzburg, inviting them for his State affair.

One doesn't get a letter from the Chief Executive every day. Immediately the envelope made us curious. A deep silence followed, after Georg had read the letter aloud. A pained expression came over his face.

"That doesn't mean that we have to accept, does it?" and he looked pleadingly at me.

"Of course not," I wanted to say. But, "I don't know," I did say.

And again we went through the same agonizing procedure to find out what was the Will of God in a situation where your own wishes and likings point sharply in one way. What could we possibly say against it? There was nothing wrong, not even undignified. Together with the Vienna Philharmonic Orchestra, we would be in the best company. This invitation from the Chancellor should perhaps even be looked upon as an honor instead of as a bother. Again, the only thing against it was that we didn't want to. That settled it. On the appointed day we stood in front of an illustrious audience, having been introduced by the Chancellor himself, and sang. The applause was very warm, the interest, great. "That was something entirely different," we heard all through the evening.

I noticed a gentleman who was talking enthusiastically over there in the corner with my husband and Father Wasner, champagne glass in hand. Was it the champagne? Never shall I know, but I learned that we were going to give a public concert in the Kleinen Musikvereinssaal two months hence.

Now our singing evenings at home turned into rehearsals, our hobby changed into a profession.

On the appointed day we arrived at the ancient building which housed the large, the medium, and the small auditoriums. Rows and rows of cars were parked outside. All those people couldn't possibly have come for us! No, they hadn't. There was a sensational attraction, a guest from faraway America, a world-famous Negro contralto, Marian Anderson, giving a concert in the big hall. The whole press had turned out; and during intermission, as they were there already, they casually looked into the small hall to see what was going on. The next morning we read in the newspapers that they had all enjoyed immensely the first concert ever given by the Trapp Family. And so had the audience. A little bit in a daze, a little embarrassed, a little bashful, and already a little proud, we received congratulations afterwards in the artists' room. Slowly, slowly, Georg lost the intense feeling that he was sitting on the dentist's chair while he listened to his family from among the audience; and when somebody said, "You really should sing during the Festivals in Salzburg," he even smiled instead of getting excited.

It was the highest dream of every artist all over the world to be allowed to give a concert during the Salzburg Festivals. But there were many sopranos and basses, tenors, violinists, pianists, so they had to wait their turn patiently—maybe until next year. But there was only one singing family anywhere around, and this was not a concert; it was a feast. In the first row sat Lotte Lehmann with her husband! During the intermission people stormed backstage, and at the end of the concert managers came from practically all

European countries with contracts and invitations. Lotte Lehmann kissed us and was proud of us, and we were truly happy. We bought a scrapbook and pasted in the criticisms from Vienna and Salzburg and the picture of Lotte Lehmann and us. Then we put the contracts, to which one from an American manager had been added, into a drawer and retired into private life. For us this was the end of our concert activities.

Little did we know that it was the beginning.

Those ladies and gentlemen from France, Holland, Belgium, England, Italy, Denmark, Sweden, and Norway had not been joking. Early in September we heard from them that their respective countries were expecting us with great anticipation.

Now it became clear that what had started in a playful way, was growing into a serious activity. There seemed to be a definite plan behind it all, leading to some distant goal, which we could not perceive as yet.

A European concert tour, the possibility of showing our children the beauty of God's world and the wonders man has made: cathedrals and palaces, art galleries and museums—it was exciting and breathtaking. At first it all seemed impossible with the children in school and Father Wasner teaching at the Seminary and editing a newspaper. In such moments this is a most consoling thought: only one thing at a time can be the Will of God. If He wants us to act in a certain way, He has to help us with the obstacles. He always does—we can count on it.

The difficulties melted away like snow in the April sun. Rupert, who had started his medical studies at Innsbruck, and Werner, who was in practical training for agriculture, could arrange a few weeks' absence; Father Wasner, with permission readily given by the Bishop, found a substitute for all his activities; friends of ours, a married couple, would take care of house, little children, and guests. Even the order of the invitations worked out ideally, except for the Scandinavian countries. These had to be postponed for another year.

In preparing the programs for this first concert tour Father Wasner went to archives and libraries to copy unpublished works. There he discovered that the ancient masters had written great music to be played on the instruments of their time, the recorder, viola da gamba, and spinet, the forerunners of our flute, string quartet, and piano. Instrument makers in Munich and Kassel made for us a set of violas in different sizes, a spinet, and also a set of recorders: soprano, alto, tenor, and bass recorders. Very serious practicing started now.

In December we started out. We sang in Paris, London, Brussels, and The Hague. Everywhere an enthusiastic audience greeted us. Newspapers talked about the musical miracle of a singing family. People said how different it was from any other concert, and managers talked about return engagements; we saw the cathedrals and castles, the galleries and museums and the wonderful countryside of France, England, and Belgium; the second part of the trip took us to Italy. We sang in Milan and Turin, in Assisi and Rome. If sight-seeing had been interesting before, now it became really breathtaking. Besides those unique treasures of art stored up in the churches, palaces, and galleries in Italy, there were also many holy places to be visited. It was a combination of concert tour, sight-seeing trip, and pilgrimage.

We sang for kings and queens; we had an audience with the Holy Father, Pope Pius XI, and sang for him the *"Ave Verum"* by Mozart; we spent ten happy days in Assisi in the steps of Saint Francis. We walked on the Via Appia, whose cobblestones had been trodden by the feet of the Apostles, into Rome, and knelt in the Colosseum and the Catacombs. These weeks were filled to the brim with happy and holy excitement, and success—success everywhere. We were "a rising star on the musical horizon."

A great thing we had learned on this trip: that music is an international language which speaks from heart to heart and doesn't need the medium of a human tongue. Whether our audience was French, English, Dutch, or Italian—in our music we could talk to them across the barrier of a foreign language. We sang to them what our hearts were so full of: "God is so good! And He is so good to us all! Let us forget all quarreling in the world and be happy together. Let us love one another as He loves us!"

Music—what a powerful instrument, what a mighty weapon!

And the Lord Said to Abram . . .

"And the Lord said to Abram: Leave thy country and thy people, go out of thy father's house and come into the land which I shall show thee." (Gen. 12, 1)

IT WAS March 11, 1938. After supper we went over to the library to celebrate Agathe's birthday. Someone turned on the radio, and we heard the voice of Chancellor Schuschnigg say:

"I am yielding to force. My Austria—God bless you!" followed by the national anthem.

We didn't understand, and looked at each other blankly.

The door opened and in came Hans, our butler. He went straight to my husband and, strangely pale, said:

"Herr Korvettenkapitän, Austria is invaded by Germany, and I want to inform you that I am a member of the Party. I have been for quite some time."

Austria invaded. But that was impossible. Schuschnigg had said it wouldn't happen. He had said in public that Hitler had promised not to invade Austria. It must be a mistake, a misunderstanding. But the voice of this very same Chancellor had just announced: "I am yielding to force."

At this moment the silence on the radio was broken by a hard, Prussian-sounding voice, saying: "Austria is dead: Long live the Third Reich!" Then it went on to announce the title of a Prussian military march.

We all went into the chapel silently. And there in the dark you could hear only sobbing and deep sighs. It was as if we had read, without warning, the death notice of a dearly beloved one.

Still in a daze, we gathered together. The birthday was forgotten. We followed Georg's eyes. He was looking at the flag from his submarine, which was hanging above the mantelpiece, surrounded by pictures and trophies from old Austria.

"Austria," he said, and tears choked his voice, "you are not dead. You will live on in our hearts. This is only a sleep. We promise you to do all we can to help you wake up again."

No eye remained dry. The little girls, huddled in my arms, cried loud and bitterly. They didn't understand what it was all about, but the young hearts felt the weight of the hour.

Georg went to the telephone, and I heard him say:

"I want to send a telegram. The address is: Dr. Kurt Schuschnigg, Bundeskanzleramt, Wien. The message: May God bless and protect you always."

I doubted very much whether by this time any telegram would reach our Chancellor, but still I was glad and proud of Georg.

"Listen," said Werner, opening a window, and in came, in rich, heavy waves, the sound of numerous bells. We could distinguish the Cathedral, Nonnberg, Saint Peter's, the Franciscans, but there must have been many more. Father Wasner called a priest friend of his, inquiring about the bell-ringing. The Nazis were marching into Salzburg. A Gestapo man with a gun was supervising the ringing of the bells in every church.

"Close the window, it's cold," said Georg. But I knew it wasn't because of the cold; he didn't want to hear the bells. But what was that? The window was closed and the bells seemed to grow louder—really—they came out of the radio now, and before we could catch our breath, the sharp voice announced:

"Now we want the whole world to hear how the people in Austria greet their liberators. They rush to their church steeples, and all the bells in the whole town of Salzburg are ringing out their grateful joy."

Such a mean lie! Werner jumped up, his eyes flashing, his fists clenched. But what could you do? Nothing.

This was only the first lie in an endless chain. From now on we led a double life. Whatever we had lived through during the day, we listened to in an altogether different description in the evening over the air—until you wanted to take an axe and smash the radio; and that is about all you could do.

"Will you do me a favor and promise me something?" asked Georg next morning. "Please don't go into town for the time being."

"All right," I answered.

He was worried enough as it was, and I didn't want to increase his anxiety.

The very next morning the children coming back from school told me that the whole town was like a lake of red, huge flags with the Swastika practically covering the fronts of the houses all over the place. The next thing we learned from friends downtown was that every house owner had been told how many flags to put out, what size, and where. Over the radio the world was informed that not even during the Festival time had Salzburg looked like that. "The happiness of its inhabitants is insuppressible."

Lunch. Supper. Nothing had changed outwardly. Everybody was sitting at his usual place, Hans coming and going with plates and dishes, serving noiselessly. Hans was much more than a very good butler. After the loss of the money, he had stayed on at a much smaller salary. He seemed to be as genuinely attached to us as we were to him. All the children were very fond of him. He was their confidant. He always seemed to have a solution to their problems. Now there was a strained expression on his face as he walked around the table.

He knew why Georg had said so pointedly at the beginning of the meal: "I think we are going to have a late spring this year. Have you seen any bulbs coming out in the garden?" and then continued to talk about flowers and the weather. He knew that we didn't trust him any more, that we were afraid of him. He didn't belong to us any longer; he belonged to the Party.

And this was only the beginning. Soon you didn't know whom you could trust. You might rush in to see a friend and blurt out your indignation, only to discover by his raised eyebrows and strange silence that he didn't share your opinion. That was bad, because at the same time he might feel it his duty to inform the authorities about your lack of understanding.

The town looked like a military camp, German soldiers on every street corner and, so the radio told us, the German Army advancing towards Vienna, wildly greeted by the people of every village or town through which they came, Austria in an ecstasy of jubilation. To this we didn't pay much attention. We knew by now how that worked. It only hurt to know that the whole world was listening to these broadcasts, and the people in foreign countries did not yet know . . .

Weeks passed, and it was as if you were living at the open tomb where they had buried your dearest one. We hadn't known until then how strong the love for your homeland could be. When we learned that it was forbidden by penalty of death to sing the Austrian anthem, which had to be replaced by the Nazi song; that it was a "must" order from now on to use as the sole and only greeting, "Heil Hitler," and nothing else; that Austria was wiped off the map, incorporated into the Third Reich, that its very name had disappeared, even in its compound forms, and been replaced by "Ostmark," "Niederdonau," "Oberdonau"—each time a dagger seemed to go through our hearts.

We learned that the love for your homeland comes even before the love for your family. Automatically we went through our days. No one was concerned about anyone, but all of us were deeply concerned about Austria and her fate. Our cheerful house of song had become a house of mourning.

For days there had been a great anxiety in the air: would there be war? The last request of the old Chancellor had been: no shooting. After all, when the big brother, eighty million strong, falls upon the little one, with only six million, what good does it do to fire a few guns?

Easter had passed, but the "Alleluia" had not resounded in our hearts this year.

May came. The ban had been lifted from me. I could go into town. But after the first time I had had enough. I was on my bicycle and wanted to go shopping. At least five times I got caught. The new government had made every other road a one-way street, and one wasn't allowed any more to go this way or that way. The places and streets had new names, too, and with all that superabundance of red material hanging down from the houses—you simply didn't recognize your own home town any more.

One day in May a tall gentleman came in a Gestapo uniform and informed us that the Führer would visit Salzburg, and every single house or dwelling must be hung with flags.

"I have been told that you do not even own a Swastika flag. Is that true, Sir?"

"That's correct," answered Georg.

"May I ask why?"

With a dangerous twinkle in his eye, Georg replied:

"Because it's too expensive. I can't afford it."

Shortly the gentleman returned with a big package, a brand-new, huge red flag with a black spider in the middle.

"Oh, thank you," said Georg.

"Won't you put it up right away?" inquired the zealous one.

"I don't think so."

"And why not?"

"You know, I don't like the color. It's too loud. But if you want me to decorate my house, I have beautiful oriental rugs. I can hang one from every window."

I didn't have a quiet minute for days after this interlude, trembling whenever the telephone or the doorbell rang. Amazingly enough, nothing happened.

How long would this go on? The children came home from school saying that this or that old teacher wasn't there any more, new teachers, even a new principal taking their places.

"This morning we were told at the assembly that our parents are nice, old-fashioned people who don't understand the new Party. We should leave them alone and not bother. We are the hope of the nation, the hope of the whole world. We should never mention at home what we learn at school now."

"Mother, listen what I learned in school today," and little Rosmarie's eyes looked frightened. "The teacher said Jesus was only a naughty Jewish boy Who ran away from His parents. That's all. That isn't true, is it, Mother?"

"Mother, the teacher wants you to see her in school," announced Lorli, the proud first-grader. I went the next day. The teacher, a strange lady, was quite friendly.

"You must do something about your little girl, or you will get into serious trouble soon," she warned me. "When we learned our new anthem yesterday" (how hard it was not to wince visibly at the word "our") "she just didn't open her mouth. When I asked her why she didn't sing with us, she announced in front of the whole class that her father had said he'd put ground glass in his tea or finish his life on a dung heap before he would ever sing that song. Next time I will have to report this"—and her eyes, all of a sudden, didn't look friendly any more. I thanked her and went home with a heavy heart.

That same evening I took Lorli on my lap and tried to explain:

"Look, Lorli. You must never, never, do you understand, never tell anything at school what you hear at home. If you do, Father will be put in a concentration camp, and Mother will be put in a concentration camp, and so will Rupert and Agathe and all your sisters and brothers. We'll all be put in a concentration camp if you don't keep silent. Do you understand me?"

Wide-eyed, she listened and nodded.

A few days later: "Mother, the teacher wants to talk to you again."

"What is it now?" I thought, and went with heavy misgivings.

"Madam, this is the last warning. When we practiced our new greeting, 'Heil Hitler,' your little girl wouldn't raise her hand, and pressed her lips together. I had to ask her repeatedly what that meant, and then she only answered, 'Mother said if I tell in school what is going on at home, Father will be put in a concentration camp, and Mother, and all my sisters and brothers!' Madam, you will understand that this is going too far."

Yes, I understood. I went home and told Georg.

"Well," he said, "only a few more weeks to go until the end of the school year. Don't forget, we are right in the middle of an unbloody revolution. Things like this are expected to happen. They will calm down. By next fall everything may look different."

So said his lips, but his eyes betrayed him.

We went to visit some friends. First we parents were alone together and carried on a whispered conversation, emptying our burdened hearts. All of a sudden our host beamed and exclaimed, somewhat unnaturally, it seemed to me:

"What a lovely performance that was last night. I have never heard 'Fidelio' so well sung."

I didn't know what to make of it and felt a little stunned, when I heard a young voice behind me say:

"Yes, Father, I think so, too."

Oh, I hadn't noticed, the youngsters had come into the room. From now on the topic of conversation was "Fidelio," but even that got painful very soon.

"Bruno Walter will never be allowed to conduct Aryan music again because he is a Jew."

How strange these words sounded from the lips of an eleven-year-old!

"It's better to stay at home," said Georg that night, and for the first time I noticed that he looked old and worn.

School was over, and Rupert came home from the university. The stories he had to tell didn't cheer us up, either.

The "thousand-mark barrier" had been lifted with the invasion, of course. Since little Barbara had announced her coming, I was not feeling so well. My old ache in the back flared up worse than before. There was a good specialist in Munich, and Georg wanted me to see him. So we set out one day for Munich. Had I known what the doctor was going to say, I most certainly would never have gone.

"Your wife cannot have another child," he informed my husband; "at least, not until the kidneys are back to normal. They are both badly infected."

"But what can we do now?" and Georg sat down on a chair as if his knees had grown weak. He looked frightened, and I was getting mad at the doctor. I tried to motion to him behind Georg's back.

But he didn't even look at me, and simply said in a very insistent tone of voice:

"The child has to be removed, of course, immediately."

This made me indignant.

"What do you mean, 'of course'? That is not 'of course' at all. On the contrary, it is absolutely out of the question—we are Catholics, you know."

Now the doctor seemed seriously worried.

"The child won't be born alive; this much I can tell you. I just hope," and he turned to Georg, "I shall be able to save the life of the mother. She has to go to bed and stay there and keep a very strict diet," and he started scribbling things down. "Keep her absolutely quiet—no excitement—the blood pressure is very high."

Outside in the street I said: "I don't believe a word of what he said; but if it makes you feel better, I'll keep to the diet until Barbara is here."

"But think of the other two times," and Georg looked so worried. Yes, it was true. Since Lorli's birth in 1931, I had lost two children for the same reason, the bad kidneys.

"All right, I'll do everything the doctor said: keep quiet, diet, and all. That's all we can do at the moment—besides pray. Oh,

Georg, let's pray especially hard that God may let us keep this little one, our Barbara!"

In the midst of all his worries Georg had to smile when he heard me talk with such assurance of "Barbara." From the first moment we had known about it, we had decided that this child would not have five or six or more first names like the others, but only one single one: Barbara. Saint Barbara in heaven would have to recognize the fulfillment of Georg's promise way back, and from then on she could send boys into this family.

"And now I would like to do something," I said. "Let's go and see the 'House of German Art.'"

That was a new picture gallery only recently opened in Munich at the edge of the English Garden, and there was a lot of talk about it. The Führer, who surprised his people every so often with new talents, had taken care personally of the selections for this exhibition. He had also chosen the color of the geraniums around the building, and in the opening speech which, of course, had been broadcast, he had stated that in the past the German people hadn't produced any art—until he had inspired them; but from now on they would look to it, and they would soon be leading all nations.

We went and saw for ourselves. This exhibition proved all kinds of things, but not what the Führer had indicated. There wasn't a single masterpiece among the selections, but there were many pictures of such crude reality that my heart ached when I saw one school class after the other, girls and boys, walking through. We learned that it was obligatory for all schools to visit this exhibit. Then we came to the most famous picture in the House, for which a whole wall was reserved: the Führer in mediaeval armor on horseback, sword in hand. In passing by this picture, one was obliged to salute it with raised arm, pronouncing enthusiastically: "Heil Hitler." Georg didn't want to pass by; he didn't want to see any more. He had had enough. Seeing me linger behind, he said impatiently and dangerously loud:

"What are you hanging around here for—come, let's go."

I certainly wasn't hanging around for the pictures, but I had discovered something.

"Georg," I said, "I smell something: frankfurters and beer," and I sniffed, looking searchingly around.

And beyond, there was a sign: "Restaurant." Never before in

any of the great galleries of renown in Vienna, Paris, London, or Rome, had we seen this combination; but when you thought a little bit, you could understand the point. In the Louvre or in the art museum in Vienna, Palazzo Pitti in Florence, a restaurant wouldn't have made any money at all, since the works of Raphael, Rembrandt, Michelangelo, and Fra Angelico made your forget hunger and thirst. This was altogether different in the "House of German Art."

Frankfurters and beer or a cup of coffee and cake were a most necessary antidote to what you had just gone through. Gratefully we followed the smell and found ourselves in a very elegant, rather crowded restaurant. We were shown to a table, and very soon we noticed two things. Although the big room was full, there was only a distant murmur to be heard, everybody was talking low, and the unavoidable smoke lingering in all other eating places in Munich was absent here: no one smoked.

When the waiter came to take our order, he whispered: "Have you seen him?"

"No," I said, and then, "whom?"

"But look! The Führer! At the next table!"

And so it was. At the very next table sat the Führer of the German people, surrounded by six or eight S.S. men. They all were drinking beer, and Hitler, raspberry juice, because one of his innumerable virtues was that he didn't touch alcohol, nor did he eat meat. For the next forty minutes we had a first-class opportunity to look at the Messiah of the Third Reich. Among his body-guard there must have been a very good joker, because every few minutes they all roared with laughter in a way which is not accepted as good manners among educated people. The gayest of all was "he." He slapped his thigh and roared so heartily that twice he started to choke. He rose from his chair, only to fall backwards in helpless merriment. His thin hair fell over his forehead, his arms waved in the air, his world-famous moustachelet quivered—he was an embarrassing sight. If one hadn't been so deeply impressed by the fact that this man held the fate of many millions in his fingers, one wouldn't have looked a second time at him. He seemed to be very, very ordinary, a little vulgar, not too well educated—no resemblance to the hero in silver armor on the wall. What a precious opportunity, though, to watch him so closely at the moment when he seemed to be perfectly at ease! One couldn't stand it too long, however. Knowing who he was, it became too depressing.

Outside again, we walked in the English Garden, a very large and very beautiful park. After a long silence Georg remembered the mail in his pocket and started to open it. Suddenly he stopped, and very excitedly handed me a letter.

"Read this!" In very polite words the Navy Department inquired whether Commander Trapp would be interested in taking over one of the brand-new huge submarines and establishing a submarine base "eventually" in the Adriatic Sea, and later in the Mediterranean. Georg was speechless. His own submarine had been forty feet long, had leaked, and could hold only five men. These new ones—it was like comparing Noah's Ark with the *Normandie*. He started walking fast. I could hardly keep up with him. We were on the main avenue of the park lined with red-flowering chestnut trees in full bloom.

As Georg stormed full speed towards the other end, he said: "Listen. This is the chance of a lifetime; this really is. Just think what can be done with such a submarine. It is perfectly incredible. I am sure you could even cross the Atlantic without refueling!" And, chewing his moustache, he reached the other side of the park, firmly convinced. "Of course one has to accept such an out-of-the-world offer."

We turned back, and suddenly he said: "But what do they mean, 'eventually in the Adriatic Sea and later in the Mediterranean'? They must be pretty sure of going there some day. That means war. I can't run a submarine for the Nazis, can I? Of course not. It's out—it's absolutely out."

We were on the other side and turned again. On the way back: "But perhaps it's wrong not to do it. After all, he is the head of the State now. I am a Navy man. This is really the only thing I know and can do well. Perhaps this is the Will of God!" and he waved the letter. "Everybody is warning me to think of the future of my children, which is gravely endangered, the way we live now. . . ."

Once more we turned. I knew there was nothing I could say. This is one of the times when a man is all alone—just he and his God. It is one of those dangerously precious moments when he has to say yes or no, and only he can make the decision. I prayed silently and fervently: "Thy Will be done."

Our speed slowed down remarkably. We were heading for the exit of the park. Before we reached it, Georg came out of deep, deep thinking and, a little woefully, he said: "No, I can't do it. When I took my oath on our proud old flag, I swore: 'With the Emperor for God and my country.' This would be against God and against my country. I'd break my old oath." With this we went to the station and home.

Rupert was waiting for us at the train. Our brand-new doctor! Two days before the invasion Rupert had graduated from medical school.

"Look what I've got here!" he said, and handed a letter to his father.

"Another letter!" I thought, and closed my eyes. I could hear my doctor: "Absolutely no excitement." Barbara had chosen the wrong moment, of this I was sure. This letter was also an inquiry. Would Rupert be interested in coming to Vienna and taking a responsible position in one of the big hospitals? They needed doctors.

Of course they needed doctors. All during the last months they had in a most shameful manner persecuted, killed, and imprisoned thousands of Jews in all parts of the country, and now they were short of doctors, lawyers, dentists; no wonder the young fledgling doctors advanced in a hurry.

"Of course, I can't accept," Rupert said. "The only question is how to word it politely enough. They'll be quite offended. I'd have to consent to all kinds of treatments and manipulations which I am not allowed to as a Catholic—and as a man. So far, I haven't used the Hitler greeting once, and I'd like to keep out of it."

"How do you intend to earn your living?" asked his father dryly, but also proudly.

A stubborn expression came into the young face.

"There must be a way somehow. It's worth trying."

And that matter was settled.

The week was not yet over when a long distance call from Munich stirred us up from our quietude for good. The Trapp Family had been chosen as representatives from the Ostmark (formerly Austria) to sing for Adolf Hitler's ("our beloved Führer") birthday.

That meant that we were made. From then on we could sing morning, noon, and night, and make a fortune.

Hans had his day off. After Rosmarie and Lorli had been put to bed, Georg called the family together. He told them about the offers he and Rupert had received and about the great temptations of both, and also the very glamorous possibilities opening up before our eyes through this flattering invitation to us as singers: and what did the family think about it?

After the first minutes of stunned silence, voices were heard.

"Will we have to say, 'Heil Hitler' then?"

"Will we have to sing the new anthem on the stage?"

"How about Father Wasner? The Nazis don't like priests."

"In school we are not permitted to sing any religious songs with the name of Christ or Christmas. We can hardly sing any Bach for that reason."

"I am sure we'd have a tremendous success in Germany with our program, but will it be possible to keep up our ideas and remain anti-Nazi when we take their money and their praise?"

Silence.

"We just can't do it."

"This will be the third time we say no to a distinguished offer on the part of the Nazis. Children," and their father's voice didn't sound like his everyday one, "children, we have the choice now: do we want to keep the material goods we still have: this our home with the ancient furniture, our friends, and all the things we are fond of?—then we shall have to give up the spiritual goods: our faith and our honor. We can't have both any more. We could all make a lot of money now, but I doubt very much whether it would make us happy. I'd rather see you poor but honest. If we choose this, then we have to leave. Do you agree?"

As one voice came the answer: "Yes, Father."

"Then, let's get out of here soon. You can't say no three times to Hitler—it's getting dangerous."

The next morning saw my husband and me at the Archbishop's palace.

"Your Excellency," he said, "this is a secret, and I ask you to treat it as such. My family and I have decided to leave the country secretly very soon. Father Wasner has become like one of us. He is in the same dangerous position we are, since we declined the offer to sing for Hitler and he is our conductor. Furthermore, as editor he has stuck out his neck many times. It might be wise for him to leave, too. We have nothing to offer him. He would have to share whatever will be our part. We go—for better, for worse— but we want to extend to you the invitation to send Father Wasner along with us if you so see fit, for we have asked him, and he is agreeable."

The Archbishop had become very, very serious. After a long while he got up and said:

"Will you please come again tomorrow for the answer?"

When we were ushered into the large audience hall at the Archbishop's palace the morning after that, where many portraits of former Princes of the Church greeted one from the walls, the door opened and in came His Excellency in his red cassock.

"I haven't talked to anyone, nor asked anybody's advice. I only prayed for light; and now I tell you this *as your Bishop*: It is the Will of God that you leave now and take Father Wasner with you." Then the elderly gentleman raised his eyes and looked out through the window, where one could see the dome of the cathedral, and slowly he added: "It may be that some day this will prove of great value to this diocese."

Visibly moved, he gave us his blessing and left.

Once more their father assembled the whole family, little ones and all, Father Wasner included, and related what the Archbishop had said "as our Bishop." We all felt that herewith we were beginning a new chapter of our life, to which their father seemed to give the outline when he said at the end:

"We have now the precious opportunity to find out for ourselves whether the words we have heard and read so often can be taken literally: 'Seek ye first the Kingdom of God and His justice: and all these things shall be added unto you.'"

Part Two

Part Two

On the "American Farmer"

IT WAS September, 1938.

"And this is the *American Farmer*," said the friendly bus driver who had taken us to the docks in London, pointing to a rather small white ship.

"How many passengers will be on board?" Georg asked the steward who showed the Trapp Family to their cabins.

"Seventy, Sir. It's a nice number. I've been on big boats but I prefer this one. You get to know all your passengers. It's almost like a big family."

"How long will it take to reach New York?"

"Eleven days, Sir. We are a small boat, only seven thousand tons. But you'll enjoy your trip, I'm sure."

And we did, very much so. From the first day we felt the friendly spirit on board. The passengers were mostly Americans going home. Our cabins were close together, and in the dining room a large round table had been reserved for the Trapp Family.

"Children, I can't believe it," said Georg when we all met for supper; and with this he spoke for all of us; we couldn't believe that we were really on our way to America.

"I feel almost dizzy, so much has happened in so short a time," I said. "It all seems like a dream. Just imagine: six weeks ago today . . ."

"We left home for . . ."

"Mountain climbing in South Tirol, Italy," said Werner.

"Yes, and in order not to make anyone suspicious, we had to leave in our usual clothes; and now when people on the boat see our Austrian costumes, they want to know whether we are Dutch or Norwegian," said Hedwig laughing.

"Then came the anxious weeks of waiting," continued Rupert.

"What waiting?" Lorli wanted to know. The little one had followed our conversation, wide-eyed.

"Don't you remember, Lorli," Agathe explained to her little sister, "when we were in the mountains in St. Georgen, how we prayed every morning: 'Dear Lord, let us get safely to America'? You see, such a trip is very expensive, and we had no money. There is a man in America who wants us to give concerts there, so Father wrote to him and asked him to lend us the money for the trip and send us the tickets for the boat. That's what we were waiting for in St. Georgen."

"It's only a week since the tickets arrived," said Father Wasner. "It seems so incredible to me that I got the permission to go to Italy. Do you remember the feeling, Rupert, when we read in the newspaper that the very day after we all left, the border was closed, and nobody could leave the country any more?"

"Yes," said Rupert, "I remember. And how lucky we were, Father," and he turned to Georg, "that the Italian Government had not allowed your Navy pension to be paid outside of Italy. In that way enough back pay had accumulated to pay for our stay in St. Georgen and our tickets to London."

"I can't get over it," I said, "how nice it was of Mr. Wagner to send us the tickets."

After we left the English coast, we came into rough waters. The population in the dining room diminished overnight. Where were all those gay people chatting happily in many different languages, who had been enjoying last night's supper? At breakfast the very next morning the waiters in the dining room had hardly any work to do. I had come down with Georg, but the rest of the large round table which had been reserved for the Trapp Family remained empty. Right after breakfast I went around from cabin to cabin, and I found my poor children in all stages of wanting to be dead, the truest sign of seasickness.

"And you'll be next. You'd better lie down," said Georg, and looked at me worriedly. "By the way, how is Barbara?"

"Oh, just fine," I replied, withdrawing obediently to my cabin, which I shared with the little girls. Lemon-colored, they had been tucked away by their father in deck chairs. In spite of all prophecies of the doctor, Barbara didn't seem to have minded the excitement of the last months, nor my inability to keep to the diet and ed rest. She was supposed to come some time after Christmas, and she seemed to have decided to keep her date.

Back in my cabin, I went to bed as I had been told to, and waited to get seasick. For a very long time I sat there, paper cup in hand, but nothing happened. The boat was thrown around like a little ball. It moaned and cracked, it bent over from one side to the other, but my stomach seemed to be undisturbable. Nobody came, and I was getting bored. And hungry. When the gong sounded for lunch, I got up and placed myself as the lone representative of the Trapp Family at the large table. Georg, the other survivor, went from one cabin to the other, holding heads.

After three days the storm was over, and the deck became populated with greenish, hollow-eyed figures, who recovered speedily in the warm sun. The sea was now like a mirror.

It had become clear to me that we had to learn English, as in America all the people talked that language.

"All right. If I have to learn English, let's go!"

When my husband noticed my eagerness, he said teasingly:

"Do you know how you can learn English in twenty-four hours? You learn every hour one-twenty-fourth!"

This was about what I had in mind when, on the first clear, sunny day with people on deck, I came along, fortified with a pencil and a pad, listening a little while to the people talking. When I had discovered a group of English-speaking ladies and gentlemen, I approached them and said, with the politest inflection of my voice, the only phrase I knew:

"Please, vat is fat?" pointing to my watch.

"A watch," a gentleman answered, looking very friendly.

"E Votsch," I wrote down seriously. "And fat?" pointing to my ring.

"Ring," he answered.

"In English, please?" I asked.

"Ring," he repeated and smiled.

And this was the beginning of a unique English course. These people saw my serious desire to master their language in as short time as possible; they also understood the necessity, and they turned out to be perfectly wonderful about it. After we had pointed all over me, them, and the immediate surroundings, I filled my little notebook with such precious words as:

E Neiff	Dschuhss
E Spuhn	Refjudschie
Dschentlmän	bjutifull
Tscheild	ei
Manni	juh

Soon we proceeded from mere words to little phrases, like:

| Haudujudu | Haumatsch |
| Denkswerrimatsch | Hooatsdeteim |

One day dear Miss Powell, an English actress and a very lovel
lady, started to work on my pronunciation.

"You must not say 'vat,' darling," she told me. "Say 'Hoo-wat,'
and she brought forth a little mirror; "'Hoo-wen, hoo-were.'"

Most eagerly I "Hoo-wat-ed" into the little mirror a mile a min
ute, feeling very English.

One of the group, an American doctor, was a great wit. He als
took me alone for private lessons, and without warning, taught m
a lot of slang. With a serious face I wrote down: "If somebody
very excited and you want to calm him down, just say . . . If yo
want someone to leave the room quickly, just say . . ." I was deep
grateful to Dr. Johnson, but especially so some weeks later whe
situations arose in which his advice came in most handy.

Our Americanization process took on speed. Our friends invite
us for some real American drinks: ginger ale, Coca-Cola, and ro
beer. Ginger ale was fine, but Coca-Cola and root beer I decline
decidedly, after the first taste.

"That's too American," I protested.

We learned from Dr. Johnson the American currency: pennie
nickels, dimes, quarters, and bucks.

We learned our first American songs: "My Old Kentuck
Home," and "Old Black Joe," in new settings by Father Wasne
and we liked them very much. On the last evening there was
great party on board ship, and already I could understand a goo
deal of what people were talking about, thanks to our new friend
Victoria Powell; Dr. Johnson; Mary Hugo, a teacher from D
luth; and the nice American consul who was going home to Ci
cinnati from the South Seas. They say that the first impression
a person is the real one, and you will come back to it time an

again. This was our first meeting with the American people, and our impression was that they are kind, generous, and helpful.

When we woke up on the last morning, we were passing Nantucket, and soon we would be in New York. Everybody was at the railing and there, like a mirage, the tremendous towers of Manhattan emerged out of the fog.

This—was—America!

The First Ten Years Are the Hardest

BEWILDERED—completely bewildered—that's what we all we[r]
when three taxis spilled us out on Seventh Avenue at 55th Stre[et]
in front of the Hotel Wellington, us and our fifty-six pieces [of]
luggage: all the instruments in their cases, the spinet, four gamba[s,]
eight recorders, the big trunks with the concert costumes, and o[ur]
private belongings, one of the bags marked "Barbara von Trapp[,"]
containing all the dainty little things our babies had worn.

While I was standing on the sidewalk waiting for the unloadin[g]
I spelled slowly what the huge lighted letters said: "D-R-U-G-
S-T-O-R-E." It was the first time that I had met the word. [In]
Europe we didn't have drug stores. How relieved I felt!

"That's good," I thought. "I am living in the hotel with th[e]
drug store. I can never get lost in New York!"

The tallest houses in Vienna have five or six stories. When th[e]
elevator took us to the nineteenth floor, we simply couldn't belie[ve]
it, but rushed immediately to the windows and shudderin[g]
looked down into the deep gorge, at the bottom of which crawl[ed]
little cars and tiny men. That was the first thing we report[ed]
home: "and we live on the nineteenth floor!"

The friendly gentleman from our concert manager's office wh[o]
had helped us through the Immigration and installed us at t[he]
hotel left us now with a friendly, "See you tomorrow."

Our last meal had been lunch on board. It was around eig[ht]
o'clock and we were all hungry. But we were not on the bo[at]
any more, where we had just sat down to a full table three tim[es]
a day. The cruel question had to be raised now: How much mon[ey]
do we have? After all the pockets had been emptied and eve[ry]
nickel and dime from all twelve of us had been collected, it showe[d]
the fabulous sum of four dollars. That had to do for supper an[d]
breakfast, and tomorrow we would ask Mr. Wagner, our manage[r]

132

for some money in advance. The boys were sent downstairs with two dollars to buy bread, butter, and fruit. Fresh fruit had been scarce on board, but on land the fall is a good time to buy fruit cheaply, and so we feasted on quantities of apples, plums, pears, and grapes.

As we were all very tired from so much standing around and waiting, we soon went to bed. After putting our shoes outside the doors of our rooms, as was done in all European hotels, we retired, only to be awakened one by one by the night watchman, who informed us that our shoes most certainly would not be shined next morning, but they might not be there any more, and we'd better take them in. Funny.

Next morning I wanted my husband's hat ironed before he appeared at the manager's office in it. To my great astonishment I learned in the lobby that for this I had to go to a shoemaker's.

Georg and the boys brought back the startling news that their shoes had been shined at the barber shop!

What a strange country!

Now I went out to look for that shoemaker to straighten the hat. I went around the block and around another block, and around a third block, not paying any attention to the numbers of the streets. I didn't have to. Just in case I should get lost, I knew where I belonged. It hadn't occurred to me to remember the name of the hotel. I was so impressed by the fact that I lived in *the* hotel with the drug store. After quite some searching I found my shoemaker. The hat was ironed, but I discovered that I was completely lost. Never mind. I stepped up to the next policeman and said very politely:

"Dear Mr. Cop, where is hotel with drug store?"

To this very day I have a tender affection for those tall New York policemen, because this one got me back safely to the Wellington.

Then we went to see Mr. Wagner. The nice gentleman had come again to guide us. First we walked over to Sixth Avenue, which at that time had an elevated, also the first of its kind in our experience. I was deathly afraid, and clung tightly to Georg's arm when I had to cross the street with trains roaring over my head.

"The quickest way is the subway," and our friendly guide dived at once into a staircase, which obviously led under the street. This was really frightening. What a noise! On one side of the platform express trains thundered by, while on the other, locals came and went. The very air was in vibration, and I, simply rooted to the ground, decided not to take one single step in any direction. I was sure I would die there. Neither I nor Barbara could stand a second more of this. Then I found myself in the inside of a howling train, from which we were spat out a few stations farther along. When we reached daylight again, I was near tears.

"Georg," I pleaded, "promise me that we will never do that again."

But before he could do so, our guide had another good idea.

"This is Macy's, one of our largest department stores," he announced beamingly. "On the eighth floor they have a wonderful toy department. Let's take a quick look. The kids will like that."

And in the store we were, and for the first time in my life I was confronted with a staircase which moved by itself. First I stared at it, thinking this in itself was an exhibition piece; but when I saw people step on it and be moved upwards in front of my very eyes, I got an uncomfortable feeling, as though I were witnessing witchcraft. When invited, however, to take the fatal step myself, I most vigorously declined. Meanwhile, a number of people had gathered behind us. We were obviously blocking traffic.

"Go ahead, don't be silly," whispered Georg encouragingly. With a lump in my throat, I put out one foot hesitatingly, but when it touched that moving thing, I quickly drew it back as if I had been bitten by a snake. Now good-natured, kind-hearted Americans gathered around me, and good advice from all sides made the situation more embarrassing by the second.

Behind me my little girls giggled: "Look, Mother is afraid," and I wished I had never landed on this continent.

"Close your eyes, lady, and take a step."

This was the best advice given so far. Now I was on it. How would I get off? That is easier. The staircase just slides you off, whether you want to or not. And this repeated itself seven times: "Close your eyes and take a step." Seven times? Oh no! Up to this day whenever I have to use an escalator, I close my eyes and take a deep breath.

Finally we left Macy's, and were seated in Mr. Wagner's office; and the elderly gentleman with the round, pink-cheeked, apple face looked like a very nice grandpa. We thanked him again for sending us the tickets for the *American Farmer*. He most willingly let us have money in advance. The concert tour would start in a week. So far, he had eighteen dates from the forty promised. His diction was not so clear as Victoria Powell's, so I had difficulty in understanding him. But this I did understand when he said in parting in a very comforting tone and with a twinkle: "The first ten years are the hardest!"

My greatest worry had been: how to keep Barbara's presence concealed from the world. At home I had had Mimi, a seamstress in a near-by village, a smart little woman. To her I had confided my secret problem.

"Oh, that's very easy, Madame," she had said right away. "All you have to do is see to it that you are always a little fuller above than below. Then you will just look stout, that's all."

"But, Mimi, how can I possibly arrange that?" I had asked a little helplessly.

"Let me do that for you," she had answered somewhat cryptically, and told me to come again in a week.

On the appointed day she had presented me with three sizes of supplements to my upper width. Number 3 was perfectly enormous. Unbelieving, I glanced from the pinkish things on the table to Mimi, who nodded approvingly.

"Yes," she said, "I mean it. You put them on in due time. Number 3 will even take care of twins, and no one will ever get an inkling."

It was now September, and I was wearing Number 2. With a sigh of great relief, I noticed that the contraption seemed to work. Mr. Wagner didn't give the slightest sign of astonishment at finding me so portly. Three cheers for Mimi!

Very happy, with money in our pockets, we took our leave. No, thank you, we would not need a guide any more. We had learned how terribly simple it was to get around in New York. After Fifth Avenue comes Sixth, and Seventh; and the streets are not named after flowers, birds, trees, or famous people as they are in Europe, but they are numbered.

Now we were out for a really good meal. Months ago we had learned to read a menu from right to left; and whatever it said on the menu of the hotel dining room, which was fastened inside the elevator, it was too much. We discovered an eating place opposite the hotel called "Cafeteria." The prices were very reasonable, and the people who owned it were Chinese and very friendly. There we assembled three times a day. The limit we could each spend for lunch was thirty-five cents; breakfast, fifteen cents; and supper, fifty cents. But at that time, in choosing wisely, one could get plenty—except me. I was always hungry. I tried so hard to restrain my appetite because a glance in the mirrors and the show windows had shown me that I was slowly taking on the dimensions of a chest of drawers. But on that first afternoon I soon felt ravenously hungry again, and went out to look for some inexpensive food. In the window of a delicatessen it said: "Sandwiches five cents." The size of a sandwich in Europe is decided by the degree of elegance. The more elegantly you want to serve it, the smaller it will be, until it reaches the size of a silver dollar. Thinking of the size of an elegant European sandwich, I ordered ten. I had to wait a little while, and then a friendly girl came with a big tray holding ten American sandwiches! Ashamedly I must confess, I ate six.

Next morning we couldn't find Rosmarie and Lorli. They were in none of our rooms, they were not in the lobby—where could they be? After half an hour's frantic search, when we had almost reached the point of announcing to the police that they had been kidnapped, one of the bellboys came and notified us that they were riding up and down in the elevator.

"Yes, Mother," and Lorli's eyes sparkled, "up to the twenty-seventh floor. Now I can write to Susi, this is nine times as high as she lives!"

None of the people we had met on the boat lived in New York. We had no acquaintances and no friends, no letters of introduction to anybody. We discovered the New World by ourselves. We learned the difference between uptown and downtown. We found out that museums and galleries could be visited free of charge. We discovered the vast possibilities in a drug store, where on a Sunday, when everything else was closed, you could buy anything from pencils and stationery to hot water bottles, alarm clocks, and jewelry of any kind and description. We learned to sit at the counter with poise and order in the tone of an old-timer: "Ham on rye," or "Two soft-boiled medium."

Wherever we met fellow countrymen, we learned of true adventure stories. There was, for instance, the lady who wanted to buy cauliflower.

"How much?" she asked the grocer.

"Ninety cents," was the answer.

"What?" She was outraged. "Behold your cauliflower. I can become cauliflower myself for forty cents around the corner!"

(Such things happen when you take words from your own language and translate them into similar-sounding words in English, thinking they mean the same thing. The word for "keep" in German is *behalten,* and if we want to "get" something, we say *bekommen.*)

Another incident happened to a priest friend of ours. When he first arrived in this country, he went to a religious house.

The lay brother who showed him to his quarters asked:

"Is there anything else you would need, Father?"

"Well," said Father thoughtfully, "a set of new bowels every Saturday. Just hang them on the doorknob."

The lay brother seemed so startled by this request, that Father had to point to a towel in his room to illustrate his wish.

Every morning we walked through the ravine of 55th Street out into Fifth Avenue and over to Saint Patrick's Cathedral, which is as large as one of the largest cathedrals of Europe; but there on the corner of 50th Street, it was overshadowed by skyscrapers. After Father Wasner's Mass there, we walked back to the Chinese Cafeteria.

We needed a laundry. As with everything else, it was a question of money. One morning the boys, who had walked back from Mass a different way, told us triumphantly they had discovered the cheapest laundry in town, a Chinese man who asked six cents for a pound. We collected all our dirty laundry, the Chinaman came and smiled and nodded. Two days later he came back, and we couldn't believe our eyes. He must have boiled everything at once in one tub, and since one of our blue aprons was not color-fast, everything, every blouse, every white shirt, every handkerchief, was of the same deep blue.

We didn't want to take the little girls on the concert tour. We looked for an inexpensive boarding school. Mr. Wagner's office helped us. We found the Ursuline Academy in the Bronx for thirty-five dollars a month apiece. For the second time in my life, I took a trip on the subway, with fingers in my ears, eyes closed for entry and exit. When we left Rosmarie and Lorli in their new school, we felt sorry for them. They had grown up in the country surrounded by meadows and trees, and there in the Bronx there was only asphalt; not a single blade of grass was to be seen. But the Sisters were very nice and kind, and the children would learn English faster than we.

Once I wanted to visit the children and find out how they were doing; and in a transport of courage, I walked myself down to the subway. Although I had learned that there was more than one drug store, I had not learned that there was more than one subway line in New York. I also disregarded the warning signs: "Uptown—Downtown," and felt proud to see myself finally sitting in a fast train because, so I decided, that would bring me there quicker. When the train stopped for good and all the people got out, I learned that I was far away from the Bronx. The funniest thing of all was that the subway had been metamorphosed into an elevated, and instead of walking up to the street, I had to walk down. There I was completely forlorn. But again to my rescue—a policeman. This time he was sitting in a car.

"Dear Mr. Cop Inspector," I said confidently, "help! Children in school. Bronx. How come?"

This he couldn't possibly know, but he understood me perfectly.

"You want to go there? Come on, get in my car."

We drove and drove.

All of a sudden he turned around and said:

"Tunnel, river above."

I closed my eyes, and I'm sure I went pale. What a terribly dangerous place this New York was with elevateds, escalators, subways, and tunnels. He got me safely to my Bronx convent, and the New York policemen had another jewel in their crown.

This whole trip was a mistake. When my little girls saw me, they clung to me and didn't want to let me go, crying bitterly at the final farewell so that I could hear them for more than a block. It was heart-breaking.

We really didn't need any organized sight-seeing trip through New York. Every time we stepped out of the hotel it became a sight-seeing tour. There were, for instance, the fire escapes, those enchanting, winding stairs outside of the houses. The trolley cars and the buses were different from the ones at home. There were news stands with so terrifically many different papers and magazines, and the newspapers themselves of the size of sheets for a baby's bed. Enchanted, we watched men climbing on something like a throne and cute little colored boys falling over their shoes in a holy fury until they were as shiny as mirrors—and this right on the street! Why didn't the people all stop and watch? Well, and then the people! There were Negroes, men, women, and children. Oh, and what cute children! There were Chinese people— maybe they were Japanese, one didn't know. Most of them talked English, but we also heard Italian and German, Yiddish and Greek. And there was the climate. Although it was now October, it was hot and damp, quite different from Salzburg. Then there was the speed. What an experience to go down Broadway for the first time when the movies were over. What a noise, what light, what a rush; or to cross Fifth Avenue around noon, or Wall Street at five o'clock. All this first and most overwhelming sight-seeing in New York didn't cost much. It was thrilling and frightening—it was wonderful and terrible—these first steps into a new continent: *our* discovery of America!

While the others explored the city, finding places like the Public Library, Central Park, Radio City—Barbara and I preferred to stay home in the hotel. My mind was stubbornly set on learning English. I read every advertisement in subways, on buses, on street corners, and in elevators. I memorized the menus, and with the help of a small dictionary, started to read a copy of *The Reader's Digest.* I was envious of Father Wasner, who already read without a dictionary. Rupert was outrageously good. He had been presented by one of the ladies on the boat with a fat book, called *Gone With the Wind,* and he was already half through it. I wanted so badly to catch up with them.

I invented a method all my own, in which I wanted to apply what I had learned about one word to as many like-sounding words as I could find. This proved later to be fatally wrong, and it still haunts my English of today. For instance, I had learned: freeze— frozen. I wrote underneath in my precious little notebook: "squeeze —squozen," and "sneeze—snozen." Proudly I talked about someone being a "thunkard," explaining wordily that I had thought if drinking much makes a person a drunkard, so thinking much, like that professor I had in mind makes him a "thunkard." When I admired the tall "hice" in New York, I got quite offended because they seemed to overlook the logical similarity between "mouse— mice" and "house—hice." I talked about the "reet" of my teeth, feeling perfectly correct in doing so. Wasn't it "foot—feet," after all?

Especially is it bad if you translate the Bible literally. The effect was tremendous when I informed a group of people with whom I had come to talk in the lobby, that: "The ghost was willing, but the meat was soft."

But what a triumph you have after so much trouble and work, after so many unexpected fits of laughter, after hours of spelling and learning by heart, when one day the nice colored man in the elevator says to you:

"Ma'm, yo' English is getting better every day."

From then on you can hardly discover any trace of an accent in your speech. You feel rewarded for all the blood, sweat, and tears of the last weeks' English battle.

Then comes the great day when you feel like graduating. The man at the desk asks you sincerely and confidently:

"How many years did you study English before you came to this country, Madam?"

Mr. Wagner must have made a mistake when he said, "The first ten years are the hardest." He must have meant the first ten *days!*

Getting Settled

THE day arrived when a big blue bus with the inscriptions "Special Coach" and "Trapp Family Choir" quivered in front of the Hotel Wellington, swallowing the fifty-six bags and the ten members of the Trapp Family Choir. As we had no home in America, we had to take all our luggage with us. A friendly, broad-shouldered driver greeted us. Very soon he grasped the idea that his was the noble task of introducing us into American ways of thinking and living, as we were the greenest greenhorns he had ever driven over American soil.

He did a perfect job. From time to time he used to holler:

"Let me explain something to you!"

That was a warning which made everyone stop doing whatever he was doing whether it was eating, sleeping, reading, or merely looking out the window, and listen enraptured to an explanation such as, for instance: "This is the largest airplane factory in the world"; or, "Now we are coming into Kentucky—hillbillies and moonshine." Remarks like this were somewhat mysterious to us. In my little dictionary I could find neither "hillbillies" nor "moonshine," but somehow it was an impression of the State of Kentucky which stuck with me for years.

But all that came later. First the blue bus drove to Easton, Pennsylvania, up the steep hill to Lafayette College for our first concert. Mr. Wagner and all his office staff had come. All of a sudden we became conscious of the fact that this was not just another country—this time we had crossed an ocean; this was now a new continent, and tonight was the first concert. Would it be a success or a failure? These reflections made us more and more solemn, and when finally the great moment came and we had to step out into the footlights, we felt again as miserable and self-conscious as we had way back in Salzburg. But there was no Lotte Lehmann sitting in the first row. A thinnish applause greeted the bashful new-comers.

Applause! A whole book could be written about it. The innocent reader might think that applause is applause. How wrong he is! If he only knew how many shades of applause exist, and how finely the ear of the artist is tuned to it. There is the thunderous applause of the later years, when you come back to a hall which is packed with people who are looking forward to your return. How heartwarming and inspiring! There is the polite, thin applause, lasting not long enough to let you get to the middle of the stage to make your bow—the mild applause for the newcomer or begin-ner—not very helpful. There is the hardly audible applause de-livered by society ladies in gloves at morning musicales, and sustained by politely covered yawns. You don't care much because if you have advanced to morning musicales, you don't mind any more. There is the warm, lengthy, enthusiastic applause after a good concert from a sincere audience, demanding encores. That makes you forget your tiredness and makes your encores the best numbers of your program. There is the routine applause of well-educated people, the concert public, people whose ancestors had attended the goings on of Symphony Hall, Orchestra Hall, or Town Hall; who, while they applaud, mildly and steadily, gaze with raised eyebrows into their programs, questioning: "Who was that fellow Palestrina, or Vittoria, or Thomas Morley? We have never heard of them before, but it was quite nice." These are the staunch supporters of musical life, the ones who give a newcomer a chance.

Later you learn to accept applause as a challenge, and to work up a concert from the "thinnish" to the "enthusiastic" response—at all cost.

But that is later, and this was our first performance in the New World. In looking over the program now, we know: first, it was much too long; second, too serious. What helped us to perform the miracle, to reap at the end some really enthusiastic applause, must have been our wholehearted sincerity. The people in the packed auditorium simply couldn't help feeling, whatever they saw and heard on that stage—brilliance of performance or mistakes in stage presence—it was all a hundred per cent genuine. It came from the heart, and that's why *they* took it to heart. After each group when we came backstage, Mr. Wagner's face looked a little less tortured, and Georg finally even whispered:

"He said it's going fine."

But at the end of this evening we were perfectly exhausted. After a whole concert tour nowadays we are not so "out" as we were in Easton, Pennsylvania, on that memorable October day.

But you get *that* excited only once. Slowly it becomes a routine, the bowing and smiling, coming and going.

Very soon we found out that the concerts were not the hardest part of the evenings. That started with the receptions. The very word we learned to dread. We were lined up in a row, and people started to file by, murmuring their names and insisting that they were very glad to meet us, or that they had enjoyed every minute of the concert. You try very hard to meet each remark with a genuine smile and say something intelligent. After a few dozen times you have exhausted your meager vocabulary, and even the smile on your face freezes into a permanent wave. You forgot to change the rings from your right hand to your left, and you don't dare do it now, but regret bitterly this grave mistake. You wonder how many inhabitants Roanoke, or Springfield, or Lexington has. You start wondering whether these are all newcomers, or whether the first ones have lined up again and are coming for a second round of hand-shaking. You inhale deeply the fragrance of fresh coffee, and you become conscious of the queer varieties of ladies' hats. All of a sudden you feel a deep affection welling up in your heart for the one person whom you see approaching: the last one.

For a moment you look down on a limp member of your body which was once your right hand. The ordeal is over.

Georg especially hated that kind of torture with all his heart. I hardly dared look at him when, after a concert, the chairman of the Ladies' Committee would announce cheerfully:

"And now we have a little reception."

Who could describe my astonishment, however, when one evening as we were lined up as usual, I noticed a mischievous light in my husband's eyes after we had already greeted at least a couple of hundred ladies. He simply beamed and said something to each one. I had to find out, and moved closer and closer, until I had, all of a sudden, to use my handkerchief to suppress a severe attack of coughing. I had heard him say in our native tongue:

"376, 377, 378 . . ."

And each lady answered, quite flattered:

"Oh, thank you!"

He was counting them! When we finally met, coffee in hand, all he said, with a twinkle in his eye, was:

"611!"

Once we gave a concert in a small college conducted by Sisters in the south. It was their first concert, and Reverend Mother, a tiny, elderly nun, was nervous. She was bustling around backstage with eyes like a frightened bird. I felt sorry for her, and wanted to console her. Then it flashed through my mind: "If somebody is very nervous and you want to calm him down, simply say . . ."—and I said it as friendly and reassuringly as I could:

"Oh, Reverend Mother, please keep your shirt on."

She did.

Another time—this was in the middle west—we were invited to a Bishop's house. By that time we had learned that there are Bishops and Bishops. Some are informal and paternal, so that you can almost forget who they are and say, full of confidence, "Father." Some, however, can never quite take off the mitre, so to speak. They are Bishops every inch of them. There you meet all the dignity and authority of the Church. It is quite breathtaking. Such a one had invited us to dinner, and, of course, it was a formal dinner with speeches and so on. There were also his Chancellor, a few Monsignori, and other dignitaries, and, sitting next to the Bishop, I was exhausting my best English a mile a minute. After grace was said, on the way from the dining room into the library, the Bishop and I met in the doorway. Politely he motioned me to go first, but, of course, I knew better, and wanted His Excellency by all means to precede me. Motioning to each other, we caused a traffic jam. Then that same spark enlightened me (hurray for Dr. Johnson!). "If you want someone to leave the room quickly, just say . . ." And so, looking up into the Bishop's eyes, I said confidently and with my best enunciation:

"P-lease, Bishop—scram."

The effect on his entourage was absolutely petrifying, and only the Bishop's hearty laughter prevented some sure collapses.

It was in Roanoke, Virginia. We came back to the hotel rather late after the concert. Rupert, the gadget-minded, immediately turned on the radio in his room, and his blood curdled when he heard a voice announce that all New York was in an uproar.

Rupert notified Georg and Father Wasner. They told me. How terrible—our little girls were in the Bronx! We called the desk. They had heard about it, but didn't have any recent news. A long bad night followed. Next morning we read in the newspaper the explanation. It had only been an imaginary invasion from Mars, a play produced by Orson Welles, so realistically presented that people really got into a panic. But our little ones were safe in their convent.

It was now December, and I was wearing Number 3. The newspapers mentioned the "stately" mother, the "majestic" figure, but that was all. I avoided looking into mirrors or show windows, and was wondering whether it wasn't perhaps twins, and whether the other one would be a boy. It didn't occur to me, however, to ask a doctor. After all, I wasn't sick; not really, at least, because very swollen feet and a severe ache in the back I had learned to get used to.

Barbara and I had it a little harder each day of this tour. It was not exactly fun to be jostled for hours and hours in a bus, to change clothes several times each day before, during, and after concerts, to rehearse every morning and sing every evening, to climb in and out of the bus, to sleep each night in a different bed, and to eat those strange new kinds of food, such as mayonnaise on a pear (pooh!), or that funny coffee, a whole big cup full and only a drop of cream, when one was used to the opposite, a whole cup of hot milk with a little coffee added, very black; or ham cured with sugar, or melons with pepper and salt. On the other hand, it was absolutely impossible to procure for love or money a single bite of one of the special dishes for which I longed with my whole being. It seemed so silly, but often for hours and hours I would dream of Schinkensemmel, or Apfelstrudel. But Barbara and I didn't have time to pay too much attention to these little hardships.

Everything went along smoothly until a certain evening, the last one before reaching New York. We had given a concert in a very small town in Delaware. We had stopped at the one tiny hotel in the place, which was built alongside the railroad tracks. With no presentiment of what was to come, I said "good-night" to my family and went to my room, which was the only one on the fourth and top floor.

I had hardly fallen asleep, when I dreamt I heard a lion roaring. I tried desperately to run away, and it seemed as if I couldn't. In the moment of utter desperation I woke up. But what was that? Wide awake, I could still hear the lion, and his roar came nearer and nearer. I was scared to death. Now something terrific was right beside my bed, roaring and thundering. The whole house was shaking. My bed was shaking. Barbara and I were shaking, too. Then the noise faded away, and with a heart pounding loudly, I listened until everything was quiet. Just as I was about to settle down to sleep, the whole thing started all over again, coming now from the opposite direction. Now I was really quite frightened. I wanted to call for someone, but there was no telephone in the room, and besides, just that night I had forgotten to inquire the room numbers of my family.

And so the night crept on with a crescendo and decrescendo of the lion's roaring, and with Barbara and me becoming more and more frightened all the time. Toward four o'clock in the morning I felt an unusual pain. Now I became really alarmed. What if something should happen here and now in this lonely little hotel room?

In moments of extreme danger you become supersensitive. Out of the gray past pictures arise going way back to your childhood days perhaps, and you are able to understand voices which, in everyday life, you are too busy to hear. "Maria has helped—Maria will always help." Have you ever been in one of the famous pilgrimage churches in Austria, Italy, or France—in Lourdes, for instance? Have you seen there the hundreds of little votive pictures, crutches, silver hearts, waxen hands and feet—the words repeating themselves all over the place, scribbled on the wall, embroidered in old-fashioned style, painted simply or artistically: "Maria has helped—Maria will always help." Such places do not grow overnight. They are the result of the tears and prayers of the centuries. If you have knelt in such a house of prayer, if you have ever taken your troubles and worries there—when you are thousands of miles away, a grown-up person, all of a sudden the image of all this will come back to you in a moment of severe fright.

I sat up in bed straight, folded my hands, and said aloud:

"Dear Blessed Mother, help me. Let nothing happen to this child. I promise to bring her in my own arms to your chapel in St. Georgen, and a large candle, too."

How I wish that no one were too grown up to understand what inexpressible peace can settle down on a troubled heart. It is that peace which is promised to them who "become as little children." I lay back and fell asleep almost immediately, sleeping calmly and long into the next morning.

When I awoke, my entire family was assembled around my bed, looking weary after a sleepless night, and highly astonished to find me sleeping so soundly. They, too, had been disturbed by the roaring lion which, on investigation, proved to be nothing more than the trains between New York and Washington.

While passing through New York, we wanted to report to "Grandpa Wagner" how nicely everything had gone with the concerts. This was Barbara's eighth month, and by now I was convinced that anyone had to be unconscious, blind, deaf, and dumb *not* to notice "it." In the course of the conversation I remarked casually:

"Of course, I shall be happy when the baby is finally here."

The old bachelor jumped up as if stung.

"Whose baby?" he asked.

"Why—mine—" I said innocently.

The effect was tragic. He canceled immediately all of our remaining concerts, and our tour came to a sudden end right then and there. He really had had no idea—wasn't that too bad! What a blow! Fewer concerts meant less money, and we needed every cent.

What next?

A little depressed, we went to the Hotel Wellington.

There we met Mrs. Pessl, the mother of Yella Pessl, the harpsichordist, and a former acquaintance from Vienna. She and Professor Alexander Wunderer, the first oboist of the Vienna Philharmonic, had already encouraged us greatly during the first stages of our musical life back in Austria. It was good to see her again.

"Well, children," she said, and came directly to the point, "there is only one thing to do if you want to have success in America. You have to give a Town Hall concert. Every artist who wants to make his way has to do that. And for that you need a publicity agent."

"A what?"

"Why—don't you have someone to do publicity for you?" she asked, quite astonished.

"To do what for us?" we asked lamely.

That was too much for the kind-hearted lady, mother of an artist, who knew what was what.

"But children, children, this is terrible!" And right there and then she called the girl who did all the publicity for Yella, and had her come over to the Wellington. We shouldn't lose a day, Mrs. Pessl insisted.

Edith Behrens came, and she and Mrs. Pessl explained to us the meaning and importance of a concert in Town Hall, New York. It would cost us $700, and at this thought we shuddered, but it might be worth millions, and this made us hopeful again. It should be soon, as soon as possible, and Mrs. Pessl's eyes wandered over me. No Number 3 could cheat her, I could see that. The first date available at Town Hall would be in two weeks, Edith learned on the telephone. Father Wasner approved the idea most heartily, and with a deep gulp we accepted.

"That gives us time for publicity," Mrs. Pessl said, very satisfiedly; and so it did. Our peace and our privacy were gone. Edith followed us with one or more photographers wherever we went, whatever we did, and pictures appeared in the newspapers: The Trapp Family Eating at the Chinese Restaurant; The Trapp Family Sight-Seeing; Craning Their Necks at Rockefeller Center; Window Shopping on Fifth Avenue; Looking Out of the Bus; Getting into a Trolley Car; Crossing the Street; Coming Down Steps. We got used to the idea of jamming up steps in stores, hotels, movie houses—everywhere—to be photographed while doing so. The Trapp Family Rehearsing in Their Hotel Room; Father Wasner (oh, how he hated it!) Directing, Reading a Score, Eating English Muffins (his favorite breakfast dish); Getting a Shoe Shine.

Then came the interviews by *Time* and the *Times, Life,* the *Herald Tribune,* the *Sun,* the *Daily News, P.M.*: "When did you arrive in this country?" "How do you like America?" "Why did you leave Europe?" "What is the difference in the food?" "Why do you wear those funny dresses?" We tried desperately to talk about music and our program, but Edith assured us that the public was much more interested in the other questions.

One single consolation there was to this—by now—awful Town Hall project: that we could make our very own program; and we did. For the first part we chose the three hardest madrigals we knew (after all, we wanted to show what we could do!), and the second part was devoted to the whole motet: *"Jesu Meine Freude,"* all forty-five minutes of it. That was a program to our heart's delight.

As we were completely unknown, Mrs. Pessl had suggested that her daughter, then already quite well known as a harpsichordist, should join us in this recital, taking turns with us, in rendering pieces on the harpsichord.

The great day came, and with it our great chance. Earnestly and solemnly we stood on the stage in Town Hall: no make-up, no unnecessary smiles, all worthy of the occasion of performing Bach's great motet. The hall was three-quarters filled. Much of it was "paper" (tickets given away), much of it was curious managers from all over the place, listening to this new attraction, a singing family. How good were they? Would they appeal to the broad public all over the country? Was there any money in them? Many of them left before the last chorale sounded solemnly through the air: *"Jesu—meine—Freude!"*

Some people, however, were seriously touched, and some even came to tell us so. A tall, young-looking man rushed backstage, and with moist eyes, taking my hand in both of his, said in a very moved tone of voice:

"This I am sure was exactly as Johann Sebastian would have wanted it to be. You must come and see me at the Public Library. I am Carleton Smith."

Now came a sleepless night of waiting for next morning's news-papers, which would present our fate in print. Either we were made now, or . . .

But next morning Edith, Yella, Mrs. Pessl came excitedly, each waving newspapers, exclaiming: "Wonderful! Excellent! Grand!" They read to our buzzing ears that we were "like no other family alive"; that "when eight members of one family sing and play as did the Trapp Family ensemble at Town Hall on Saturday afternoon, music would seem to have achieved one of its miracles"; "as a choral group the Trapps proved admirable. They evidently possess either perfect pitch or an extraordinary memory for tonality. The effects achieved in Praetorius, Lechner, Isaac numbers were already those of musicians of discriminating taste. Their work in the difficult Bach motet was accurate and veracious in the conveyance of the composer's intentions. It was all-around musicianship"; crowned by an important daily which gave two long columns and said, among other things: "There was something unusually lovable and appealing about the modest, serious singers as they formed a close semi-circle about their self-effacing director for their initial offering; the handsome, portly [!] Madame von Trapp in simple black, the others in black and white. It was only natural to expect work of exceeding refinement from them, and one was not disappointed in this"; and so on, a long column. By now, most of us were hopping around in joy and jubilation. Finally someone intoned: *"Nun Danket Alle Gott,"* Bach's great hymn of thanksgiving. We were so terribly happy that we were "made," although we didn't know yet what that meant.

On Monday morning we paid the promised visit to the Public Library to see Carleton Smith. He was talking to a gentleman whom he introduced to us as Professor Otto Albrecht from the University of Pennsylvania in Philadelphia.

"Otto is a music lover, and I told him all about you," Carleton beamed. "By the way, what are your plans?"

"We are looking now for a place where we can stay for the next weeks. The hotel is so expensive," said Georg.

Professor Albrecht's face lighted up.

"I know a furnished house which is for rent, not far from where I live."

And, in a genuinely American way, he made a couple of telephone calls and everything was fixed. The rent was one hundred dollars a month, and we could come right away.

Georg and the older girls went ahead with Otto Albrecht to fix up the house. It was very close to Christmas now, and Barbara and I simply loved the idea of settling down and having nothing moving under us for a while. The house was in Germantown, Philadelphia. When we got out at the North Philadelphia Station, there

were Georg and Otto Albrecht and several cars waiting. On the
way from the station to Germantown Georg said:

"It is perfectly incredible. Absolute strangers, friends of Otto Albrecht, stop with their cars, come in, find out what we don't have
enough of. Then they return with spoons, forks, and knives, glasses,
blankets, one brought a bed, another one pots and pans, and one
even came with a carload of records. There is a victrola in the
house. Now they have come with their cars to help me to install
my family. They are Quakers, from the Society of Friends, as we
used to call them in Europe."

The Society of Friends. They were not new to me. After World
War I when I was in my teens, a student in Vienna, the famine
had gotten so terrible that it was impossible to study or do any
work. For a bite to eat one would have sacrificed everything. In
that most crucial moment the Society of Friends came to Vienna
with food, and every student and every school child got one hot
meal a day. If it had not been for that one hot meal a day, I might
not be alive now. Such a thing one never forgets; and there they
were again crossing our path—the "Friends."

When we entered "our" living room, the fire was burning in the
fireplace, and from the victrola sounded the great *"Hallelujah
Chorus"* from *"The Messiah."*

Georg, noticing how tired I was, took my hand and said reassuringly: " 'And all these things shall be added unto you.' "

Yes—even friends—one of the rarest gifts in the world.

Barbara

THE very next day was Sunday, and in the evening two cars stopped before our house. Out came Otto Albrecht and Rex Crawford, a friend of his.

"We want you to meet Henry Drinker," said Otto, and told us to get into the cars. "He is a great music lover, and once a month he has a big party in his house, singing *a cappella* music just the way you do. I am sure you'll like each other." And off we went.

In a very large music room there were about a hundred and twenty people gathered around a tall, boyish-looking gentleman. We were too far in the rear and couldn't hear what he was saying, but that wasn't necessary. He was simply radiating enthusiasm. Then he raised his hand—silence fell upon the hall, and he conducted his guests in the *"Requiem"* by Johannes Brahms. We had been given the music, and we sang with them. Mr. Drinker was neither a great conductor, nor had he any outstanding voice, but never mind all that. He was as sincere a lover of music as we had ever seen. When an especially beautiful passage had just finished, he interrupted the music, dropped his hands, and said with contagious fervor:

"How marvellous! How simply wonderful! Oh, let's do it again!"

And we did it again. After an hour of such intensive music-making everyone seemed to be ready for the buffet supper. During this intermission we were introduced to Mr. and Mrs. Drinker. Otto told them about us. At the end of the evening, when most of the people had gone home, Otto asked us whether we would sing one number for our host. We gladly did, and chose our favorite Bach chorale: *"Wie schön leuchtet der Morgenstern."* With this one number we sang our way directly into the innermost heart of the Drinkers. We didn't know it then, but on that evening one of those friendships had started which have a beginning but no end.

Christmas passed quietly and peacefully. Dorothy and Rex Craw-ford, Miriam and Otto Albrecht, our neighbor, Mrs. Hurlburt, and some more of their friends, the Drinkers included, dropped baskets and packages at our door, and the poor refugees from Austria saw themselves confronted with six turkeys and baskets with pies, fruit, and other edibles, books and toys for the little ones, and books and records for the grownups. When Georg had seen my tears at the mere prospect of having electric lights on the trees, he went all over Philadelphia, and finally found real candles and candle holders. Now the last cloud had vanished, and it was the most beautiful Christmas we could remember. With Peter and John we had to say to our friends: "Money we have not, but what we have, we give you." This was our music and our prayers. We invited them on Christmas day for a party to help us with our many cakes and pies, and sang for them for two and a half hours —the best we had to give. And every morning and every evening we reminded Our Lord of His promise that He would reward every drink of water a hundredfold because what should be done unto His least brethren, He would count as having been done unto Him; and would He please, Who had promised such a generous reward for a simple drink of water, look upon all these turkeys, pies, and other gifts, and fulfill His promise?

Slowly we discovered that it was even beautiful at times to be regarded as poor, because one discovered such riches in one's neigh-bor's heart, and there was so much genuine love all around.

The day after Christmas I figured it was time for Barbara and me to get ready. I asked Rupert to bring me Barbara's suitcase, and emptied its contents on my large bed—all the numerous pre-cious little things: shirts of fine muslin with tiny shirrings and pleatings; costly embroidered coverlets; delicate little silken gowns; fancy show dresses; every item with a tiny embroidered monogram and coronet. I had just laid them out all over the room when Mrs. Drinker appeared on the scene—she with the loving heart but a very practical mind when needed, whose eyes could flash green lightning, and who was always sober, never a victim of sentimentality. Not without pride I showed her these little treasures.

Quietly her eyes wandered over my exhibition, and perfectly unmoved, she asked dryly:

"And who is going to wash and iron all this every day?"

I hadn't thought that far ahead yet. When Mrs. Drinker noticed this, she took over immediately. With eyes and mind of a general she surveyed my almost desperate situation: a battle to come, with no ammunition to fight it.

"Pack that silly stuff away and come with me. We'll go shopping for some sensible things." I tried hard to swallow my hurt feelings, while she tried just as hard to drive home the point. While driving over to Germantown she said: "A baby doesn't need all that. Three shirts, a couple of dozen diapers, and a pair of rubber pants is enough. You have to become practical now—practical, don't you see? You are poor, don't forget." The words sounded hard, but the eyes betrayed a deeply concerned heart. In looking back over the years I can see now what she went through in watching this newcomer waste her time and her little money on things of the past which had only sentimental value. How lucky I was to have such a sturdy friend to put things straight for me in those confusing and bewildering days! How often did we meet refugees who had arrived in this country at the same time as we without such a friend to guide their first steps. They never really "made it"; they live unhappily between two continents.

But at that moment I didn't see how you could possibly bring a baby into the world with just three shirts, a couple of dozen diapers, and a pair of rubber pants. But there is no use arguing with a general. That much I felt right away.

Of course, I had expected that we would go to a baby store, as I would have done in Europe. But, oh no! It was one of those hopelessly big department stores, in which I always felt so absolutely lost. I never could find my way around or my way out again, and I was always tempted to take along a spool of thread, tie it to the doorknob, and then go light-heartedly off from counter to counter, feeling sure I could always spool my way back.

But Mrs. Drinker didn't need a spool of thread. Straight away she headed for the baby counter. There we bought a few very sober-looking knitted things, which I didn't even recognize as shirts at first. Mrs. Drinker took no notice at all of my reserved, almost hostile silence towards American baby clothes. She did all the shopping necessary, and in no time we were sitting in the car again and driving home. She was very pleased. It was a "White Week," and everything was marked down.

"Aren't you glad?" she said. "You have saved more than three dollars on the whole deal!"

"Yes, Mrs. Drinker," I answered meekly, but unconvinced.

There wasn't much time to lose now, and I went out to find what, with the help of my dictionary, I recognized as a "midwife," like the indispensable Frau Vogl. After asking around, I learned that in the whole neighborhood there were only three midwives to be found, all of them Negroes. At that time I was a little afraid of colored people, whom we had never seen in our country, and who still seemed to us a little legendary; people out of *A Thousand and One Nights,* interesting to look at and to talk to, but a little scary to have around too close.

Oh, time and again, Mrs. Drinker told me that one *had to have* a doctor and one *had to go* to a hospital to have a baby. I was finally persuaded to make one concession: the doctor. But go to a hospital—that was ridiculous. Why? What for? I wasn't sick. In Europe you went to a hospital when you were dangerously sick, and many people died there, but babies were born at home. Would they in the hospital allow my husband to sit at my bedside? Could I hold his hand, look into his eyes? Could my family be in the next room, singing and praying? The answer to all these questions was "no."

All right, that settled it. I tried to explain that a baby had to be born *into* a home, received by loving hands, not into a hospital, surrounded by ghostly-looking doctors and masked nurses, into the atmosphere of sterilizers and antiseptics. That's why I would ask the doctor to come to our house.

But I had to find the doctor first. I tried many, but each time I mentioned the word "at home," they didn't want to take the case.

When I was very tired and discouraged, I found a young doctor in our neighborhood, young and a little nervous about the whole idea, but he said he would come.

I consoled him.

"Don't you worry. There is nothing wrong. I know all about it. It is the most natural thing in the world. You just have to sit in the next room, and I'll call you when I need you."

His eyes widened, and he opened his mouth to speak, but closed it again in utter amazement.

And so it happened. The evening came when I knew it was time. Everything went the old way. The family gathered in the living room, reciting the rosary aloud. Then they sang hymns. Then they prayed again. The doors were open, and I could hear them. Georg was there next to me, and his good, firm hands patted me once in a while, as he repeated: "Soon she will be here, our Barbara," and then we both smiled. The doctor had not come yet.

Then it had to be: "Call him now and tell him to be quick!"

When he arrived, he looked troubled. He had a nurse with him—a sweet-looking young girl. They were washing their hands when all of a sudden I had to squeeze Georg's hand very hard, and time seemed to stand still. Then I heard a funny little squeak. The doctor, pale, beads of perspiration on his forehead, turned to me and said—I couldn't understand what—and then carried something in his right hand through the room. It was all over. At that minute a full chorale downstairs started: "Now thank we all our God!"

The doctor, in the middle of the room, turned around.

"What's that?" he gasped.

And then I saw what he was holding: my precious baby—head down!

My heart almost stopped. I was sure he would drop her.

"Watch out—don't break her!" I cried.

"Her! Why—it's a boy!" he said reproachfully.

What? I must have misunderstood. Georg bent over me.

"Barbara is a boy," he smiled.

My heart started singing: "Now thank we all our God!"

Many years later I happened to learn about planned parenthood and birth control to guard against unwanted children. I must say, Barbara, whom we now had to call Johannes, had not been exactly planned for that very moment, and as far as being wanted is concerned, I would have gladly said many times, "Oh, won't you please be so kind as to wait for just six months." Yes, many times on the flight, on the boat, on the bus, on the stage. But thousands of years ago God assured us—it's in the Book—"For My thoughts are not your thoughts, nor your ways My ways." So if there is any planning to be done, why don't we let Him do it? Looking back now, I know that He chose the only right moment for Johannes' arrival. The predictions of the doctor in Munich proved beautifully wrong, and Johannes promises to be a fine American boy.

What Next?

THE little baby boy was almost twins. He weighed ten pounds two ounces when he was born, and never could wear size one.

When the baby was three days old, he was carried into the parish church, where Father Wasner received him into the fold of Christ in the Sacrament of Baptism. He was given the names Johannes Georg. That was the first great family feast in America.

From his tenth day on, he cried bitterly almost day and night until I desperately called the doctor. He discovered that there was nothing wrong with the precious boy; he was only hungry. I felt guilty and ashamed. But how horrified I was when I learned that I should give him orange juice—raw orange juice! and squeezed bananas—raw bananas! With my European upbringing that meant almost murder. But Johannes was an American boy, and throve very soon on carrots, spinach, and juices, and there was no more crying to be heard.

The next weeks were a wonderful change. For months we had been living out of a suitcase, every day in another hotel. Now we were all together again. The little girls were back from the boarding school in New York, and we had our own household. The older girls took turns in kitchen and household duties, and Martina helped me with the baby. The lovely young nurse, Anne, showed us how to do things in America. There were, for instance, the diapers. In Europe they are square. You fold them so that they are three-cornered and knot them around the baby's legs. In America the diapers are oblong, and you pin them with safety pins. That and the raw orange juice took me a long time to get used to. Soon, however, we found out that those practical little knitted shirts, which washed like stockings, were a grand invention. No ironing was necessary, and what I wouldn't have believed would ever happen: I didn't open Barbara's suitcase a single time.

Almost every day we had company: the Albrechts, the Crawfords, the Drinkers. They took the family to the symphony concerts on Friday afternoons; to the Franklin Institute; to the Art Museum; for rides through beautiful Fairmount Park; to parties at this or that friend's house.

Through Mrs. Drinker we got acquainted with Ravenhill Academy, where the little girls went to school from then on. Unlike the school in the Bronx, it was situated on the very outskirts of town, surrounded by big gardens. Very soon Rosmarie and Lorli felt very much at home with the Sisters and the new schoolmates.

The question arose now: what to do next? Much of the money we had earned with the concerts had gone into the boat tickets, which Mr. Wagner had advanced, and the daily living expenses, plus the Town Hall concert. Our first contract had been for forty concerts, of which we gave only eighteen, but Mr. Wagner said he could easily have gotten the other dates after Christmas if it hadn't been for the baby. There was nothing we could do about that. The contract had expired anyway.

We had arrived in America on a visitor's visa, which expired in March. Our friends advised us to apply for an extension, which we did right after Christmas. Everybody assured us that these extensions were a mere formality: they were always granted. But our visitor's visa only allowed us to earn money by giving concerts; no other way. The money which was left would carry us, if we were very thrifty, perhaps into the summer.

What next?

These were the things we talked about, Georg, Father Wasner, and I, in these days, but as we didn't find any solution right away, all we could do was go on with *our* part of the program: to seek the Kingdom of God.

Every morning we walked to the parish church, where Father Wasner said Holy Mass.

The weather can be disagreeable between December and March. The house was a little small for our large family, and it was very meagerly furnished. There wasn't enough of anything, in spite of the Friends' help. We simply were too large a family. Most of all, there was never enough food; and if you are hungry and sitting on one another's lap, you easily get irritated, especially so when the immediate future looks insecure and veiled. So for the moment, to seek the Kingdom of God was, for us, to take it all with a smile and in genuine gratitude, because weren't there many others much poorer than we?

One day in February Mr. Wagner arrived unexpectedly at our house. He brought with him an agreement, again for forty dates. Since the baby was here, there would be no trouble, he promised, and happily we signed our second American contract. The tour would start in September. One great worry was lifted off our shoulders. From September on, we would be secure again—and until then? Oh, there would be a little concert here and there, our friends assured us, and if there was only one a month, we could keep alive on it.

Then one morning came the fatal letter. The U. S. Immigration and Naturalization Service informed us that our application for extension of temporary stay was not granted, and we had to leave the United States at the latest by March 4. This was a cruel blow. We had burned all our bridges behind us, and would never dare go back home again, and now America wouldn't allow us to stay here.

Now—what next?

It was such a shock that for the moment no one could say or think anything. Each one swallowed his private disappointment and fear.

One thing was certain: we had to leave. There wasn't much time to secure tickets for so many people on one boat. In the newspaper we saw that the *Normandie* would leave New York on March 4. Georg went to the French Line and was able to secure twelve tickets third class to Southampton. After these tickets were bought, there wasn't much money left, and what would we do in Southampton?

Then it came to us: A year ago we had had an offer from a Danish impresario for an introductory tour of Scandinavia; two concerts in Copenhagen, two in Oslo, and two in Stockholm.

"Let's get in touch with this manager to see if he can take us now."

It had to be done by cable, although that again was expensive.

Then came fearful days of waiting. And what if he did not accept us? There was an absolute blank in our mind.

We started to dissolve our household, giving back the borrowed

lankets, beds, spoons and forks. The Crawfords had kindly offered
to store in their attic things which we didn't want to carry with us
twice across the ocean; so we started dividing our goods into "tak-
bles" and "leavables," as Hedwig said. But the usual cheerfulness
was missing. Everybody went about his duties rather silently.

About two thousand years ago something similar had happened
to a group who left their homelands, merely following an idea
represented by a star: the three Holy Kings. When each one of
them notified his people that he was about to set out on a long
journey to go and find somewhere a newborn King, their friends
must have shaken their heads in disapproval: "I hope you won't
regret it." Then for weeks and months they followed the star,
which guided them into the land of the Jews, into the very capital,
Jerusalem, and then—it disappeared; and when they thought they
had reached the goal, they found themselves in complete darkness.
Nobody knew anything about a newborn King, and the words
were ringing in their ears: "I hope you won't regret it."

What a temptation to wish never to have left. But after God
had tried their faith and their patience, He came to their rescue.
They were shown the way, and the star appeared again. "And seeing the star, they rejoiced with exceeding great joy."

That was the story we talked about on March 1. Only three
more days to go, and still no answer from Europe. It was a dark
moment, and no star to be seen. Then we chose the three Holy
Kings for our special patron Saints. We promised them to imitate
their faith and patience. Would they please ask God to have the
star appear again?

It did. Next morning came a night cable:

EVERYTHING READY FOR FIRST CONCERT MARCH
TWELFTH COPENHAGEN.

Our new faithful friends helped us in closing the house and
getting the family on the right train to New York. The Drinkers
sent their chauffeur with the car for Georg, the baby, and me.

When we came to say good-bye, Mrs. Drinker took both my
hands in hers and said:

"Now, why don't you call me Sophie?"

In New York we all assembled at Carleton Smith's house, and
from there we went to the boat. Last kisses and good wishes, then

shouting and waving, and then the *Normandie* was towed out int
the open sea. Soon the skyscrapers disappeared in a golden mis
and we found ourselves on the way to Europe.

The *Normandie!* What a noble boat, and what a wonderf
crew! Although we were only third-class passengers, the Frenc
Line went out of its way to make our stay as enjoyable as possibl
We got a pass with which we could stroll at any time all over th
boat and use all the social rooms and facilities of all classes. W
were invited to eat in the tourist class, and for our rehearsals
special drawing room on the first-class deck was assigned to u
adjoining the wonderful winter garden. The third-class cabi
were much more luxurious than our places on the *America
Farmer* had been. But the nicest of all was the behavior of th
crew. The stewards and stewardesses, the waiters and officers we
of such tact and politeness that for four short days we almost fo
got that we were poor refugees with a very uncertain future. C
board the *Normandie* we were treated as celebrated artists. Peop
knew about our Town Hall concert and we were asked to give
gala performance on the last evening together with René Le Ro
the flutist. Champagne was served free of charge afterwards. Th
boat itself was a dream of beauty, and the size was such that
took me eight minutes from my cabin if I wanted to reach th
upper deck with Johannes for some fresh air. Long corridors ha
to be traversed, different elevators taken until we finally reache
the "seashore." There was only one disadvantage: there were fo
thousand people, and four days was too short to get really a
quainted. I felt like asking: When will this town arrive in Europ
When we had just barely learned which passage to take to reac
the Chapel Number 1, the Movie Number 2, or the Swimmir
Pool Number 3, it was time to get ready for Southampton. B
four days was not too short to create a warm feeling for the bo
and its crew, and when, years later, we learned of the dreadf
disaster the *Normandie* had suffered in New York, we felt as
something terrible had happened to a close friend of ours.

In Sight of the Statue of Liberty

FROM the day in March when we left on the *Normandie* to that day in October when we set foot on American soil again we learned a lesson, the greatest of them all. In Bible English it is called: "Be not solicitous," and translated into everyday language, it means: "Don't worry."

We started out by worrying.

"What shall we eat, what shall we drink, what shall we put on?" These must be the very elements of human worries, as Our Lord picks them out when He says: "Be not solicitous for your life, what you shall eat, nor for your body, what you shall put on." Then He explains how useless it is if we *do* worry, how it gets us nowhere; "Can any of you for all his fretting add an inch's growth to his height? And if you are powerless to do so small a thing, why do you fret about your needs?" After having told us how senseless it is to worry, He tells us what to do. We should look at the lilies, how they grow. They don't work, nor do they spin, but not even King Solomon in all his glory was clothed like one of them. Now—if God clothes the grass, which lives today in the fields and tomorrow is cast into the oven, will He not be much more ready to clothe you, oh you of little faith? You should not be asking then what you shall eat or what you shall drink and worrying about them. The heathens may do that, who don't know about God. You, however, must know that your Heavenly Father knows well that you need all these things. Therefore, seek first the Kingdom of God and all these things shall be added unto you.

And this half year was set apart for teaching us this lesson, that we should never forget it in the future.

There we were, a group of twelve people and a little baby who, for the next seven months, had no home, and except for six concerts, which would provide for three weeks' living, did not know

163

the answer to the question: what shall we eat, what shall we drink
The political horizon was filled with dark clouds; the outbreak o
the war seemed imminent; the atmosphere in Europe was full o
suspicion and mistrust; we didn't know a soul in the Scandinavia
countries, nor any of the languages; the permission to stay wa
carefully restricted by every country to the time necessary to giv
our concerts. Europe was just waking up to recognizing "tourists
as "fifth columnists."

It would have been easy for God to show us the plan for th
period, as He had it all fixed up, how there would be enough co
certs, enough money, extensions of our stay, helpful people, gen
erous invitations, new friends, and new love. But then we agai
would not have learned that most valuable lesson, so He left u
in the dark, and gave us only one thing at a time. We alway
spent the cent before the last before we got a new engagement.

In this way we passed the time until the end of May in Den
mark, Sweden, and Norway. When our prolonged extension ha
almost expired, an invitation from Holland with permission t
stay for twenty-eight days at the country home of friends took car
of the month of June. In July we dared to pay a short visit t
Austria. The men of our group, however, stayed away. Back i
the old home we learned with horror what one short year can d
to an invaded people, how it had embittered the ones while
changed, imperceptibly to themselves, the others, and falsified the
way of thinking and living. We learned the shocking truth tha
"home" isn't necessarily a certain spot on earth. It must be a plac
where you can *feel* at home, which means "free" to us. Soon w
met the men in St. Georgen, south of the border, where I fulfille
my promise and carried little Johannes up the hill and lit a bi
candle in the shrine of Our Lady. For August and September w
had our engagements in Sweden. But, mind you, not all of ther
were neatly put down on a list in advance. No, each conce
brought forth the next one, when an excited member of the aud
ence invited us to his home town for a performance. By then w
were well advanced in our course: "Don't worry." It really wou
have been a waste of time. All the practicing and rehearsing c
this new art we needed badly when in September, 1939, the wa
broke out. All borders were closed, foreigners were asked to d
part, concerts already promised were canceled. But we had learne

by then that the Heavenly Father knows what we need. More than before, we tried to concentrate on "Seek ye therefore *first* the Kingdom of God" in doing our daily duties, rehearsing the program for the next American tour, taking care of all the little chores of everyday life, and trying most conscientiously *not to worry*. At the moment before our last permission to stay in Sweden expired, Mr. Wagner again advanced the money on the next concerts and sent the tickets for the SS. *Bergensfjord*.

When, on October 7, 1939, we finally docked in Brooklyn, Hedwig said with disappointment in her voice:

"In spite of the war, this crossing was not dangerous and not a bit exciting. Nothing unusual happened."

Photographers and newspaper men crowded on board, searching for sensational stories. Our picture was taken, too: The Trapp Family Alone, and The Trapp Family With Kirsten Flagstad, who also happened to be on the *Bergensfjord*. Then we saw Mr. Snowden, our friendly guide of the first year, in the crowd. He waved and called, "Welcome home!" and then it was our turn with the Immigration Officer. Rupert had an immigration visa this time, whereas the rest of us were all on visitors' visas.

I was so relieved and so grateful after all these months of uncertainty to have reached the haven again, that when my turn came and the Immigration Officer asked me the fatal question: "What time do you intend to spend in America?" I didn't answer as I was supposed to: "Six months, Sir, as my visa says," but I simply blurted out: "Oh, I am so glad to be here—I want never to leave again!"

Their whole attitude changed. The members of the Trapp Family were held for the very last, and then they were questioned and questioned again; but nothing we said could undo the dangerous impression my most unwise outburst had created: these people don't want to leave again.

Everybody was gone; we were the only passengers on board. But we were not allowed to leave. A tall policeman came and watched us, and all we could do for the rest of the day was play shuffleboard among ourselves and admire beautiful Brooklyn. We didn't understand yet why, but we were prisoners, and so Hedwig had gotten her highlight for this trip after all: tomorrow we should be taken to Ellis Island.

A large motorboat came, and our policeman took us over to the island with the large prison building, where the doubtful people from foreign countries were scrutinized. Lucky Rupert went to the Hotel Wellington and started from there to try to get his family out of jail, because jail it was. When the huge door was closed behind us, the door which had no knob on the inside, we were led into a hall as big as the main waiting room in Grand Central Station.

It was one of those beautiful, hot October days, Indian Summer, but tradition on Ellis Island has it that on October 1 the central heating has to be started. The windows, high up and barred, could not be opened, and the temperature was around eighty degrees.

"Could I get out with the little ones into the fresh air?" Martina approached a warden.

"Every day for half an hour after lunch," was the answer.

We still didn't understand what we were doing there. We had been told by some officer of the ship that our papers were not quite clear, and it was only for some formality that we were being taken to this place. But we couldn't remember having done anything wrong. It must be a misunderstanding, and Rupert would come in the afternoon and get us out. So we tried to make ourselves at home on two large benches facing each other. With the help of our suitcases we boarded up a corner, and as there was absolutely nothing else to do, we started to sing. It is always good to rehearse. Soon people grouped around us, and it seemed that their strained faces looked less worried after listening for an hour to our music. Then we started to talk. There were Spaniards, Jews, Greeks, and a large group of Chinese. We learned that the Chinese had been here already for eight months. Most of the people had been here for weeks. Goodness—and our first concert was supposed to be on the fifteenth. A lady from Poland said:

"At least it doesn't cost anything; it's all paid by the State. And if America doesn't let you in, the ship line on which you came has to take you back in the same class, at its own cost, to the port where you started out. It won't cost you a cent."

How terribly consoling! That meant another third-class passage on the *Bergensfjord* to Oslo!

"And if that country in Europe doesn't let us in, what then?" asked Werner.

"Well," said the lady cheerily, "then the ship has to keep you. There is an Italian family on the ocean traveling for the eleventh time between Le Havre and New York. And it doesn't cost them a cent."

What a prospect!

One of the wardens came, a fat lady with greasy hair and a stern look, and handed each one of us a sheet of paper where it said in German:

"Information: You have been asked to come to Ellis Island as there is some doubt concerning your passport. You will come before the special hearing as soon as possible, and you can plead your cause. If you can't speak English, you will get an interpreter. There is no reason to get excited. You will be treated very politely." Then it said in capitals: "DON'T TALK ABOUT YOUR AFFAIRS WITH YOUR FELLOW PRISONERS"; and at the end it added: "Please be patient. We don't want to keep you a moment longer than we absolutely have to."

Then it was time for lunch. We were lined up by twos and filed through the door, which was opened with a special key from the inside. As we passed by, the fat lady tapped each one of us on the shoulder, counting. Georg disliked this extremely.

On long tables the food was served in tin plates, everything on one plate.

After lunch we were taken out into the yard by twos. The yard was closed in by a very tall wire fence, and what should we see greeting us through the bars from a very short distance, but the Statue of Liberty! The half hour was very short; the whistle blew and we had to go back in.

Finally Rupert came, and he didn't look very cheerful.

"One of you must have made the remark that she wants to stay in this country. That makes you all suspicious, and the authorities don't want to let you in. That's what Mr. Wagner was told."

Soon Rupert had to leave. The visiting hour was over. We asked him to call our different friends to help us out.

Johannes had started to walk while we were alone on the *Bergensfjord* on that last day. Now he practiced walking all day long. He was not quite nine months old, but was very strong.

Between singing and playing around with Johannes the long hours passed. We filed through the door again for supper, and right afterwards we had to take all our luggage and were led upstairs into a large dormitory. The windows were small slits high up on the wall, and the door had no knob on the inside. The very bright lights were left on the whole night, which made sleeping hard, and every so often the door opened and the warden came in and counted noses. Each time Johannes woke up and cried unhappily.

Next morning we were awakened at six o'clock. The newspapers had heard of the Trapp Family at Ellis Island and sent reporters and photographers. From time to time a policeman came in and called a name, the name of the lucky one who should go to his hearing. In the afternoon Rupert reported that he had called Mr. Drinker, who had promised to do what he could. How quickly one gets used to things: to be marched by twos, to eat from tin plates, to be counted numberless times day and night, to windows next to the ceiling and doors without knobs. Father Wasner could say Mass each morning, but only we were allowed to attend, no one else.

Mr. King, the big boss of Ellis Island, came to visit us. He was especially nice and said that even Toscanini had been here briefly, and many other famous artists, and we should not worry. In the afternoon Elizabeth, Carleton Smith's wife, came with a big basket of fresh fruit and newspapers with our picture: The Trapp Family Playing Recorders on Ellis Island. What publicity! Elizabeth assured us that our friends were working busily to get us out.

We were singing a good deal now, because the people were so happy about it. It took their worried thoughts away from their own problems. We were getting very popular on Ellis Island.

On the fourth day we were pretty much at home, with a daily routine: *ora et labora*. Mass in the morning and rosary in the evening, during the day rehearsals, recorder practice. Father Wasner was working on a new composition. We wrote letters back to Sweden, letters of thanks. Quietly we waited for our hearing. We had been told from all sides that this was merely a formality; we just had to wait for our turn. An extremely nice letter from Mr. Drinker helped a great deal to cheer us up. In the afternoon the door opened again, and this time *our* name was called. The policeman led us over to the courtroom. There we took a solemn oath that we would tell the truth, the whole truth, and nothing but the truth, and then the long questioning started. For two and a half hours we (I particularly) were questioned. Why had we come? What did we intend to do? Where did we intend to live? On what boat did we intend to leave again? We didn't know? Didn't we have return tickets? How come? Didn't we intend to leave? And so on. After we had told the truth, the whole truth, and nothing but the truth for two and a half hours, the judge said he didn't believe us, and we were dismissed.

"And the *Bergensfjord* is sailing tomorrow," went through my mind.

Our companions were eagerly awaiting the outcome, and when they heard what had happened, all looked very gloomy. Each time a prisoner is released, they all gather around him and applaud heartily while he is let out the door. This they had intended to do with us. But quietly we all sat down again and—started to sing. It was the only thing to do if we didn't want to cry. In the middle of a song Georg was called out. He came back shortly afterwards, and his beaming countenance spoke the word: we were FREE. Our friends had approached their senators and congressmen, vouched for our honesty, and word had come back from Washington to Ellis Island and the misunderstanding was cleared up.

It was touching how our fellow prisoners selflessly shared in our joy. First endless applause while we got hold of our bags; then one more song; more applause; another song, and finally our best *Jodler* at the end. Outside Rupert was waiting, and in the motorboat we waved over at the Statue of Liberty, this time from the other side of the fence. The second dove had returned into the ark with a branch from an olive tree. It was safe to set foot on land. And this must have been the feelings of Noah, his wife, his daughters and sons, when they sang their hymn of thanksgiving after the tempest was over.

Learning New Ways

NOW we were really in America, and although I wouldn't even have dared to whisper it to myself on the top of the Empire State Building or in the middle of Central Park at midnight, for fear the Immigration Officer could hear it again, I knew this was for good.

A touching reunion with the Hotel Wellington! For the first time I noticed that there were green carpets in the lobby and the nice bell captain with his bellboys and elevator boys wore a handsome purple uniform.

A great many other things I seemed to discover all anew, and many times my family exclaimed:

"But, Mother, don't you remember from last year?"

No, honestly, I didn't. It seems that an expectant mother is more occupied within herself, taking in from the outside world merely the bare essentials.

The first concert was in Town Hall, New York, on a Saturday afternoon. It was a weekend, and what is more, it was one of those balmy days in the fall where the foliage in the country is a riot of color, and people simply didn't feel like staying in town on such a day and listening to Palestrina. Result: a small audience. Further result: a disappointed manager, who had thought we were a better "drawing card" than the box office receipts showed.

For the weekend of our Town Hall concert our Philadelphia friends had come to New York. How wonderful to see them again! The Crawfords offered most kindly to take the little ones into their home. Rosmarie and Lorli could go to their old Academy again, which was not too far from the Crawfords' home. The parting was always a very bitter moment for all of us; but at that time I still thought children had to go to school, and everything else had to be sacrificed to this fact. Later I should learn better.

That was the year of the World's Fair, and we spent some most exciting days on the grounds, which seemed like a whole book of fairy tales.

What that word "drawing card" meant, we should discover in a painful way during the next weeks.

In a short time we learned to know some of the largest auditoriums in this country with a seating capacity of between 2,500 and 4,000, and we always had ample chance to meditate on the color of the upholstery; in one place, a silvery gray, in another, a deep red, or a warm golden yellow; because it was not disturbed by human forms—the huge halls seemed practically empty. (And the artist said to his audience: "Come into the front row, both of you.")

An otherwise large audience of eight hundred or nine hundred got almost entirely lost in that vast space. What was the matter? Well, Grandpa Wagner had "invested quite some money in the Trapp Family Choir," and now he wanted it back. That's why he had them sing in large halls; but he forgot to tell the people about it. From our short meeting with publicity we had learned sentences like this: "You can't tell the people often enough. You just have to rub it in, or they forget." For these people in Hartford, Connecticut; Harrisburg, Pennsylvania; Raleigh, North Carolina; or Washington, D. C., it was not a question of forgetting, but of getting acquainted with the fact that their presence was requested at the first concert of the Trapp Family Choir in their town. But aside from a meager notice in the rear of the local paper, we couldn't find any window cards or photographs, no "three-sheets" glared from the walls; no interviews, no photographers made our life miserable. Quietly we came and quietly we left, and Mr. Wagner got more and more disgusted. At that time he used pink stationery. At each hotel and at each concert hall those pink envelopes awaited us, filled with gentle reproaches about how badly we had done the last time. This is not exactly a tonic before a concert.

We got more and more nervous and discouraged. We knew we had rehearsed very conscientiously. This "Missa Brevis" by Palestrina *was* a masterpiece, and we *did* sing it well. You just feel such a thing. We also knew that the people who had come to our concerts went away deeply moved, and their words of appre-

ciation were sincere. But something seemed to be wrong with us
—what was it? We tried so hard, even if ever so tired, to be nice
and peppy at the receptions—to please everybody; still, the pink
envelopes came in greater numbers.

At our first visit at his office Mr. Wagner had received us with
the news that so far he had been able to arrange only twenty-four
concerts out of the forty. This time it was due to the war. But
there wouldn't be any difficulty to book the rest as soon as we had
started to sing. Now the pink letters threatened there would be
no more dates if the halls continued to remain empty. It was very
disheartening.

Otherwise, we had a wonderful time. There was the big blue
bus again with the same driver, who continued in his friendly
way: "Let me explain something to you." But this time with our
advanced English we understood much more of what he explained.

He noticed with satisfaction that in another point, too, we were
advanced: that was our luggage. In vain he had tried to explain
to us that when he had driven the Don Cossacks from coast to
coast, each one of these grown-up men had carried only one suitcase.

"And these kids don't seem to get along without three bags
every night," he had sighed.

I hadn't argued more about this with him for the simple reason
that I hadn't enough English words to argue with. Otherwise I
would have tried to make him understand that I had to unpack
my three suitcases every night, put the little stacks of nightgowns,
shirts, panties, etc., neatly into the drawers, my different framed
photographs, alarm clock, New Testament, Missal, rosary, candle
holder, and little vase with flowers (fresh ones if we could pick
any from the bus, otherwise a little bunch of pussy willows and
evergreens, which had to be packed carefully in tissue paper)—on
my night table; hang the dresses in the closet, and so on. It is just
as well I didn't even try. I am sure he would never have understood that. But now with the help of the Crawfords' attic, a lot
of stuff was left behind, and each one of us made his entry into
and exit out of the daily hotel with only one big, and one small
bag. And the big one didn't even get emptied every evening any
more; only when we were in a place more than one night. Well,
and the driver didn't even know that my little overnight bag was
only one-fourth the size of the one which had accompanied me

over Europe, that expensive, heavy leather affair, in the lid of which were the two score crystal flasks with silver tops, containing everything from a toothbrush to shoeshine equipment, with heavy silver mirrors, tortoise-shell comb, jewelry box. He also didn't know that our neighbor at home in Salzburg couldn't possibly travel without taking her own bed and night table along with her. She couldn't fathom the idea of how one could sleep in a strange bed. Baroness M. M.—— was a widely traveled lady. When she went to India tiger-hunting, among other things she took along three of her own milk cows, which saved her from the strain of getting used to different milk, and about seventy hats, to be up to every occasion. Compared with all this, we were fast approaching the example of the Saint of Assisi.

This time my camera was not packed away, but at my right hand always.

"Please—stop!" I could cry at the most inopportune moments, when the driver was just overtaking a big truck on a well-populated highway. Then when we finally managed to halt, I ran back and took a picture of such an exciting item as a huge roadside advertisement, shouting to the world that you can't live without a Ford. I asked my family to pose in front of it. We would send the photograph back to Europe, where they would gasp at such a thing, which was four times as high as Rupert, and wider than the row of Trapps holding hands with outstretched arms in front of it.

Or I took an American graveyard on the roadside: simply stones stuck into the grass—no little hills covered with flowers, no shrines, no iron or carved-wood crosses; these cemeteries didn't look as if they were frequently visited and tended. There were no seats or benches beside the graves. There was no wall around the graveyard, and no tender love hovered around the place, all of which made Martina exclaim:

"I wouldn't want to be buried in America."

Then there were the rows and rows of cars. When entering a city on a weekend, time and again I had to take a picture of the four-lane highways filled with solid rows of cars with people leaving for the weekend; or a parking place near a factory or a big school. In Salzburg we could count the people who owned a private car, and one of the spectacles of the Festivals had always been the strangers driving up in their limousines to the opera. No one seemed even to waste a look or a thought on this pageant of cars here. They had become a piece of daily necessity, but not yet for us; that's why I took their pictures.

In Gettysburg we took snapshots of the battlefield. Of the monuments and cannons. In Europe every ancient town has such a memorial as this, but in America it is the only one we remember.

In the South we were enchanted with the Spanish moss and the cypress trees growing out of the water. And with the Negroes. Bashfully and embarrassedly at first, later more and more encouraged by the always hearty and kind reception, I asked whether I might take a picture of this old grandma rocking on the porch with the cutest little darky on her lap, or of that group of sturdy colored boys picking cotton or harvesting peanuts.

What a different kind of sight-seeing! This time it was not cathedrals, galleries, or museums. This spectacle was prepared directly by the hand of God: these huge oak trees, these cypress swamps, these endless woods in the Blue Ridge Mountains. They were not man-made, and neither was the Natural Bridge, nor the caves in Virginia, nor Niagara Falls.

"How does it happen," mused Agathe thoughtfully one day while we were riding through the endless pine forests in North Carolina, admiring the bright red soil, "that I feel fine and at peace and quite at home here in America as long as I am in the wilds? The minute, however, traces of men show up, these roadside advertisements, for instance, these ugly wooden houses with their scales [she meant clapboards, completely unknown in Europe], the dump heaps around the huts, the car cemeteries [she meant auto dumps]—oh, it makes me so unhappy! It spoils the countryside, it doesn't fit; then I don't like America."

Funny—I felt the same way, and we found out the others did, too. There was some disharmony which man had brought into the ravishing beauty of this country.

"If I think of the villages in Europe," Rupert entered the conversation, "in the Alps or in France or England or Scandinavia, there the houses fit into the landscape, and the people do, too. They seem to be a part of it."

"Yes," said Werner, "that's true; and those old farms at home look so nice and homey and well-kept, with flowers all around. Look!" and he pointed through the window. We were just passing a run-down farm with rickety barns. "Why don't these people take better care of their houses for their children and grandchildren?"

"Ah," put in our driver, who had listened to our spirited conversation, "that's where you make a mistake. Who wants to live in the country with children and grandchildren? They just want to make some money, for instance, cut a wood lot or get a few good crops, and then move back to town and take it easy."

"You mean," gasped Hedwig, "that the people on these farms won't live there forever?"

"Sure not," he laughed, and his mere tone of voice said "you crazy Europeans."

"Who wants to work hard from dawn to dusk if you can make more money much easier in a factory in the next town?"

Well, of course, that solved the riddle why so many houses were not painted.

Anyway—this side of America was very strange to us. We had to learn much more about this country and its people before we could fit the many little pieces together. At the moment it was puzzling.

Our next stop was Hartsville, North Carolina. There we would learn some more. There was no Catholic church at the place, but on Sunday morning the priest came from the next parish in his car and said Mass in a private home, and we assisted at it. Afterwards we all had breakfast together, and Father Plicunas, the friendly priest of Lithuanian extraction, wanted to show us his church.

"Come on, let's run over. It's just around the corner," he insisted, and packed his car full of as many Trapps as possible. Off we went at hair-raising speed, forty-five miles to his rectory.

"But you said it was . . ."

"Yes, just around the corner. Why—that's nothing. My parish is . . ." and he quoted a fabulous number of miles, length and width, which would have taken care of at least three dioceses in Europe.

More and more as we rode along we were impressed by the foremost quality of America; its terrific size.

One day in December as we drove through the most beautiful winter woods and were admiring the increasing beauty of the landscape as we came farther north, the "Let me explain something to you," was heard again all over the bus.

"Now we are entering the State of Vermont. No use looking out the window. This is not a progressive State. All they raise is gravestones."

The last of our twenty-four concerts was in Philadelphia in the Academy of Music in the afternon. It was two days before Christmas. Afterwards we were invited to dinner at the Drinkers'. Harry Drinker received us radiantly.

"I have a house for you right across the street."

After supper we all went to look at the house. It was furnished, and he really meant it, we could move in immediately.

"Instead of paying me in cash, pay me in music." And so it happened: a most perfect exchange of goods. Each one gave what he had; and we sang for him and with him the master works of the sixteenth and seventeenth centuries which he hadn't discovered yet, and both parties were truly happy.

The Miracle

THE inevitable happened. After Christmas came one more pink letter containing the check with the rest of the money due to us, and notifying us how much Mr. Wagner esteemed us as artists of first rank, but that he did not think we were made for American audiences, and he did not see his way clear to the renewal of his contract, but he wished us God's choicest blessings for a successful future.

That was a deadly blow.

Georg and I went to New York to talk to Mr. Wagner, but he only quoted sadly a five-figure number, the money he had lost on us.

You will never be a hit in America. Go back to Europe. You will be a great success there."

Back to Europe, with the Swastika stretching its black spider-legs all over the map.

Very depressed, we went to the Wellington after a little supper at the Chinese cafeteria. In the lobby we met the husband of an artist whom we knew. They also had come from Austria some time ago. Perhaps he knew the secret of appealing to the American public, and we confided to him our troubles. Something gleamed in his eyes which now, years later, I can distinguish as the genuine joy of getting rid of a rival. He talked very earnestly and very persuasively.

"Mr. Wagner is perfectly right. You must go back to Europe. Let me advise you: go right away before you spend your last dollar. Your art is too subtle. People here will never understand it. This is no place for you. Go back where you belong and be happy. In three days the *Normandie* sails again. Let me help you to get tickets. May I call for reservations?"

This was perhaps our darkest moment. The star had vanished

altogether. But how grateful was I when Georg said: "No, thank you, I can do that myself," and rather stiffly we parted.

Then we sat upstairs in our room and looked at each other. What now?

"Our Bishop said that it was the Will of God that we go to America. So many people have told us since that our music is more than just earning our living. It has turned out to be a mission. We must keep on singing. Let's look for another manager."

Around the time of our first Town Hall concert we had made the acquaintance of several managers. One of them I still remembered very clearly, a Mr. F. C. Schang from Columbia Concerts, Inc. When we had met him, he had talked about the English Singers, whose manager he had been. The very way he spoke of them impressed me. It was not cool and businesslike, but warm, personal, respectful.

"It must be nice to work with a manager who feels that way about his artists," I had thought then. Now this came to my mind.

Next morning we called Mrs. Pessl to find out how one approaches a manager. So far, managers had approached us, and we didn't know anything about the other way around.

"Well, that's easy," she answered. "All you have to do is ask for an audition," and she explained to us what that was.

With trembling hands I dialed CIrcle 7-6900 for the first time and asked for Mr. Schang.

"Am mother of Trapp Family Choir," I informed him in my halting English. "Want to ask audition. Will be possible? When?"

"Georg, he sounds awfully nice," I said happily. "Right away he said a week from today."

Quite consoled, we went back to 252 Merion Road, which from now on was our address. No more "c/o Management Charles Wagner"; a real address of our own.

Anxious faces awaited us, and great was the joy when we told them: "A week from today."

We rehearsed as never before. Three hours in the morning, three hours in the afternoon, and an hour after supper. We chose the most difficult and intricate pieces, and perfected our performance in most conscientious work.

The big day came, and we stood on the stage of Steinway Hall. Our audience consisted of Mr. Schang and Mr. Coppicus, the two managers of the Metropolitan Musical Bureau, a division of Columbia Concerts, Inc. Mr. Coppicus had heard us once in Vienna.

We sang the very best music in the very best way we could, as solemnly as possible, as was fitting for Bach and Palestrina. We sang for half an hour; then the gentlemen arose and went out. They sent word back that they felt very sorry indeed, but they did not think they could manage the Trapp Family Choir.

Silence.

In the train going home we discussed what it might have been that made them refuse us.

"Perhaps we should have sung Josquin des Prés instead of Palestrina. That's even more difficult and would have shown better what we can do."

"Or we should have played more on the recorders. Mr. Schang seemed to like them."

"Next time let's do . . ." I said.

"What do you mean, next time?"

Into Georg's tired eyes came a faint hope.

"Surely you don't want to give up now," I said belligerently. "What else is there to do? We'll study some more, ask them for another audition, and next time they'll take us!"

It didn't even occur to me that we could have given auditions to other managers in New York. Two weeks passed in which we rehearsed "*Alle Psallite*," an organum from around 1500, the motet "*Ave Maria*" by Josquin des Prés, one piece by Dufay, and a difficult trio sonata by Telemann for alto and tenor recorders and spinet. Then we felt up to the occasion and wrote to Columbia Concerts, attention Mr. Schang, for another audition. We held our breath waiting for the answer, which came by return mail: the first envelope with the weighty words, "Columbia Concerts, Inc." The answer was most cordial: "Come any time. Let us know twenty-four hours ahead."

We fixed the date. The evening before, we couldn't go to sleep, it was so exciting. Tomorrow our fate would be decided. If they refused us again, we would have to ask the Department of Labor for permission to earn our living as maids and cooks.

Again we stood on the little stage in the Steinway building. This time there were more people present: girls from the office and others. If a shy smile had crept in between numbers the first time, it certainly was suppressed on this occasion. The quaint chords of the sixteenth century couldn't afford such worldly gestures.

My heart started sinking when one girl after the other quietly left the room. Also the gentlemen left. We were waiting. Then I was called out and informed by Mr. Coppicus' secretary that it was definitely "no."

I just couldn't believe it, and I couldn't bring myself to break this cruel news to my family.

"Will you please wait for me at the Wellington," I said to them cryptically and disappeared. This was my very last chance. I at least had to find out *what* was wrong with us. I asked my way through to the nice young lady who had just talked to me.

When I had found her, I said: "Why Mr. Coppicus not take us?"

She looked so kind, so sympathetic; she took me over to the window and explained in a low voice:

"Mr. Coppicus said the Baroness has absolutely no sex appeal. They will never be a real attraction."

"Oh," said I, and looked blank, and then quite hopefully, "thank you very much indeed."

"Sex appeal." I memorized the words. For heaven's sake, I mustn't forget the precious phrase before I found out what it was. I had been too proud to admit to the girl that I didn't even know what it was that I lacked so badly, but I would find out.

But how? Well, in a book store. Around Christmas I had been in Scribner's on Fifth Avenue and remarked on their vast music department. It must have to do with music, of course. "Sex appeal," I murmured from time to time as I walked the blocks over to Scribner's. Now after Christmas it was quite empty, and right away a nice-looking young man wanted to know what he could do for me.

"Music," I said, and he led me over to the big alcove which was lined from floor to ceiling on three sides with books on music. After a little searching, I discovered that they were arranged alphabetically. Quickly I moved over to "S"; "Shostakovich; Sibelius; Strauss, Johann; Strauss, Josef; Strauss, Richard; String Quartet; Symphony." I read all the titles aloud to myself, but "it" was not there.

The young man came.

"Can I help you with anything?"

"Yes," I said somewhat haughtily. "Book on sex appeal, please. Need it for concerts."

Why did he disappear so quickly and never come back?

Scribner's had disappointed me. I really had thought they had a book on *everything*. All I could do now was go into the lion's den and find out right there. So back I walked to Steinway Hall. On the way I mused to myself whether "sex appeal" was something you put on your head, whether it is part of your appearance, whether you buy it by the ounce or by the inch. Shortly afterwards I found myself on the fifteenth floor of 113 West 57th Street, face to face with Mr. Schang.

After having shown me to a seat, he was leaning back in his swivel chair, and with a big cigar he produced a smoke screen between us. What a moment! All of a sudden I became conscious that this was my last, my very last chance, and there was my bad English.

"Why you not take us?" I started out.

He didn't answer right away. Then suddenly he sat up and, taking the cigar out of his mouth, he started to explain.

"It has nothing to do with your musicianship, I want you to understand. Already at your Town Hall concert I recognized you as good artists. Still, it's the worst program I've ever heard. That program. *That program!* That piece by Bach was forty-five minutes! That's for a few music enthusiasts, but do you think people across the country want to listen by the hour to quaint ancient tunes? And the recorders! They sound like a calliope. But by far the worst thing is your appearance—solemn and deadly serious, you come and go like a funeral procession. No charming smile and no good looks, either," and he continued in real disgust: "those long skirts, high necks, hair parted in the middle, braids in the back, shoes like boys, cotton stockings! Can't you get decent store clothes so one can see your legs in nylon stockings, get pretty, high-heeled shoes and put a little red on your face and on your lips?"

"No," I said gravely, "we can't." And I was choking-full of explanations as to why we couldn't, but I knew I would get hopelessly tangled in long English sentences without the right beginning and the right end.

Silence.

"This is—last word?" I finally ventured to ask.

"Yes."

The battle was lost. All of a sudden I felt very tired. The strain had been great; the rehearsals of last week, the excitement of the morning, and the tension of the last minutes. And this was America, of which everyone had told us—here you can say what you want, do what you want, wear what you want. An urgent desire took hold of me to let this man in front of me know how I felt. All was lost; I couldn't spoil anything any more. If I couldn't say it in words, I'd say it anyhow.

And I took a thick book lying on his desk, slammed it on the table, looked at him as crossly as I could manage, and said:

"I thinked—America free country. *Is not!*"

After this annihilating speech, I turned and walked out. My tears he should not see.

While I was waiting for the elevator, the nice young secretary tapped me on the shoulder and asked me to come back into Mr. Schang's office.

"Maybe after all you'll make it all right," said an altogether different Mr. Schang—"win over the American audience at large, I mean. I'd like to try for one year," and he sounded genuinely interested. "But it will need a great deal of publicity and advertising, and that is expensive. Could you spend—let's say—five thousand dollars on advance publicity?"

"Will try," I said, and then we shook hands.

All I let them squeeze out of me at the Wellington was: "Mr Schang is almost sure that he will take us; not quite, but almost."

Then I lapsed into silence and prayed for the money. In the bank we had exactly $250. That much I knew.

The same evening we went over to the Drinkers' and sang with them for two hours. Afterwards, over some ginger ale, I told my story.

"If we can advance five thousand dollars, he will take us," I finished, avoiding looking at my family, but looking pleadingly at Mr. Drinker. Would he have an idea?

There—while Sophie was still laughing to tears about me at Scribner's, Harry Drinker's voice could be heard:

"I'll lend you half the money if you find somebody for the other half."

I closed my eyes in excitement, and also in order to think hard

When I opened them again, I said: "Mrs. P."

That was a rich lady whom we had met at a concert at the Cosmopolitan Club in New York, and she had said with such genuine cordiality: "If you ever need any help, let me know."

Mr. Drinker went to the telephone and called Mrs. P. She said "yes." The miracle had happened.

The very next morning—he had said there was no time to lose, it was late in the season—I stood in Mr. Schang's office and handed him two checks, each one for $2,500, and said simply:

"Here, borrowed for a year."

There was great quiet in the room until a warm and sincere-sounding voice came from behind deep blue clouds:

"Congratulations!"

Again I wanted so very badly to "say something." I pressed his hand, and he must have seen in my eyes what was in my heart when I said:

"You not regret—never—I r-r-really mean it!"

When he walked with me to the elevator, he said:

"I believe in you as musicians, but now we have to try to coin the gold lump of your artistry into practical currency, so that everyone may take something home from your concerts.

"For this we shall start by changing your name. 'Trapp Family Choir' sounds too church-y. I am the manager of the 'Trapp Family Singers.'"

Merion

WHEN I arrived in Merion Station, I didn't go straight home, but stopped first at the Drinkers' house. The last twenty-four hours I had lived—we all had—in a pink fog. Things were too good to be true, and didn't yet register completely. As they slowly began to sink in, a deep gratitude took hold of me, and not only gratitude, but also a new feeling of responsibility. There were people —Mrs. P., Mr. Drinker, Mr. Schang, who, while believing in us, risked something. Not only should they not be let down, but some day they should have real reason to be proud of us. Now we simply *had* to become the best artists in our field for the sake of these people who trusted in us.

And this I had to tell the Drinkers before going home.

There we experienced in our own life what other people's trust does to you. It releases new powers; new depths in your soul open hitherto unknown to yourself. It sharpens your will and fixes it on the goal—it helps you to do the impossible. That's the way God works with us. He always gives us another chance. Why do people use this magic wand so little? It would transform this world into a paradise. Communism would not be a threat, and United Nations would not be needed. The brotherhood of man would be lived, not just talked about.

A new life had started for us when we entered the "house across the street." Our application for extension of temporary stay had been granted this time on account of war conditions in Europe. It had to be renewed every six months, but no one would be forced to leave the United States during the war. And we had a new manager in whose hands we felt secure. Those troubles of last year did not cloud our sky any more. With new strength and vigor we reorganized our life. Johanna took over the kitchen; Hedwig

184

was in charge of the laundry; Agathe started to sew; Maria took charge of the mending and darning; Martina, the housecleaning; the boys brushed the shoes of the entire family and helped with the dishes; Georg did the shopping; I took care of the correspondence; and Father Wasner, of the bookkeeping. From the day we had left Austria Georg had asked Father Wasner to take over the handling of the money. During all those critical years when we were in debt, we felt we didn't have the right to own anything individually until we had paid back every cent we owed. Therefore, the incoming money and the incoming bills went to Father Wasner, and everyone, Georg and I included, who needed money for one thing or the other, went to him. That guaranteed, so we felt, the best use of our money.

At that time the little girls wanted to start learning to play instruments, which didn't seem to go with their being in school. At that very moment I happened to meet right in Philadelphia a former teacher of mine from Vienna. Now she was over here, a refugee, too. It was almost incredible, but how lucky we both felt! She was looking for a home, and I, for a teacher. So she came and stayed with us and grew right into the family as Tante Lene. Very soon we noticed with amazement how much time the little ones had to practice the piano, the violin, the recorder, and still spend hours every day out-of-doors.

Mr. Schang had suggested that we give two Christmas concerts in Town Hall. That meant an entirely new program, and we started right out working on it. Father Wasner went to the big libraries in search of Christmas motets. When he brought them home, the different parts had to be copied before we could start working. Then we had to get acquainted with English and American Christmas carols, for many of which Father Wasner made new settings.

It was the day before Christmas when we moved into our new home, the little house with the blue shutters. Very kindly, a neighbor came over to find out whether she could do anything to help.

"Yes," I said, "can you please tell me where I can get a goose? You see, at Christmas one has to eat a goose if one can afford it at all."

Good-naturedly the friendly lady, whose name was Betty, herself drove me to the Reading Terminal Market in Philadelphia to get that indispensable Austrian goose. She obviously didn't want to spoil Christmas for me. But that was my last day of vacation.

Right after Christmas school started. This was not grade school any more with our bus driver as teacher; this was high school, and these were the subjects: American Past, American Present, American Living, American Thinking; and Betty was the teacher. Soon we were good friends. From what I had told her in my halting English, she had made the hair-raising observation that I was floating around in a dream world, in which money and what it stood for had no part. As far as Americanization went, Betty saw with sharp eyes that we were freshly hatched baby chicks with eggshells still sticking to us: eggshells of European thinking and believing, European dos and don'ts. Out of pure helpfulness she decided that something had to be done about it. First she took care of my English, which still showed strong traces of my two first teachers: Dr. Johnson and the driver.

"Betty, who are the two guys over there?" I asked the very first morning, pointing to two most dignified Main Liners.

She almost fainted.

"But—Maria! You can't say that. That's very poor English."

Oh, I was sorry, but I definitely remembered Dr. Johnson having told me that "guy" is just another word for "gentleman."

"And do never say 'O. K.' That's vulgar."

"O. K., Betty," I said.

"But Maria—that's very vulgar!"

How often would she have to say that!

Now I would have to learn to unlearn. No more "gee whiz," "golly Moses," "jeepers creepers," "gosh," "oh shucks," "boy oh boy," "jump in the lake"—at least not when Betty was around. But how many more times poor Betty almost fainted, as for instance, that afternoon when she had company for tea and looked somewhat blue, and I remembered suddenly one of Dr. Johnson's most helpful suggestions if I wanted to cheer someone up:

"Oh Betty, don't be a cranky old hog."

But this was only one part of my education, and at that, a minor one. To make, eventually, a good citizen out of me, she would have to make me money-conscious, to teach me to appreciate the nickel, of which there were twenty needed to make a dollar.

"Don't say 'buck,' Maria, that's very vulgar."

Desperately she tried to explain:

"You are not rich any more, Maria. You are poor now, don't you see?—poor."

What a sad truth, and how cruel to state it aloud like that! And, quoting Dr. Johnson once more, "If I never see you again, it's too soon!" I went into my room and bewailed my fate with real tears, that these Americans were just hard-boiled, hard-hearted, didn't understand us, never would, and wasn't it awful! Betty with her sound common sense never even dreamed how my sensitive heart shrank each time at the word "poor," and how I cried my eyes out after each application of the remedy.

Another thing we had to learn from scratch: that no work, as long as it is decent, can ever disgrace anybody. We were still so Europeanly prejudiced, that we didn't want to be caught at manual labor. When company came and we were busy in the kitchen, pantry, or basement, we went out the back door and came in the front door, not to give away the secret that we had been working. What a blessing, however, that we had no money at all, and simply had to jump in and swim. I remember the sad number of fellow refugees whom we met occasionally in New York. One such refugee had been a director or inspector or professor in Europe, and now, of course, he was waiting for a "leading position." He had brought with him a little money, too much to die with, and too little to live on; but it kept him, unfortunately, from starting all over again from the bottom. And there they were, huddled together in shabby apartments, starving, cold, but still wearing old fur coats and leather gloves and wasting precious time waiting for that "leading position," which might never come. This misfortune we were spared. We just had to learn the hard way, and that is one of the things we are most grateful for now. Now when we are driving the manure or lime spreader on our farm and see a fancy Cadillac drive up with some unexpected company, we only wave and shout: "We'll be right with you!" without the slightest shade of embarrassment on either side.

But that was not so on that morning in Merion. The night before, we had been invited for dinner at a friend's house, and my partner on the left had been an extremely nice-looking young man in evening clothes. The next morning a coal truck came with a load, and who can describe my horror when my elegant left-hand neighbor, black all over, started to shovel the coal into the cellar. I was all bewildered and looked away discreetly, not to embarrass him. Embarrass him? Why?

"Good morning, Baroness. Don't you remember me?" he shouted through the rumbling of the coal. Well, he wanted to get into the coal business, and had started from the bottom. What a completely different world, but what a wholesome one!

Betty rejoiced when I cheerfully announced one day that I would rather *walk* into town (ten miles!) to save the fare, and almost tenderly she started to caution me not to overdo my thriftiness, only to be most cruelly disappointed by the finishing of my sentence: because I wanted to buy a color film.

"But you can't afford that, Maria. Don't forget, you are poor."

And now something funny happened. I must have shed the last tear which was in me for that particular subject. Without being the slightest bit offended, I looked at her triumphantly and said sweetly:

"No, we are not poor. We just don't have any money."

In this moment I had somehow passed from freshman to sophomore.

Johannes was so cute now with his blond curls, waddling like a penguin all over the place. If I wanted to take colored pictures of him in that state, I just had to do it then, and couldn't wait until we might one day have real money in the bank. Johannes might be in college then. This I tried to explain to Betty in the most poetic terms, but didn't succeed. I thought if I showed her my colored slides, that would make my point clear, but—wow!

"You have a projector, Maria, and a screen?"

"The screen was a present, Betty, but the projector—" and I lighted up with eagerness to show off what I had learned most recently—"the projector we bought, and the sewing machine, and the victrola, and the washing machine, without any money. American installment plan buying is something wonderful. Only five dollars a month—just imagine! In three years they will be really our own."

Betty was torn between feeling proud of her hopeful pupil and mad at the projector. The sewing and washing machines she let pass right away. The victrola I had to explain as being absolutely necessary in our business. We *had* to listen to other choirs. All right then. But the projector remained a sore spot.

But how many delightful hours we spent together, teacher and disciple, between tears and laughter, as I slowly advanced into the senior class.

Our life did not allow much social activity, but there was a small circle of real people with whom we loved to spend our Sundays and free evenings. And there were the Drinkers across the street. Nothing was more gratifying to us than to have found such genuine music-lovers. Harry's enthusiastic "Let's do it again!" still sounds in our ears, and his radiant smile whenever we performed for him for the first time one of our newest motets or songs was applause in itself.

Nothing demonstrates more his sincere love of music than the fact that he had made, besides other translations, new English translations of the entire vocal works of Johann Sebastian Bach. These translations are a more correct rendering of the German originals, especially those taken from the Scriptures, and are more singable.

Another dear friend whom we met in those days was Madame Marion Freschl, a famous voice teacher with a most superior grasp of the problems of the voice. In those critical moments which occur in every singer's life she always came very efficiently to our help.

Again we were fortunate at this time in beginning an association with Miss Alix Williamson who has since handled our publicity so well.

At that time trouble started in the nursery. How comparatively easy it had been to bring up the older children. Of course, there were stormy times when a little liar had to be punished, or, for instance, when I had my one and only battle with little Martina. That had been soon after my wedding. I had told the three youngest ones, Martina, Johanna, and Hedwig, that they could play any place in the big park whenever they had free time, and with whatever they wanted, except with knives, scissors, and matches. "And whoever doesn't obey will get spanked," I had said. The very next day I found tiny little Martina with the largest knife we had in the kitchen, carrying it like a bouquet of flowers

before her. I took it out of her hand, turned her around for a slap.
She departed seriously. Not long afterwards I ran across her dragging the large scissors from the sewing room on a cord behind her
on the way to the garden. Again, without saying much, I took the
scissors, and Martina was turned around for her reward. Now I
was on my guard, and sure enough, I discovered in her little apron
the whole kitchen supply of matches, destined to be buried under
a tree for the future, as she confessed. Now I took the little sinner
upstairs and gave her a good spanking. Not a tear. The serious
little face with the tiny frown between the brows lit up when she
told me with a genuine sigh of relief:

"You don't have to worry from now on, Mother. I won't be
disobedient again. I just had to find out whether you really meant
it."

She has kept her word.

But now after all these years there was real trouble brewing.
Lorli was becoming the naughtiest little girl in Merion, Philadelphia, and perhaps the whole United States of America. Those few
weeks in school had made a little wild Indian of her. Fresh as a
monkey, she always had an answer ready, and unfortunately, they
were most of the time so unexpectedly witty that one had to be on
one's guard not to laugh out loud. Poor Rosmarie suffered a Purgatory from that sister of hers. Rosmarie was the kindest, mildest,
most good-natured soul, and let herself be dominated and tortured
by that wild little creature.

Sadly I remembered a scene in my own school days. I wouldn't
have dared even to whisper it in front of Lorli, but I myself had
been much worse than she, the very despair of my teachers, full of
tricks and mischief. One day the teacher called me out in front
of the whole class and solemnly pronounced this curse:

"I wish you may sometime have a daughter exactly like you.
Sit down."

For a little while, I remember, Lorli had attended a kindergarten
in Salzburg. There she had made the fatal acquaintance of scissors
and learned what wonderful patterns you can cut out of a folded
piece of paper. The first item on which she tried it was her beautiful, new, fluffy pink blanket. I admonished her earnestly never to
do that again. She promised, and must have meant, never again
on a blanket, because the next victim was one of the precious bed

PHOTO: ROBERT LEWIS — ALIX WILLIAMSON

BUILDING THE NEW HOUSE AT STOWE, VERMONT

" 'Can you tell me what one does with a fallen-down house?' "

THE AUTHOR AND HER HUSBAND
Georg and Maria Trapp.

cade curtains in the living room. Now she was told that under no circumstances might those scissors cut anything which was not strictly her private property. She promised, and looked, oh, so sincere! Her left hand took a firm grip on the curls above her forehead, and before I could cry "no," the scissors had cut what was strictly her own. But she hadn't disobeyed.

When she started going to school, she never came home. Hours passed every day, and I got worried. So I explained to her she must always keep going and never stop. The very next day I was waiting again, and finally I went all the way into town to find her walking up and down, chatting cheerily with a policeman, who said to me when I took hold of my daughter:

"Yoor little girl kept me very nice company. She said I should walk up and down with her because she wasn't supposed to stop, and she told me all about her home."

That I could believe.

But now she had new ideas. One day I found her posing before a mirror, making lovely faces.

"Mother," the little angel said, "where do I have my complexion? Patsy's mother said I had such a lovely one. Do you really think I'm pretty? A girl from the twelfth grade said I'm the prettiest girl in school. Can you show me where the sparkle is in my eyes?"

"Oh, oh!" I thought.

The same evening we were mending stockings near the fireplace, and I seemed to have forgotten Lorli's presence in the room.

"It's really a pity," I said to Agathe, "that beautiful babies usually grow to be ugly little ducklings. Poor Lorli! What a horse-face she's got now, and what a pretty little thing she was in Salzburg! Too bad."

It did the trick.

Long afterwards, when Lorli was to appear for the first time on the stage, she came and said:

"Honestly, Mother, I'm so sorry that I'm spoiling the picture on the stage, but I'll try to play extra well to make up for my looks."

For years she had avoided even looking into a mirror. She came to one of her sisters to part her hair.

One of her weak spots at that crucial time was her nibbling at everything edible she could get hold of between meals. Outside of

Christmas, Easter, or birthdays, there were no candies around, and one night while we were out singing with the Drinkers, Lorli simply couldn't withstand the temptation to look for something in the line of sweets. The most thorough raid all through the house didn't produce a single candy. Finally, she landed in Father Wasner's room, which was strictly forbidden to begin with, and there she found in a drawer a little box with hosts to be used for Holy Mass, *and she ate them all!* On that evening a little girl wept herself into slumber after the most awful spanking of her life, and, oh cruel fate, no birthday celebration the next day. For a while there was hardly a day without a spanking, which was the most awful moment of the day for Rosmarie, who cried bitterly, whereas the proud little sinner pretended not to mind. How many times in later years has Lorli flung her arms around her mother's neck, thanking her with all her heart for the great lessons of discipline and self-control.

And one day something else happened. Johannes had strewn all his toys all over the living room floor, and when it was time for lunch, I said casually:

"Now, Johannes, pick up your toys."

Well, lo and behold, the little fifteen-months-old pulled himself up to his full height, looked right into my eyes, and said:

"No."

"Oh, yes," I assured him.

"Oh, no," he answered.

And "yes" and "no" went back and forth several more times, and then it had to be.

After these first spanks of his young life, he stamped his fat little foot and said crossly:

"No, no, no!"

So the first spanks were followed by the second, and by the third. All of a sudden the tear-stained little face brightened. He climbed on my lap, put his soft little arms around my neck, whispered sweetly into my ear, "Yes," curled up, and was fast asleep. That experience lasted him for many years.

This is one of the most subtle moments in bringing up children, I guess: to sense when to spank and when not. Some of the dear little ones do need it, and no substitute will do. Others, however, must never be touched harshly. With Lorli's sister it was enough

o say reproachfully: "But Illi!" (our nickname for Rosmarie) and
he sensitive little soul dissolved into a lake of tears. The old say-
ng: "Spare the rod and spoil the child" seems like a translation of
he Bible: "Who loves his son does not spare the rod." It is to be
oped that the world will soon turn away from its experiment in
he realm of progressive education where poor, unhappy children
lways have to do what they want; the young will is then crippled
y its own whims.

One morning in early May Father Wasner in his office as finan-
ier, remarked at breakfast:
"We have not quite fifty dollars left in the bank."
There were still four months to the next concert tour, and one
hing was sure: fifty dollars wouldn't get us to September. Next
hing: family council. Recently we had seen an exhibition of Penn-
ylvania Dutch handicraft, which had been very interesting, and we
ad noticed that the items sold fast. As there was nothing and
obody to sing for at that moment, the only other suggestion we
ould think of was: "Let's have a handicraft exhibit, too."
The different Christmas and birthday presents had shown that
there seemed to be talent for handicrafts in the family. Let's find
out. The next two weeks were devoted to the most concentrated
work in leather, clay, wood, linoleum, paint, and silver. At one of
the Drinker singing parties we had learned to know the sisters
Smith, one of whom was a sculptor. Eleanor and May became the
most faithful and devoted helpers now. Where to get the materials
downtown; where to have the clay baked; how to find a place for
the exhibition; how to advertise it; they helped us with all these
most practical factors. The exhibition proved such a success with
so many orders coming in, that we were seriously advised to repeat
it in New York.
Reverend Mother from Ravenhill lent us the station wagon in
which the whole Trapp Family Handicraft Exhibit drove to New
York. With the children's furniture, the carpentry work of which
had been done by Georg and the painting most successfully by
Martina, who showed great skill in peasant art (she was also the
creator of lovely trays, wooden bowls, and boxes); really artistic
work in clay by Johanna; very original jewelry by Werner; leather
work of all kinds by Hedwig; wood carving by Maria; linoleum

cuts by Agathe, we felt we had an unusual collection of objects
sell. Rupert and I were the unskilled ones. We did the exhibitin

Soon there were more orders than time to fill them, and Se
tember was reached without our having had to contract more debt

Now we were well on the way. We had learned that work-
whatever it may be—honors you and makes you free. Further, w
had found out that as long as you are willing to work, America
still the land of unlimited opportunities. It is up to you to us
them. And we had also found out that this was the only way t
become American, a part of this nation of pioneers: to be a pionee
yourself.

The Fly

EPTEMBER came, and one day a big bus stopped in front of the ouse on Merion Road. This time it was a red one, the newest ype with a motor in the rear. The same bus driver was here again, e old faithful, and started to load. To his great delight, we had ecided to take Johannes along with us. He loved the baby dearly nd rearranged the bus for him.

Tante Lene and Martha would stay behind with the little girls. Martha was a close school friend of our Maria from Salzburg. She ad been with us in Sweden as a baby sitter to take care of young ohannes during our lengthy rehearsals. When the war broke out, he couldn't return home, but came along with us to America.

By then we had found out that school can be taken care of at ome, but we still thought that it was bound to a house. Later we would learn that it can very well take place on wheels.

A friend of the family had offered to come along and help us ake care of Johannes while we were rehearsing, and during concerts.

How altogether different was this farewell from the other years! he first time we had had to lug around all our belongings with us nd deposit the children in a strange boarding school; the second ear we could leave them in the house of friends, and a corner of heir attic housed part of our goods; this time, however, we left hem in our own home, surrounded by friends who would keep n eye on things. Slowly, slowly, the tree with the ten branches which had been plucked out by the roots and taken across the cean into a new soil, started to root again. It is always an experiment to transplant a full-grown tree. One doesn't know whether he roots will take to the strange soil. What a relief when it shows hat they do!

After a tearful farewell we went first to New York—Hotel Wel-

lington, of course! This year the carpets were red and the uni
forms, bright frog-green. The next day we were to give a concert
in a New York college, and Mr. Schang would be present. This
was the first concert under his management, and the first one of a
tour of sixty-five, which would lead us from coast to coast. What
an important and exciting moment!

F. C. Schang was no stranger to us any more. We had seen him
several times in his office, and he had also visited us in Merion.
Out of his vast experience in the concert business he had given us
the most valuable advice in building up new programs which
would contain something for everybody, for the housewife in Mich
igan, the farmer in Kansas, the rancher out west as well as for the
music scholar. Our programs in the past had been mostly in Latin
and German. Now we added English numbers. Among the Eng
lish madrigals and folk songs we found some wonderful pieces
like "Sweet Honey-Sucking Bees," "Early One Morning," and "Just
as the Tide was Flowing"; and among the old American folk songs
we found hidden treasures. Our program now had five parts: first,
sacred music, selections from the ancient masters from the sixteenth
and seventeenth centuries; second, music played on the ancient in
struments: recorders, viola da gamba, spinet; third, madrigals and
ballads; fourth, Austrian folk songs and mountain calls; fifth, Eng
lish and American folk songs.

I had admired Mr. Schang many times for his unique ability to
master every situation. It was perfectly incredible how he could
always say the only thing which should be said at the moment.
How finely he could choose the nuance of what to say, to whom
and when. Whether it was Grace Moore or Lily Pons, the girls
and I, or Mr. Henry S. Drinker, I was always stunned by the
finesse he displayed on each occasion.

Now we were at the college, and Sister Mary Rose, a saintly nun,
was in charge of the concert; I felt genuine curiosity creeping up
within me: what would Mr. Schang do to make Sister Mary Rose
happy? He couldn't kiss her hand, he couldn't tell her how much
he liked her gown—*what* was he going to say? This would be his
first meeting with a nun.

There he was.

"Sister Mary Rose, may I introduce Mr. Schang, our manager?"
A few nice words went back and forth, and look—here we go!

In a voice vibrating with genuine admiration, F. C. uttered the weighty words:

"Sister Mary Rose, in all my life I have never heard such perfect diction!"

We got a return date.

This concert was a new experience. We tried very hard to put into practice the very good admonitions our new manager gave us before the concert:

"Don't be formal; smile, relax, forget about the audience. Simply sing for the fun of singing. Be at ease; don't look so pained; relax, don't worry."

But if you have to try hard to be informal, if you have to force yourself to look relaxed, that to begin with is not the real thing. The worst of it was that *he* was in the audience; he, the one person among all the people of the U.S.A. whom we wanted most to please and satisfy. But all the same, the concert turned out to be very successful. Mr. Schang smiled all over, congratulated us time and again on the great difference in our stage appearance.

But the next day when he came to the Wellington to say goodbye, as the bus was waiting outside all ready to take us to the West Coast, he added:

"There is something you are lacking, and I can't put my finger on exactly what it is. There is something between you and the audience; but I trust, I just know, that if you try hard, you will find what it is."

That word "lacking'" stuck with us. From now on we watched for what we should do; most critically so. After every concert we sat together and discussed it. Was it the coming and going, the standing, the smiling and bowing? Georg, our most faithful helper and companion in the concert business, sat in the first row every evening and added his observations. But all along, we knew we still hadn't found it. The concerts were good, very good; the people liked them and said so; but . . .

We were heading for Los Angeles and driving on Highway 66. The great highlight of this trip was for us our first meeting with the Indians, the real Indians, about whom we had read so much in Europe. We had all been brought up on Carl May, a German, who had written many books about those great heroes of the Wild West. His books were devoured by every boy, and also by many a girl, and every one of us had once cried over Winnetou, the great chief of the Apaches. And now we would meet his blood brothers. Our hearts beat higher long before we came to New Mexico; but finally it said on the map: "Pueblo Laguna," and I was ready with cameras for both moving and still pictures.

Finally I said to the driver: "When is Pueblo Laguna coming?"

He answered casually: "Oh, we passed it a good ten minutes ago. Why?"

"Passed it? The Indians? Our first Indians? Just passed it like that?"

I was so disappointed, I could have cried. I went back to the very rear of the bus to hide my sentiments. But above the driver's seat was a big mirror, and the driver's eye could see easily what was going on within me. He was sincerely sorry. Never in his life had he thought that anyone could want to take pictures of Indians, something so unprogressive; but, well, she took pictures of Negroes, too, didn't she? He turned the bus around, and back we went to Pueblo Laguna and met our first Indians, nice, friendly people, who looked at us as curiously as we at them. They had never seen Austrians in their national costume, either. We admired their beautiful church, bought some of their quaint pottery, and sang a few Austrian folk songs for them, and I was permitted to take pictures, with hands trembling with excitement. One was a picture of baby Johannes with his white-blond curls, embracing a little Indian boy of his own age with straight, bluish-black hair. There was something about the Indians which moved us deeply that first time, and every other time, we met them, something so dignified and so sad. A strange sensation of sympathy and understanding passed back and forth between us. Was it that we had once shared their own fate of being exiles in our own home? From then on, we always went out of our way to meet the Indians again, and to spend as much time as we could with them.

On this trip we saw some of the most dazzling phenomena of nature: the Painted Desert, the Petrified Forest, the Grand Canyon, the sand desert of California. There was little time to spend in each place, but every day our admiration for this country of wonders grew.

Then we were in Los Angeles, the "suburb of Hollywood," and we were disappointed. Somehow the world of the films had enieloped the whole area around Hollywood, and the atmosphere was one of artificiality and unnaturalness. We didn't fit very well.

Then we greeted the Pacific Ocean for the first time on our way up the coast, heading for Seattle. In Santa Barbara we spent a wonderful day with Lotte Lehmann. The Indian missions, the redwoods, Yosemite Valley and Sequoia National Park, Golden Gate Bridge, Carmel-by-the-Sea, more redwoods, finally the lagoons of Oregon, the peaks of the snowy mountains, and the beautiful bay of Seattle—it was all like a dream; the vastness of the country and its riches, its wild beauty and its proud spirit—America the beautiful!

We had sung many concerts, but we were still hunting for the missing link.

Then we wound our way back and finally came to Denver, Colorado. We had been forewarned that the society sponsoring our concert was very high-brow in a musical sense, and expected a very classical program. This they would get. We omitted the ballads and folk songs and gave our best in a most serious type of music. At the end of the performance I felt suddenly sympathetic with the few among our listeners who might not have been quite so high-brow as the others.

On the way out to take a bow, I whispered to Father Wasner: "I'd like to sing a *Jodler* now."

As this was not on the program, it had to be announced. All announcing was an additional pain, accompanied by blushing each time.

I stepped forward and said: "We shall sing as an encore now one of the mountain calls from the Austrian Alps, known as *Jodler,*" and we started.

In yodeling one has to take a deep breath and then hold out for long phrases at a time. We were just in the middle of it when, oh horror! a fly started circling around my face. I watched it, crosseyed, and got panicky. I knew very soon I would have to take a deep breath, and what if . . . A simple move of my hand would have chased it away, but that's it. To move your hand leisurely on the stage whenever you want, and wherever you want, it is necessary not to be rigid with self-consciousness and sweating with stage fright. We took our deep breath, and it happened. In went the fly and, of course, down my "Sunday throat," where it got stuck.

I felt like choking. Again, a good cough would have helped. But to cough the right way on the stage is much, much harder than to sing the right way. I outdid myself in not coughing, but I couldn't help turning purple. I happened to have the leading part in this *Jodler,* the melody; but that mountain call had to be finished without it, because I was struggling between life and death. My brave children tried not to pay any attention to their choking mother, and when they were finished, I was, too—with the fly. I felt terribly sorry for everyone, but mostly for the audience, who had been cheated of their encore. I forgot that I was on the stage and embarrassed and facing people. I only felt I had to apologize and make up.

Out of this urge I stepped forward and said perfectly naturally in everyday language:

"What never happened before, has happened now: I swallowed a fly."

I was perfectly amazed at the success of this simple statement. The people laughed and laughed and laughed. When they had recovered, I informed them that we wanted to sing another encore to make up for the spoiled one: this time an Austrian folk song, and I explained:

"It describes how a young hunter climbs up in the rocks for hours, looking for, and finally finding and shooting, a . . ." I wanted to say *Gemse,* the only word for which I knew was "chamois"; but somehow I got mixed up and said "chemise."

I was perfectly dumbfounded. Was that such a joke in America? I couldn't see anything *so* funny, and looked questioningly at my children who—can you believe it?—were shaking with laughter, too. When, finally, the worst had passed, I started. For a whole line I was alone; the others were to fall in later; and while I was singing by myself in full, loud yodel tones, Rupert, the mischievous one, whispered to me what I had said. To remain serious now and go on singing was almost harder than not to choke with the fly. I could have skinned Rupert in front of the whole audience.

But—the incredible had happened. The missing link was found: the audience and we had been for some precious minutes one whole. The spell was broken. Now we had found the bridge. Very soon we could say truthfully to our audiences:

"We don't consider this a concert; but we rather feel as if we had taken out one wall of our big living room at home, and you are all our guests at a musical party."

Quite informally we explained interesting details of the numbers to be performed, and the people assured us afterwards that they had quite forgotten that they were in a concert hall.

"You have made us feel so much at home."

Three cheers for the fly!

Stowe in Vermont

WE HAD to be back East in time for the Christmas concerts. And when Mr. Schang heard us again in Town Hall, he was all smiles.

"Now you've got it—you've got it! I always knew you would," he exclaimed. "It sounds like an altogether different attraction, and looks so, too," he added very pointedly. He had finally convinced us that the artificial, glaring light of the stage required artificial means merely to make one look natural and not like a fainting ghost.

"Some of your girls look sick, green as spinach. You don't want the audience to be unquiet about their not feeling well, do you?"

No, we didn't, and so some of us with a less ruddy complexion submitted to the use of make-up in order to look natural. These Christmas concerts turned out to be a real success. Everybody was satisfied, and when the first season under Columbia Concerts' management was over, we had reached the goal. They were not disappointed that they had taken us on their list of artists. We had not let anybody down. More and more requests for concerts came in, and the second tour was already planned for ninety-six, and the third, for over a hundred concerts.

". . . And all these things shall be added unto you."

Now we were living through the second part of the promise. All these things: friends, the ability and the opportunity to work. We were able to meet our debts at the appointed times.

From September through April we were traveling constantly with only a short stop around Christmas.

In the first touring year, for lack of the necessary money, we had had to go to the cheapest hotels we could find. The mere atmosphere around these places was depressing: the dirt, the filth, and the people frequenting them. You always felt like sneaking in and sneaking out. In the second year we couldn't get ourselves to do that any more. We still hadn't any money, but we had learned of the existence of cabins and tourist homes. Of course, these places were never large enough to take care of a big group, and so we had to split up every night, which made it difficult for the bus to deliver and collect us. Sometimes there were no eating places near—it was rather complicated, although more satisfactory than the low-grade hotels. This way of traveling stopped with Schang.

He insisted: "You must eat and live decently if you want to do a good job on the stage," and he was right. Those lunches for thirty-five cents at the diners on the roadside filled one's stomach for the moment, but didn't give any energy. That's why we had been so absolutely exhausted after the first concert tour with eighteen concerts; much more so than after the one with over a hundred.

Everything was fine, except for the one sad fact that for the greater part of the year we were separated from our little girls. They had meanwhile made great progress on their instruments, and one day the question arose: shouldn't they be on the program now? Fine, wonderful. But what of school? Couldn't we try to take a teacher along and have school in the bus and in the hotels? Well, there was nothing like trying. Tante Lene had a young friend, Betsy, who was willing to try, and on the next coast-to-coast trip Betsy came along with Rosmarie and Lorli, and Tante Lene accepted a teaching position at Ravenhill, leaving Martha alone with Johannes in the house. Martha, who would have been the most logical one to come along with us, had to give up after the first cruel try because she was a victim of car-sickness to an extent which made you almost regret the invention of automobiles.

Now the whole family, only the baby excepted, was together again—on wheels—and when we came back from this fifth American concert tour, we celebrated a great feast at home: we had paid the last cent of our debts, and we still had some money in the bank, after five short years.

That meant that this summer we wouldn't have to stay in Merion. When this sentence was pronounced aloud during lunch, the whole family broke out in cheers.

These past Philadelphia summers had been a real penance for us northerners. The combination of heat and moisture is something unknown to people from the Alps; the moisture was such that the wallpaper was loosened, and the shoes under the bed became mouldy overnight. At least, the boys said so, and they must know because they cleaned them every morning. Our heavy woolen costumes with close-fitting bodices, the heavy shoes and stockings had not been designed for this climate, but they were still all we possessed in the line of dresses. So far, that had never been a problem, as the money question came foremost. We were all still wearing what we had brought from Europe, but the things were starting to get threadbare. So one day we went shopping downtown in Philadelphia, and in a wholesale place we found material and patterns almost exactly like the ones at home, in cotton. Agathe, our seamstress, opened a workshop, everybody helped, and for about twenty dollars in all everyone got two light summer cottons. Every item had to be sewn at home. The dresses, the blouses, the aprons, even the men's socks were knit at home. For our own red stockings fashion came to our rescue. All of a sudden it was the latest rage for all college girls to wear red or green stockings in exactly the same pattern we were used to. When low-heeled shoes also came into fashion, we were all right. It would have been difficult to make shoes at home, although Hedwig had already begun to try it.

Usually around this time of the year in May our friends began to talk about their summer plans, whether they would go to the seashore or to the mountains, and by the middle of June they would all have said good-bye. For us country people it got harder and harder to live in a suburb, even in such a nice one as Merion, because of the asphalt. It was absolutely impossible to discover a dirt road anywhere within walking distance. We were so used to hiking, this having been our main recreation at home. We tried to get out on the highways for a hike. Due to the genuine kind-heartedness of the average American, every other car stopped and asked whether we didn't want a lift. When we branched off from the highway on a side road and wanted to sit down somewhere for a picnic, a sign on a tree invariably said: "Private—Keep Out—No Trespassing." After several attempts, we gave up hiking.

Now a great thing happened. Mr. Schang had said right away in the beginning: "Don't you think you would save money by making the tour in your own cars?" It had taken us two years to digest that suggestion, but now, all of a sudden, two large cars presented themselves for a very reasonable price: a seven-seater 1935 Lincoln Continental for $400 and a large Cadillac for $500. For twelve people with all the concert and private luggage we needed heavy cars. Here they were, and we took them. Little did we know the difference in cost of repairs between a Ford and a Cadillac, but we would learn that in the near future. At first we were drunk with the feeling of having advanced so high as to be car owners. Georg and the boys got drivers' licenses, and the next tour would be easy.

The Drinkers had invited us before to use a cabin of theirs in New Jersey in the woods on the Rancocas Creek. We had been there once, and it was a most delightful place, that spacious bungalow on the bank of the quiet river with the strong current and the low, black cedar waters. We felt like Tarzans in the jungle. But there was always the transportation problem. Now, however, with the cars, the whole universe was open to us, and at first, we accepted most gratefully the renewed invitation and settled for a couple of weeks on the Rancocas. There we found all the possibilities for exercise: hiking, swimming, canoeing, cutting wood.

It was an ideal two weeks, but it almost meant the end of Johannes. Clad in a bright red play-suit he walked one day straight into the river, which was eight feet deep at that place, and sank immediately, remaining quietly at the bottom like a little red mushroom. Father Wasner, who had seen him, jumped in, coat, shoes, and all, and got the mushroom out, who laughed and thought it was a lot of fun. If it hadn't been for the gaudy red, we wouldn't ever have found him in the dark waters. From now on he had a bodyguard.

Back in Merion, the question arose seriously: where did we want to spend the summer? Somewhere where it was cool, that was understood—but where? On the wall in the living room was a big map of the United States with little dots all over it, showing where we had given concerts. This map was now the center of interest, everybody having his own ideas and wanting to return to the spot he or she particularly preferred from all our trips. No one was astonished that Georg wanted to go to the seashore, to salt water. My special attraction had been New Mexico and the Pueblo Indians, and couldn't we please get tents and camp in a Pueblo? Father Wasner preferred his love-at-first-sight, Kentucky.

The boys were lured by the Rocky Mountains for some climbing—everybody had his very own ideas and fought for them.

Then one day a letter arrived from a Mr. R. from Stowe in Vermont, saying he had heard we were looking for a summer place. He had a tourist house equipped for twenty people, and was sure we would like it there. The price was reasonable, just exactly what we could afford, and the plans for the seashore, Kentucky, and New Mexico were postponed for some other year.

Our two big cars were packed, the house closed for the summer without any regret, and we went up north into that State which had been introduced to us by our driver as not worth while looking out the window for, as they only raised gravestones.

The farther north we came, the more the countryside reminded us of Austria. Finally we drove into Stowe, passed through the village with the friendly white church and its beautifully pointed steeple, out towards Mount Mansfield, as the tourist home called "The Stowe-Away" was in that direction. From the moment we entered, everything seemed to be waiting for us: the score of pleasant, sunny rooms, the lawn around the house, little cabin in the rear, and the view—the view! For years we had looked onto a surburban road with limousines passing by, or into other people's windows; and now it was like home; mountains and space and sky, meadows, fields, and trees.

Across the road was a wide brook with swimming holes, and all around were woods and pastures, the most ideal hiking country. Now we could walk again. We walked the three miles into the village when we needed anything; we walked up Mount Mansfield many times and through Smuggler's Notch and down to Bingham Falls and over to Mosglen Falls, around Round Top, and into Stowe Hollow.

It was a most wonderful summer.

The longer we stayed, the more we liked it, and the more difficult it was to think that one day we would have to pack the cars again and drive back into city life.

One day a friend came visiting on his way from a lecture trip in Canada back to the States. He also had been a refugee, but he had been longer in the country than we and knew more of its ways. We told him what a nightmare it was to go back into the city.

"But why don't you buy something and stay in Vermont?" he asked.

"Just because we don't have the money," we answered.

"But you don't need money if you want to buy a farm." He seemed amused at so much naiveté. "All you do is make a down payment, and then pay by and by."

From this moment on, our life was changed.

Once more we had a short meeting, the last one on that subject. Should we buy store clothes or a farm?

"But why buy store clothes now?" asked everyone rather impatiently. "People are used to us the way we are—nobody seems to mind—America is a free country—and how much would it cost anyhow?"

When we found out that walking shoes, street shoes, evening shoes, nylon stockings, underwear, six summer dresses, four winter dresses, an afternoon tea dress, evening gown, suit, skirt with several blouses and pullovers, summer coat, winter coat, hats to match, handbag and umbrella would run up to five hundred dollars apiece, which meant four thousand dollars for us all—that settled the question. That much money we didn't have anyway, and it would be a shame to waste it on clothing.

So we decided to buy a farm in Vermont.

I read once that bees can smell flowers in bloom even across hills and dales; male butterflies find out about a female of their own kind over sixty and seventy miles; news in the jungle gets around at a fantastic speed over vast regions. Something similar must be the case with real estate people. We hadn't told a soul outside the family, but catalogues started to come in, cars stopped in front of the house with agents who had heard we wanted to buy a farm in Vermont. The peaceful days when we played croquet on the lawn and lounged in the shade of the trees, sipping our coffee leisurely, those days were now gone for good. The fever had seized the family, and our sole occupation came to be looking at the property of other people who, for one reason or the other, wanted to get rid of it.

So far, we had learned English and American, which, as I had found out, were two distinctly different languages; but now we discovered that there existed another idiom, the one used by real estate people. "Good—very good—excellent" mean one thing to you and another thing to a real estate agent. After visiting the twentieth farm, we had learned by experience. If the buildings on the place are called "in excellent condition," then it is worth while looking at them. If they are "in very good repair," you don't risk much when you go through the house. But if they are only "good," you'd better stay home. They might not be there since the last storm. Then there is the inevitable "rushing trout brook." If you are lucky, you find a thin trickle between the stones; but mostly you aren't even that lucky. You just look at the stones and they are dry. A highly astonished Mr. Smith or Mr. Jones will assure you that the last time he was here it was a roaring brook, and its present looks must have to do with the pasture conditions.

Up and down we went in the State of Vermont. We saw "a valley of your own," which was highly recommended by one of the agents; but we would have to be Indians, or Eskimos in the winter, since the whole valley was densely wooded, but didn't even contain a cottage. Then we were shown the "dream castle," an old stone foundation next to which stood a little farm house. As it was too much "dream" and too little "castle," we declined it. A "spacious log cabin nestled in woodland" was offered us. This turned out to be an old shack, uninhabited for ten years, at least a mile away from the nearest road. We saw a "charming hilltop farm" with a "sweeping mountain view." This looked fine until we discovered by chance that three months of every year the water supply ran out completely, and water had to be carried by hand from the nearest pump half a mile away. One agent heartily recommended a "century-old residence with quaint features," which with "imagination plus a little paint and fixing" would make an ideal home for us. "Come see what you can do with it!" urged the prospectus. The quaintest feature, besides the heating system, which consisted of one wood stove in the kitchen, was the floor. The ancient boards, sagging everywhere, gave way under me in the dining room, leaving me with a badly twisted ankle for my efforts.

It is perfectly amazing with what tender expressions a stony pasture can be described, so that you feel ashamed of yourself if you don't purchase this bargain for the sake of your children and grandchildren.

We almost bought something near Brattleboro, a terrific number of acres—2,800—of woodland, a road leading through a gorge-like valley with a few houses and sunshine, most probably, between June 10 and 30. We even went so far as to bind the bargain with one hundred dollars. Never did we spend one hundred dollars better than when we lost those acres and got out of the deal. In spite of the thirty-acre lake on that property, Georg shuddered when he thought of the dark, shady location.

"I want sunshine and plenty of it," he sighed.

That settled it.

Finally, when we had looked at most of the salable "bargains" and couldn't find what we wanted, we started to hate the mere words "real estate." The farms in good locations with nice houses were far too expensive, and the ones we could have afforded were in all stages of being run-down. Finally we got quite allergic to the looks of crooked barns, broken-down fences, and stubbly pastures. We gave up.

One day in August a car stopped outside The Stowe-Away, and in came a gentleman. He took off his straw hat and introduced himself as Mr. Burt from Stowe and sat down. My family was out somewhere, so I was alone for the conversation.

"Nice day," Mr. Burt started.

"Very nice," I agreed. "Wonderful haying weather. How is the haying going?"

"All right, I guess."

Silence.

"Are there many tourists in Stowe?" I didn't really want to know, but I had to say something.

"Not too many."

Silence.

"It must be beautiful up here in winter."

"Yes," Mr. Burt agreed, "it is."

So far, he had rested his arms on his knees and turned his hat one way, on and on. Both of us were watching it in fascination. Now he changed the hat's direction, turning it the other way, and said:

"Are you singing much these days?"

"No," I said, "we are taking it easy. This is our first vacation in America."

"Oh."

Silence.

What in the world could I say next?

Then something dawned on me.

"Where do you want us to sing, Mr. Burt?"

The hat stopped twirling.

"Yes," he said, "that's it." He sounded genuinely relieved. "That's what I really came for. You see, last week the Army took over a former C.C.C. camp outside of Stowe, and we have been asked to entertain the boys; so we thought of you people and wondered whether you would give them some kind of a performance."

"But surely, gladly. When?"

The date was fixed for next Saturday, and we would be called for in Army jeeps.

"You mean one of those brand-new cars which can do all kinds of tricks? We read about them in the *Reader's Digest*."

The next Saturday two Army jeeps stopped in front of the house, and a Captain Hunt and another officer drove us over Barrows Road through an enchanting little valley to the camp. What a nice place for a camp! The barracks stood together on a flat spot on top, and there was something which looked almost like an amphitheatre with a few more barracks below. Soldiers everywhere. We sang from the bottom of the amphitheatre, which was a former gravel pit overgrown with green, and the soldiers sat all over the slopes. The stars came out, and the music sounded more beautiful than in any concert hall in the world.

After the concert we were asked whether we could sing a Mass for the soldiers. Next Sunday was to be our last Sunday in Vermont. We agreed readily to come. Again the jeeps came to get us and drove us through the valley. This time it was morning, and even more beautiful. It was one of those wonderful, warm days in the fall with an incredibly blue sky. On the way back Georg asked the driver to stop for a moment.

Then he pointed up to the last sunny slope and said with emphasis:

"A place like this; that's where I'd be happy."

And five days later that sunny slope, which belonged to a large farm, was our own.

The very next morning a man knocked at our door.

"I heard you want to buy a farm," he said. "I want to sell mine. Why don't you have a look?"

Although we had closed the chapter and given up the idea, there couldn't be any harm in looking at one more place, and in the afternoon we drove behind the farmer, who showed the way. We drove as far as the little white schoolhouse, and there was a sign: "Luce Hill." That's where we branched off. Up and up it went, and the farther up we went, the more beautiful became the view. Then we were on top of the hill; and when we got out of the cars, we knew: this is the place. What a panorama! Three valleys lay open before us, and as many as nine mountain ranges we could count stretching into the blue distance. We had been in all forty-eight States; we had stood on many a top of the Green, White, Blue, Smoky, and Rocky Mountains; and in Vermont we had traveled up and down the State and seen many hills and dales, but never had we come across anything like this.

For a while we stood in silent admiration, until Georg whispered into my ear:

"For heaven's sake, look at the buildings!"

A quick glance told me that they were "in fair repair," which didn't disturb me the slightest bit.

"Oh, Georg," I exclaimed, and my arms were around his neck, never minding the farmer and his numerous family. "We can build a house and barns, but we can never build a view like this!"

"We shall let you know in three days," Georg said to the owner, and we drove back to The Stowe-Away.

For all of us it had been love at first sight, and Georg's remarks about the buildings I couldn't take too seriously. After all, hadn't he liked the location first? That was his "sunny slope." I understood perfectly, however, that he felt how serious the step was when we were about to settle down. The place would become our home, and we should never have to regret that signature.

The only thing to do was pray; only thus would we find out the Will of God. We turned an empty room into a chapel. We put up a crucifix on the wall, and two candles were lit, and one member of the family was there for an hour at a time. We all took turns for three days and three nights. Then we had one more meeting, all of us together, the family and Father Wasner, and in perfect peace and unison we all said the same: we hadn't found the place, but the place had found us.

On Thursday we met at the Town Clerk's office and solemnly

received the deed, all of us together, as a joint possession. Then we went up our hill. Rupert and Werner felled two trees from our woods and made a Cross twelve feet high. This they carried up to the highest point on the hill behind the house, and we all followed, singing and praying. On the top the Cross was planted, while we sang a hymn of thanksgiving. In California we had learned that the Spanish missionaries had thus taken possession of every new spot on the coast.

One has to have lost a home oneself to understand and appreciate what the words mean: "home sweet home."

A New Chapter

ONCE more we set out on the concert tour to the West Coast; but this time everything was different; we owned a farm! Now we had a place where we belonged; we also had pictures which we carried around with us. In the joy of our heart, we had to show them to everybody. We still have those pictures, and when I look at them now, I understand fully why a really good friend of ours in the Middle West, after careful study, said slowly and deliberately:

"I hope you like that place."

The view, which is what we really had bought, didn't come out on the photos very well, and what did come out was not too dazzling. But it was with us as with parents of a newborn baby. In pride and exultation it is shown around: "Isn't it lovely?" No, it isn't. That red-faced little dwarf isn't lovely at all, but none of the friends has the heart to say so aloud. The same was the case with our friends who had not been up on Luce Hill on that glorious September day and were confronted with only the pictures of a shabby little house and crooked barns. But they all wanted to share our enthusiasm, and bravely broke out in those exclamations which we wanted to hear.

One of the greatest things in human life is the ability to make plans. Even if they never come true—the joy of anticipation is irrevocably yours. That way one can live many more than just one life.

While riding in the bus on the way out west, this was our royal occupation. As the neighboring farm had proved to be a terrific bargain when it was offered to us for sale, we had "bought" it, too, and now owned almost seven hundred acres. And what were we going to do with them?

Vermont is a dairy country. The most obvious thing for us

would be to go into the dairy business and build—eventually—a big barn for a hundred and fifty cows, which our place could feed, as people had assured us. The first thing which we would have to decide was: which breed of cows.

"Our neighbor at the foot of the hill has Jerseys," said Hedwig. "They look lovely, just like deer; and a few of the best farms around Stowe have Jerseys, too. They say the milk looks almost like orange juice, just yellow with butter fat."

"Yes, but I have heard that Jerseys suffer a great deal from diseases. Ayrshires are supposed to be much more hardy, especially for a hill farm," said Agathe.

"Why not Holsteins?" came in Martina. "They are twice as large as your lovely Jerseys. Mr. H. told me his cows give an average of fifty to sixty pounds a day, which makes about $2, times 150, makes $300 a day, $9,000 a month, and $108,000 a year!"

"And how much do those elephants eat?" asked Maria. "I was just reading here," and she pointed to one of the U. S. government pamphlets on agriculture, "that the Brown Swiss are comparatively new in America, have practically no disease, don't eat so much as the Holsteins but give the same amount of milk, are very hardy . . ."

"But they are twice as expensive," said her father.

"Last year you sent us post cards from the West, huge herds of cows with such funny faces—a white strip down the nose. Why not those?" Lorli wanted to know.

"Or the other ones," said Illi, "the dark black ones."

"Hereford and Angus seem to be westerners. I haven't seen them anywhere around Stowe," said Georg.

This conversation was going on in the Cadillac. In the Lincoln they were discovering meanwhile that Vermont fifty years ago had been the wheat granary of the East, and in addition the sheep country. Government pamphlets went from hand to hand, and the discussion centered around different breeds of sheep.

Whenever the inhabitants of the two cars met, at meals, for instance, or after the concerts, there was always a very spirited exchange of ideas on the one and main topic: the farm.

"How many men shall we need to work?"

That important question was raised one day. Father Wasner

had been born and raised on a farm, and he knew more about farming than any of us.

"Ours was a good-sized farm," he said, "about a hundred and twenty acres. We had seven people and three teams all year round, besides my father and brother; and during haying and harvesting, we had fifteen."

"Then," I mused, "I guess with twenty-five or thirty hands and five teams around the farm we should be able to do it."

"No, I don't think they do things that way in America," said Georg, who had read more than we. "Look at this."

He also had some pamphlets from the Department of Agriculture—on farm machinery. And now our vocabulary was enriched by words such as: "side delivery rake," "hay loader," "seeder," "corn planter," "blower," "manure spreader," and "tractor."

"That way we'll do it perhaps with three men and one team."

These words merely "increased our word power." At that time they didn't mean a thing to us, since in our day those things didn't exist in Austria. Very few individuals, indeed, owned seven hundred acres. In the whole neighborhood there was one single silo, and that had turned into a point of sight-seeing. Tractors were a great rarity and much talked about.

With altogether new interest we looked at the countryside as we crossed the Middle West; and the longer we looked, the less we liked it. Miles and miles and miles of corn fields or wheat fields—always the same crop. Later we came into the ranch country, and there were thousands of acres of pasture land; and when we were in California again, we passed through orchards with thousands of apple, or cherry, or orange trees. But it was always "or"; never "and." Now we saw clearly the difference. At home in Austria a farm was a self-sustaining, independent unit. You tried to grow a little bit of everything: for the people and for the animals, and a little more than enough to sell to buy the few items you couldn't grow, such as coffee, tobacco, and cotton material. The wool of your own sheep was spun at home and woven or knitted. The pigs supplied you with smoked meat for the whole year, and lard, besides. For sweetness you had your honey. The flax of the fields provided all the linen. Eventually you slaughtered some beef cattle or a sheep or some geese, ducks, or chickens, to get variety in your menu. In the orchard behind the house you had cherry, apple, and pear trees, and in a protected corner, even some peaches and grapevines. In the vegetable garden was a berry corner for strawberries, raspberries, blackberries, gooseberries, and currants. From your own rye you baked that delicious black bread, and you always kept enough grain for next year's seed. That way, each farmer on his homestead was an independent little king in his own realm. And after we had weighed dairy farming against wheat raising, or sheep breeding, or fruit growing, we all settled contentedly on doing neither one of the "or's," but we wanted a little bit of everything as it was at home. Each one of us chose right there and then a favorite department: Martina, the pigs; Johanna, the sheep; Hedwig, the cows; Maria, the garden; Agathe, the bees; Georg, the machinery; Father Wasner, the orchard; and I, the horses.

This choice was made on the edge of the desert at Death Valley, entering California. We were eating in a nice western-looking inn, and our spirits were animated. All of a sudden I stopped and looked at the boys.

"And how about you?" I exclaimed. "What's the matter? What do you choose?"

There was a moment of hesitation, and then Rupert said:

"Mother, we have to tell you: Werner and I received a letter from the Draft Board today. We have to be ready to be called."

Deep silence followed these words. What each one of us had secretly dreaded, now had happened. I looked across at Georg; he was studying the pattern of the tablecloth.

A cloud had passed over the sun of our happiness. For a short while we had forgotten that there was raging the most cruel war in history. We had become farmers in spirit, and farm work means raising, bringing forth; not destroying and annihilating. Now we had been brought back to the present day with brutal force.

In Los Angeles we had to go to register as enemy aliens and had to be fingerprinted. Fingerprinting had so far existed in our minds only in connection with detective stories, and we felt like semi-criminals.

When we stopped at the Grand Canyon on the way back home, I heard somebody whisper behind our back:

"These are Dutch from the East Indies."

"George," I said, "please look at the newspaper. The East Indies must be invaded." They were.

That incident reminded us of the time during the war when Hitler was making such fast progress in invading country after country. We in our quaint costumes attracted attention wherever we went. Upon hearing that we were refugees, people immediately associated us with yesterday's invasion. Alternately, we were thought to be Danes, Norwegians, Poles, Croatians, or French.

One day, back in New York it happened that in an overcrowded cafeteria I couldn't find a seat. I tried to balance my tray and eat standing up. Suddenly a lady rose from her seat, silently took my tray out of my hands, indicated her vacant seat, cut the meat for me, and motioned me, still silently, to eat. Deeply embarrassed, I tried to gulp the food down at super-speed. With cheeks still full, I hastily got up and said:

"Thank you very much."

"Oh, not at all," my benefactress replied beamingly. "I was only too happy to do something for the poor Finns."

We hadn't yet reached the Continental Divide when gasoline rationing set in. There we were with those darling cars of ours, each one doing ten miles per gallon. Our allowance was only the minimum amount, allotted to all private cars. This wouldn't even get us out of Colorado. From now on we had to visit the local rationing board in each town, explain our situation, and ask them to help us to get back home.

We had reached Chicago when the local Draft Board summoned Rupert and Werner.

The boys, who felt bad about leaving the family in such a critical moment, were still the bravest ones.

"Mother, remember the old saying: 'If God closes the door, He opens a window.' You'll see that everything will turn out all right again. It seems to be God's Will that we go."

"And God's Will hath no why" went through my head.

We were back East and had finished the concert tour. Georg and I, two girls, and the two boys went up to Stowe to prepare for the family moving. The boys started immediately to make firewood before they had to report for training. It was the beginning of March and still bitterly cold. In the deep snow nothing else could be done.

On March 9 Georg and I drove the boys to Hyde Park, our county seat, where the new draftees assembled. Not much was said on that trip. Each heart was filled to the brim with the one wish: God bless you!

How dry eyes can get when they are not allowed to cry! In the silent group of elderly parents, brides, and children we watched the small local train disappear around the curve, waving "Godspeed" and trying not to be afraid of the future.

It never rains but it pours! F. C. Schang had tried for months, and not left a stone unturned, to get into the Army. When I came to the office with a heavy heart to talk over what was to be done since the boys had left, he received me radiantly in a Captain's uniform; this was his last day in the office. My knees grew weak. In this most critical moment of our career as singers we would have to do without the support of the one man who had believed in us and who, through that trust and with his personal experience and skill, had helped us to build up our nation-wide reputation. I went to a florist and came back with twelve red roses.

"That's one from each one of us, Freddy," I said; because now I was not only talking to the great manager, before whom I had once trembled in my boots—I was also talking to the man with the warm heart and the irresistible laugh, the quick wit and the brilliant mind, the personality whom you are proud to call your friend. Very European as we still were, we had many, many acquaintances from coast to coast, but only a very few whom we called friends. Freddy Schang was one of them.

When he saw now how hard it all was on us, he grew serious and came over from behind his desk.

"Thank you, Maria," he held my hand. "I feel sure that the Trapp Family Singers, who have weathered many a storm, will also survive this."

There was a request at the office for one belated single concert in Bethlehem, Pennsylvania, ten days hence. The office pointed out to us that this was a chance to try to see whether or not we would be able to sing without the boys.

Of course, we had to try. This seemed like an insurmountable obstacle: first, the finding of genuine music written for women's choir; and second, the learning of it by heart in practically no time. Father Wasner did the impossible. In one sweep through music libraries he came home with motets by Vittoria and Palestrina for equal voices, and also precious rounds by Mozart, Haydn, Beethoven, and some songs by Schubert and Brahms for women's voices. Besides that, he arranged some of our old numbers for the new ensemble. From then on, we hardly took time to eat and wash dishes. Once more the house on Merion Road resounded with music. The closer the day came, the more discouraged we grew. We missed the boys so much; not only in singing, but everywhere, all over the house. There wasn't the same joyous spirit of rehearsing. It was subdued, serious, dutiful. When the day came, we drove over to Bethlehem, knowing that if this concert was not a success, our singing had come to an end. Columbia Concerts would have no more use for us; and there was a $12,000 mortgage on our place, and a run-down farm to be built up, which would cost a lot more money.

At that time we knew over two hundred pieces by heart, but each one was for mixed voices—all of which didn't do us any good now. It added to our excitement and tension when we discovered several well-known faces from the New York office among the audience; they also knew of the importance of this performance. And all this happened not in some corner of the United States where there hadn't been many concerts before, and the people would most probably like whatever we did; no, it happened in Bethlehem, where we had sung a year before, and where the audience was composed of singers and music lovers. The world-famous Bach Festivals had educated these people to a high taste in music. If we could please them, we would be all right.

With the help of God we came through with flying colors. I was told that it wasn't an average, good concert; it was one of those outstanding, excellent ones which one remembers after years, and after having sung hundreds of times. When we sang Brahms' "The Day Has Come When Thou and I, My Dearest One, Must Say Good-bye," the audience was in tears; and when we sang finally "The Orchestra Song," it got the people to their feet, they clapped and clapped and clapped. And that makes the success of a concert: to keep the audience between tears and laughter. The art of your music must be so convincing and so strong that it makes people forget themselves. It must take them out of that everyday state of mind. They had cried and they had laughed, and they wanted more encores than we had prepared. The performance was a great success, and Columbia Concerts was satisfied. Half dead but relieved, we went back to Merion the same night, after having sent a telegram to the boys, saying:

BATTLE OF BETHLEHEM HAS BEEN WON!

Wherewith Western Union demanded to know whether this was a code.

No, it was the truth. It marked the beginning of a new chapter. God, Who had closed the door, had opened a window.

The End of a Perfect Stay

THE next days were full of commotion and unrest; the packing and moving from Merion. Three happy years we had lived in the shelter of this house, which seemed much larger inside than outside. Trying times had been followed by easier ones, and each one of us left many memories within its walls. This had not been an ordinary three years. An important metamorphosis had taken place within us. It changed us from hundred-per-cent Europeans, not into Americans yet—that is a matter of growing and developing which means time—but into people who wanted to become a part of this nation. We could never understand those refugees who seemingly had undergone a magic transformation aboard ship, which they had entered as Europeans and left as ready-made Americans, finding everything wrong which they had left behind, and everything "swell" and "O.K." which they found here. It had been a slow and almost painful process with us. One cannot love what one does not know. The more we knew about America, the country and its people, the more we felt a strong, warm love grow in our hearts. For instance: there was a war going on, and we were registered as enemy aliens; and not only were we not locked up in a camp, but we could go about our business unmolested, while wearing our foreign costumes and talking our native tongue on the street and in the trains and elevators. There had always remained some German numbers in our programs, and never had the audience minded that. This attitude was completely un-European, this lack of prejudice was heart-warming. The Americans never seemed to ask, "Who are you?" but "How good are you? Let's see." They gave you a fair chance to give your best, and then they accepted you for that, whether you came from Poland, Russia, England, or Austria. They even overlooked the language angle. With our music, that language beyond languages,

221

we had sung our way into their hearts, and on that day when the boys were leaving we felt it: that country our boys would be fighting for, and perhaps dying for, we wanted to be our country. We declared our intention to become citizens. We were allowed to go to Toronto, Canada, and enter the United States, this time not as visitors, but as immigrants. Now we had a quota number, and had to wait five years to become citizens.

The little house was bulging with furniture which belonged to us, the family who had arrived with a few suitcases and four dollars in cash.

It happened like this: Once we met the publishers Sheed and Ward, Mr. and Mrs. Frank Sheed from England, who also spent the war years near Philadelphia. We found we had many things in common, and from then on, spent many delightful hours together.

On my first visit to their house I exclaimed:

"Oh, what beautiful rugs!"

This item of furniture the little house on Merion Road didn't contain.

"Oh," said Maisie Sheed, "they are from an auction. This one was eight dollars, and this, five dollars, and this one here was the most expensive: twelve dollars."

They were beautiful old oriental rugs, one even a Bokhara like the one in the living room in Salzburg, and Maisie Sheed told me that there was a place in Philadelphia on Chestnut Street, Samuel T. Freeman's, where there were auctions every Wednesday. You got good things there very reasonably.

"I always go on Tuesday first to look over what they have. Then I mark down the numbers in which I am interested, and then take just as much money with me as I want to spend. As you have to pay cash, you don't run into temptation that way."

I could hardly wait for next Tuesday. And then I started out to investigate and discover what was behind the name of Freeman. There were three very distinct worlds: the basement, the ground floor, and the second floor. The basement contained a lot of junk. It looked like a receptacle for the contents of other people's attics: many washbowls and pitchers, mattresses, pillows, and bed springs, dozens and dozens of oversized pictures in old-fashioned frames,

HAYING TIME, STOWE, VERMONT

"... surrounded by the sweet-scented hay ... happy as a lark, freer than a queen!"

TRAPP FAMILY MUSIC CAMP

"How could we do what we are doing..."

PHOTO: SIMON NATHAN — ALIX WILLIAMSON

which, if sold by the pound, should bring good money; nothing which made your heart beat louder. The second floor—what a difference! Only high-priced articles with a high-brow audience. Ladies with the newest hats and gloves. Very expensive furniture, illustrated catalogues which showed its origin abroad, Wedgewood china, crystal glass, jewelry, and acres of carpets, shiny and expensive-looking. Then there was the ground floor, a hybrid of the other two. The majority of the items on sale was mediocre, but somehow one or two first-rate pieces, unrecognized by the crowds, always escaped. I looked all over the huge room.

I returned the next day to the auction with five dollars cash. Very soon I was seized by that special fever which comes while one is witnessing bidding. A tall young man by the name of Bill was the auctioneer. His sonorous voice held the audience spellbound. That voice had many shades. It could sound matter-of-fact, sympathetic; it could plead; it could get outraged: "What, only four dollars for this easy chair? That's a darn shame!" And sure enough, he would frighten somebody into $4.50. The voice could sound reproachful and then die down to a whisper, which it did now.

"This sideboard, genuine pearwood lined with green felt, four dollars. No one gives more? No one gives more than four dollars for this wonderful piece of craftsmanship? Ladies and gentlemen, if you go to a lumber yard, the lumber alone will cost you three times as much! Who gives more?"

"I," I said, unnecessarily loud, and when everybody turned towards me, I wished I were inside that sideboard.

A benevolent glance from Bill's eyes hit me, and "Five dollars, sold!" made me the owner of a genuine pearwood sideboard. It also started a silent friendship. Bill somehow never forgot that I had understood the disgrace that sideboard would have suffered, and had rescued it.

That was the first of many Wednesdays to come. Bill, who had learned that I was a refugee without a table or chair to my name, helped me with all the organ-like registers of his voice. Obviously I was the only refugee in the place. My competitors in bidding were mostly second-hand dealers (the antique store owners went to the second floor), and somehow I seemed to deserve preference over the professionals. When I, very timidly in the beginning, indicated by raising my hand that my heart was set on a certain bed, sofa, chair, table, carpet, etc., Bill's voice immediately dropped down to contempt:

"And here, ladies and gentlemen, is one of those pieces . . ."

"One of those pieces" seemed to mean, "whoever takes that junk home is an outright fool," and no one wanted to show such lack of discrimination. Almost invariably I got my piece for a very reasonable price, always under ten dollars. Other people go to the races or to ball games or to Friday Symphony Concerts. I went to Freeman's, whose ground floor was a heaven of bargains. It had all the flavor of a treasure hunt to search all over the ground floor, crawl behind the furniture, duck under beds and desks to look at the small pictures which were stored there until one found the disguised prince: a chest with the carved inscription "1738," which finally nobody wanted because of its size, or a beautiful rug, which a hole in its middle had gotten down from the second floor, or a heavily carved bed coming from Tirol, of all places. By and by the place on Merion Road was filled until it couldn't swallow any more. That was before we had bought the farm, and my husband got worried. Carpets, for instance, according to an unwritten law of Freeman's, came together with curtains, and I had brought home scores of curtains in all materials, among them very beautiful old brocades, silks, and velvets.

"We shall never have enough windows," Georg moaned, and he invented most artistically engagements which absolutely had to be done on Tuesdays or Wednesdays. He usually had to do without me, though.

When the family sighs became louder and remarks like: "Everybody can sleep in only one bed at a time" became more frequent, I decided to get me an accomplice, and after I had once lured Father Wasner into Freeman's, he succumbed to the charms of the place immediately. That time we bought, for practically nothing, six old carved-wood statues of Apostles, a couple of large crystal vases, and a bunch of silver spoons. When I came home that evening, I explained that for mere necessity, for lack of space, I had to buy smaller items now, and that I had, so far, strictly adhered to the principle: first the necessary (tables, chairs, and beds); then the useful (carpets and curtains); and then the luxurious (pictures, vases, and silver spoons).

After we had bought the farm, my situation at home grew no better by any means, as the house on the farm was about half the size of the one in Merion, and where, just where, would we put all these things?

There was a large cow barn on the upper farm, and that's where we were going to store the furniture for the moment. And now we were packing it into a big van, destined for Stowe, Vermont. These days we were packing from morning till night, and interrupted the packing only for a hasty lunch. We never had to prepare supper, as there was a farewell party every night; at the Smiths', the Crawfords', and at many another friend's house.

And finally, at the Drinkers'. Once more we sat around the large dining room table with Harry at one end and Sophie at the other, with me next to him, and Georg and Father Wasner next to her, the family in between; and in came one of those giant turkeys which Harry carved with such elegance that watching him was at least as much pleasure as eating the turkey. Once more we sat around the fireplace in the large music room and sang no end. This time there was no "let's do it again." We wanted to sing every piece once which we had ever done together, and that was a large order. Once more Emily came in with a tray of ginger ale, beer, and pretzels. And then there was that awkward situation which arises invariably when your hearts are full of emotions which cannot be pressed into words. We were so grateful to the Drinkers, with the gratefulness of refugees who have found what they are named for—refuge—for their trust and all their efforts; and the Drinkers, this we could feel, were pleased that we were on our own feet now, and we could sense that they would miss us, the neighbors from across the street. And that is the ingredient absolutely necessary for good parting: that you will be missed afterwards. It was the early Pennsylvania spring, forsythia blooming all over the place, all the trees budding, and the robins, fat as ducks, busy with their nests.

"Spring is such a good time to start out something new," Sophie said.

Then we grouped once more around Father Wasner and sang Bach's Chorale of Thanksgiving. This we didn't sing with the Drinkers, we sang it for them.

As I crossed the street looking at the moon which stood bright on a cloudless sky, I couldn't help thinking:

"Even if Harry and Sophie don't believe it as literally as we do, how pleased they will be one day when Our Lord says to them: 'I was a stranger and you took me in. As long as you did it to one of these My least brethren, you did it to Me. Come, enter into eternal joy!'"

The New House

EARLY next morning we left for Vermont—for home. North of Rutland there was snow; and after we had passed through Burlington and come into the mountains, there was lots more. When we reached Stowe, we came into a real blizzard.

The dark floor in the living room of our house was partly covered with a thin layer of snow, "like sugar on a cake," as Johannes remarked, because windows and doors did not shut tightly.

"That's very good for sweeping," exclaimed Hedwig, taking a broom and demonstrating how well you can get after the dust that way.

The man who had lived with his family on the lower farm, which we had bought, too, had remained there and was now our farmer. He had helped the men when they came with the furniture. All we had to do was put up enough beds for the first night. While Georg went down into the small cellar to make a fire in the one-pipe hot air furnace, we ran to and from the barn with parts of beds and mattresses and pillows. The beds *were* pretty large, and the house *was* pretty small, and it was only twenty degrees above zero and rather chilly. Johannes discovered a register in the living room floor. Lying flat on his stomach, he pulled a chain which opened the furnace, and he could gaze right into the flames. When he let the chain drop, it made a loud bang. What a delightful heating system; not dull and invisible as in a city house. Then Martina came in with a lighted kerosene lamp. My enthusiastic exclamations of how homey, how cozy it was, as in the olden days, couldn't shatter Georg's stony silence. Poor Georg. He couldn't see any of the romance of all this. In fact, he didn't see the doughnut at all—he only saw the hole. I knew he was genuinely troubled about the shabby little house, into which we really couldn't fit for longer than a weekend, "and a weekend in summer with picnics out-of-doors, I mean," he had said. The crooked barns, the boy gone, and not much money, with half a year to go before we would make any more, and how many concerts would we get without the boys—this nobody knew. It was a picnic supper that first night with paper cups and paper plates, which were burned afterward in the furnace while Johannes pulled the chain. After supper there was a knock on the door, and the farmer came in.

"The sap is running," said Theophile; "we have started to tap."

We looked at each other, and finally Georg said:

"What is running?"

And Theophile had to explain to us newcomers all about maple syrup and how it is made. Maple sugar is as distinctly American as is the skunk. We had never heard of it in Europe, and now without even a warning, we were making it ourselves.

Again our vocabulary was enriched by new acquisitions, such as "to tap," "spouts," "buckets," "evaporator," "sugar house."

The very next morning we started out on the loveliest time we had had so far in America, the weeks in The Stowe-Away included: our first sugaring season. Theophile and his oldest boy went with the team and the gathering tank on the sled. Our girls helped collect the sap, and Theophile showed Georg the more important and rather intricate process of boiling it. Georg and I were in the sugar house, and we loved it. We loved the whole atmosphere.

This was the very first beginning of spring in Vermont, much snow still around, and the horses had to force their way, breast deep when they started to break in the sugar road. But around noon the sun got warmer. It thawed from the roof of the sugar house, and little rivulets were running all around the sugar bush. Some unprotected places on the slopes were already bare, and an early spring flower raised its dainty little head. The first bird could be heard through the woods; spring was in the air and filled you with new energy and joyful anticipation. Feeding the fire with those heavy, big logs and handling the cans with maple syrup made our backs ache in the evening when we walked back toward the house, very tired but satisfied. Maple syrup is a cash crop. It was the first money we made on our farm. Then Georg counted the gallon cans as the stack grew, down in the cellar. There were already over a hundred, and each can would bring $3.60. I was so very happy, because the occupation in the sugar bush kept Georg away from the house, the sight of which was such a thorn in his side, and his work got him into better and better spirits.

Cold weather set in again, the first run was over; an awful blizzard kept us in the house. There would be no sugaring, Theophile told us, for a few days. When we were all in the house at once, it didn't need much persuasion to see the point: it was too small for us. There was an architect, Alfred, living in Stowe, whom we had consulted about the condition of the buildings before we bought the farm. He had assured us that they were in good enough repair to be fixed for our personal needs. This architect was a special godsend for us, as he had lived more than half of his life in Europe, especially in our Austrian Alps, talked our language fluently, and knew very well the part of the country where we came from. Very soon his family and ours were on most friendly terms, and everybody called everybody else by his first name.

On this particular blizzard day we called Alfred on the telephone. Although we had no electric light, we had a telephone, which we had not used so far. There was a hitherto-unseen machine screwed to the wall. One had to stand on tiptoe to be able to speak into the mouthpiece, but it was a telephone. I took the receiver as I was used to doing in Merion, and great was my astonishment when a voice said:

"And how do Grandpa's new teeth fit?"

I hadn't had any experience with a party line before, didn't know what was going on, and listened entranced to the sad story that the teeth didn't fit at all, and Grandpa was losing them all the time. Long after silence had set in on that "talky-talky machine" as Johannes called it, I tried in vain to click the receiver and get a connection—until I discovered the crank. It took some more time to find out that it only worked with the receiver on while cranking, but then I felt a little like Columbus after the discovery of America. I got Alfred on the line and informed him that our cabin was slightly too small, and what could he do for us?

"Oh, that can easily be helped," I heard his cheerful, reassuring voice. "You just raise the roof and build another storey. You'll have plenty of room."

Further, he advised us to see Mr. Sears, a very good carpenter in the village. We called Mr. Sears, who promised to come and see us as soon as the blizzard was over. That was next day. We explained to Mr. Sears our need and Alfred's advice, and asked if we couldn't start right away. He looked a little doubtful as the weather was still very cold, but when he saw our pleading eyes, he gave in and on the same afternoon we started to rip open the roof, which had to be raised according to prescription.

Georg, Maria, and Hedwig went wholeheartedly into carpentry, and soon most of the roof was gone, and a new construction of two-by-four's indicated the new lines. On the fourth day there was another blizzard, which kept Mr. Sears at home. At noon we were all sitting in the kitchen, which was in the ell, eating lunch, when all of a sudden we heard a terrific crash. We jumped up, and when we opened the door into the living room, we stepped into the open. Most of the house was gone. It had fallen, chimney and all, right down into the cellar. A few broken walls were still standing, but the roof was definitely gone. As if this had been the goal to be accomplished, the blizzard almost at once died down, after having covered the whole mess with a thin film of new snow. At this moment the telephone rang. It was our ring—Ring 3. I went out into the open air. The telephone was still hanging on a piece of wall. Alfred's cheerful voice inquired how things were.

"I wanted to say, don't open too much of the roof at one time," he warned. "On a stormy day that might not be too good."

"It won't bother us any more, Alfred," I said.

"Oh," he seemed to beam, "congratulations! Are you that far already? But that was fast."

"Why don't you come and see for yourself," said I and hung up. Then I called Mr. Sears.

"Mr. Sears, can you tell me what one does with a fallen-down house?"

"I'll be right up," said a hasty voice.

An hour later an architect and a carpenter stood at the grave of their plans and tried to hold hands with the bereaved. The whole situation was so unique that it had some of the flavor of a threatening flood or an ocean crossing during the war—some of that champagne-like tickling of the nerves. What was going to happen next? My poor husband looked broken.

"Now, Georg," I said, "I am really glad for your sake. You hated the idea of putting a new patch on the old frock, as you called it. You didn't trust the foundation, you didn't like the whole idea. Now we'll build a new house and make it exactly as we want it."

"Build a new house—where's the money, may I ask you?"

"Bah—money! Didn't somebody once say that a nation is worth exactly as much as it is willing to work? What is good for a nation is good for a family, and that way we are worth millions. Congratulations!"

Architect and carpenter agreed that the next thing that would have to be done was to tear down what little of the house was still standing.

"And now, Alfred, please make us a plan of an Austrian farm house, and if we all work together, we'll have a lovely home very soon!"

I was astonished that the always-happy-sounding, cheerful voice only said "Well," but it rather sounded like "W—e—e—e—l—l," and then: "There's a war going on and the War Production Board has forbidden any new building to be erected. We'll have to see about the regulations."

While the sugaring went on, parts of the family worked in the sugar bush, while parts learned the use of crowbars in tearing down walls, in separating boards. Under layers of wallpaper we found newspaper from the year 1832. The nails were handmade; the boards, very wide; the beams, hand-hewn. We tried to keep as much of the good old material as possible to be used in the new building. Alfred had found out that the war building regulations permitted one to build onto an existing house, and this fitted our case if anyone dared to call the remaining ell a house. There was the kitchen with a woodshed behind downstairs, and two rooms upstairs. One room was inhabited by Father Wasner; the other one, by Georg, myself, and little Johannes. These rooms were not heatable. When the snowstorms raged outside, dainty little pyramids formed on the floor, as the roof leaked. That was all right as long as what came down from the sky was snow. Later when the weather grew warmer and it started to rain, we needed an umbrella and a few buckets in each room. But that was after the sugaring season, and there were plenty of buckets to use.

We had to make an application, and the War Production Board sent a commission to investigate the necessity of the planned construction. All we had to do was show them around: first, the small kitchen, which also served as dining and living room for twelve people; then, the two remaining bedrooms; then, the dormitory for all the girls, which was above the horse barn in the hay loft; and finally, the arrangement under the horse barn, which was a substitute for the one bathroom for a mile around, which, with the rest of the house, had gone down into the cellar. The gentlemen wholeheartedly agreed that the necessity for new construction was urgent, and our petition was granted.

When the sugaring season was over, we proudly counted 363 gallons. The clearing-up of the ruins now made it necessary to carry the cans into the cow barn. Agathe had found time between chores to make a lovely woodcut for a label, saying: "Pure Vermont Maple Syrup from the Trapp Family Farm." We were deeply impressed when we read that for the first time.

Now the buckets had to be washed and stored for the next year. The evaporator was turned upside down, the smokestack packed away indoors, the sugar house closed up after a final "sugaring-off party" with Theophile and his family. It had been a lovely time. On the same afternoon Theophile broke the sad news to us that he had bought a farm of his own and was going to leave us, but he recommended that his brother be given his place. We were glad that Theophile had found a place he liked, but we were sad to lose him. A few days later Ovila came with a family of seven children, the oldest, eleven.

It was Sunday afternoon and the whole family had gone down to the farm house to help the newcomers move in. I was sitting outside just enjoying myself; I intended to go down a little later. As I felt cool, I started to go upstairs to get my jacket. When I walked through the kitchen, I could hear footsteps upstairs. I knew definitely that all our people were gone. Who could that be? There it came over to the stairs, and I could hardly believe my eyes when a tremendous big skunk came waddling down the stairs. I had heard enough about skunks to make me politely back up, almost apologizing. Slowly he came down into the kitchen but, oh horror! didn't walk out through the wide-open door, but settled under the ice box. I ran down to the farm house to tell the others, and when we all came back home afterwards, the black and white tail was still sticking out from under the ice box. We all tiptoed and whispered in order not to frighten the dangerous guest.

He apparently liked it there, and for days he came and went, so that finally he became so tame that he drank milk out of a bowl and looked for food in our garbage pail. One day he came back with a family. As the ice box was not big enough, they settled under the house. But one cannot tiptoe and whisper forever, and once in a while something dropped to the floor, which was the roof for the skunk family. Then Mother Skunk quietly gave the defense signal: "Let us spray," and unanimously we hated the one who had dropped that fatal fork, or whatever it happened to be.

Real spring came to Vermont. The last snow was gone, and after a few days of warm rain and another few days of hot sun, the whole countryside was changed within a week. A new coat of green covered everything, green in all shades, from the tender, yellowish green of the new foliage to the more intense green of the grass on all the slopes, and the dark spots of spruce and pine. The air was full of new melodies we had never heard before. Every day brought exciting discoveries. The first trillium was found in the shade, dutchman's breeches, dog-toothed violets, quaker ladies, all were new to us, new and exciting.

Spring in a suburb is tame and well-groomed, like everything in a well-kept suburb. One day the garden service arrives by truck, and out come a few men with a number of tools. In a great hurry the hedge is trimmed, the lawn repaired, and a bed full of pansies is left behind. But spring out in the country in its wild beauty is something which almost tears one's heart out. What abundance, what generosity of nature! So much of everything; of flowers, of buds on the trees, of bees and bugs, of the very water trickling in innumerable springs down the hills, making the brooks in the valleys roar with joy, of the very sunshine falling in heavy, warm folds from the cloudless sky. You feel some of this elementary renewal going on within yourself. Your chest widens and so does your heart. You are full of new plans and new life, and your heart is willing to love everything and everybody with new zeal. Our living quarters gave us plenty of chance to live out-of-doors, and that way we enjoyed to the utmost the first spring on our hill. Every morning when we saw the sun rise behind Elmore Mountain, bathing our hill in its light while the low valleys were covered with thick, white fog, and every night when it went down behind Nebraska Notch, our hearts filled with exultation and thanks that we had bought this place, this hill, this view.

All we needed now to complete our happiness was a decent place to worship. Chapels were not mentioned among necessary constructions, so we couldn't think of building one now; but next to the old horse barn was the newest building on our place, a chicken coop, uninhabited. After a lot of scrubbing and whitewashing, it looked and smelled clean, and then—three cheers for the auction house of Freeman!—there were the curtains. The walls disappeared behind heavy folds. Georg carpentered an altar and Maria made a tabernacle; we put two benches along the side, Freeman carpets on the floor, and then we approached our Bishop for permission to reserve the Blessed Eucharist. Since the days of Bethlehem, Our Lord must have a secret liking for stables. The permission was readily given, and the Feast of Corpus Christi was celebrated in joy and glory on our hilltop. The Bishop had graciously lent vestments and a monstrance for this our beginning. Two priest friends had arrived from Washington and helped now to celebrate this great event. For the first time since the creation of the world, the Blessed Sacrament was carried over this hill. When Father Wasner raised the monstrance in Benediction, he showed the Lord this corner of Vermont, and as in the very first days of creation: "God saw all the things that He had made, and they were very good."

With Holy Mass in the morning and Benediction in the evening, the days were framed from now on, and what rich days they were!

After the snow had gone, we started first to clear up around the house. Twenty-four big truckloads of rusty old wire, parts of machinery, beer and whiskey bottles, three broken-down cars, and tin cans—tin cans no end—we took down to the city dump heap, and only after the last load was there, did we learn that we were not eligible to use it. We should have made our own junk disposal somewhere on our grounds. But the good people didn't make us take the twenty-four loads back, thank goodness! After a wilderness of old fence posts and wires was taken away from around the house, it looked much better right away, especially when the old apple trees broke out in such abundant bloom. Only the old ell still looked like a broken tooth. From the left-overs of the main house Mr. Sears built a nice, roomy cabin outside on the lawn, which served as dining and living room very well all through the summer. There we could even entertain guests most successfully.

Mr. Sears had long since turned from being a mere carpenter into an all-around factotum. He knew absolutely everything, from where to buy this and that to how to make elderberry wine out of the bloom of elderberries, or how to collect and dry fresh ferns to fill a cushion against rheumatism.

During the last year in Merion when we needed more time for rehearsing, we had looked for part-time help for the kitchen, and had found a colored maid. Her name was Aunt Bea, and she was of such a sweet disposition and so lovable that we all grew very fond of her. Aunt Bea had cried when we moved away from Merion, and had said: "Whenever you need me, just tell me. I'll come with the next train." As far as help was concerned, we really needed Aunt Bea. It would have released a whole person for working on the house. But where to put her? Mr. Sears, as always, had the answer. He remade the woodshed behind the kitchen into three dear little rooms. One more thing we needed: a bed not so wide as the ones we had bought.

"Why don't you go to an auction," Mr. Sears said, and showed me how, in the back of *The Burlington Free Press,* auctions were announced daily; two, three, or four. The mere word "auction" had a sweet sound to my ears, and I picked the nearest one and set out to buy a bed. Georg had such an innate aversion to buying second-hand things other people had used, that he didn't want to come along. I would have found the place easily even without special directions by the number of cars lining the road a mile in advance; and there was the place, with all the farm machinery displayed and the auctioneer standing on the manure spreader, pointing with his stick at the various things. They were through with the cattle when I arrived. I had hardly taken a place at the outskirts of the crowd, when the auctioneer eyed me and addressed me sweetly over the heads of the others.

"And you, lady, what do you want? I'm sure we have it."

It was embarrassing to be so suddenly the very center of attention.

"A bed," I said and blushed.

His whole face was one expression of condolence.

"Oh, but we have no beds. But I have something for you, lady, I have a horse."

"But I don't want a horse," I said, horrified. "I need a bed!"

"Lady," and his voice grew stern, "I told you once already, I have no bed. But look at this horse," and he came down from his throne leading a brown horse over to me. The horse was shy and bony and very big. "This is the horse for you, lady," and that tone of voice didn't allow any contradiction. "Topsy is twelve years old, and exactly what you need. In all your life you haven't met such a bargain," and he whispered in my ear: "You can have her for forty dollars."

I was absolutely inexperienced in horse prices, but forty dollars sounded even to me very little. Taking my hesitation—I was desperately thinking how I could make it clear to him without hurting his feelings that I absolutely did not want a horse—for an assent, his jubilant voice rang through the air:

"One brown horse sold—forty dollars!"

Merely to collect myself, I bought a few other items: a few chains for a quarter, a bag of salt for a dime, loads of rope for a nickel, two more crowbars for another dime. Slowly I drove home. The family was sitting at supper.

"Did you get the bed?" Georg asked me.

"N-no."

"Did you buy anything else—antique furniture?"

"Yes—I mean, no," and a little too hastily and too exuberantly for the occasion, I told about my bargains in rope, chains, and salt.

It made Georg suspicious; he put down fork and knife, looked at me straight, and said:

"And what else did you buy?"

"A horse."

"A what?"

"A horse, Topsy. The best horse on the market for forty dollars. Twelve years old."

"And Aunt Bea? Are you going to put her on Topsy, or whatever the name is?"

Now everybody laughed, and I felt better.

"Aunt Bea can have my bed," Martina came to my rescue. "I'll gladly sleep on a cot."

A few days later we got Aunt Bea from the station in Waterbury.

We also got Topsy and put her in the stall next to Prince and Lady. I had taken over the horse barn, and jealously I cared for "my" horse now, giving her double portions of oats, grooming her morning and night a little more than Prince and Lady, the team, and very soon Topsy became fat and round and strong.

After all the remains of the old house had been cleared away, we started one bright summer morning with the new one. Alfred had made a beautiful plan of a Swiss chalet, the very looks of which made us intoxicated.

First we had to dig the cellar. The old one was much too small. Again Mr. Sears advised what to do. We needed a scraper and a man who would handle it with the team. The scraper we found on a neighboring farm for ten dollars, and the man we found, too: Cliff. He was helping his old father on the farm, but he had time to spare. Cliff knew all about horses. When he saw my interest, he showed me how to harness them, explaining the different parts of the harness and reins. After a few days he encouraged me to get a harness for Topsy and a second scraper. From then on Cliff worked with the team, and I with Topsy, who was ambitious and jealous, and wanted to be as good as the team. For a little while things went fine. The scrapers went into the loose soil as if it were butter, and the slope in front of the house vanished rapidly, until the topsoil was gone. Then came hard-pan, and it was hard hard-pan. The scrapers only scratched it. Mr. Sears sighed deeply two or three times, produced picks the next day, and from then on, all of us had to work with picks until the loosened dirt could be scraped away. That was a slow process and a backbreaking one. The summer days grew hotter, and often we were interrupted by heavy thunderstorms. There was no bulldozer anywhere near, and for eight hot weeks Georg, Father Wasner, the girls, Mr. Sears, Cliff, and I worked our way deeper and deeper until the hole for the cellar was finished.

At another auction we had brought home three lovely little pigs, as Aunt Bea had cried out about so much good garbage going to waste. These pigs grew fast into pets. They were called Petunia, Violet, and Suzy. Aunt Bea and Martina had completely lost their hearts to them, and the piglets grew almost while we watched them. The skunk family had left, as there was too much commotion around the house, but we had two cats and a dog and, on the lower farm, another team and fifty-two head of cattle.

Besides a skunk and a sugar maple, we had made the acquaintance of another American character: a stone boat, the like of which we had never seen in Europe; and nobody knows why, because it is hard to understand how anyone can live on a farm without a stone boat. You can move practically everything with it. We needed ours to move all the stones in the old cellar foundation.

Haying time was in full swing when the scraping was over, and Ovila was very glad to get the other horses to help. Now Topsy and I mounted the one-horse rake or the hay tedder, and Topsy acted very intelligently on the large meadow behind the horse barn. She worked very slowly the long stretch across to the other side, but the very moment we turned, she almost galloped back to the barn, only to be turned around and mourningly wind her way in the other direction. What a feeling that was on the rake, surrounded by the sweet-scented hay, the shiny body of "my" horse in front of me, reins in hand, happy as a lark, freer than a queen!

Meanwhile, the Trapp Family had completely dropped out of newspapers and magazines, and they had begun to wonder why. But one beautiful summer day two reporters came up Luce Hill, a lady and a gentleman. She was the writer, and he, the photographer. They wanted a story on what the Trapps were now doing.

"Come and see," I said. "We have no time for posing, but you can take pictures of everything you see." So they took pictures of the building, of Martina with the pigs, and Agathe with her beehives, and Maria in the new vegetable garden, and Hedwig in her out-of-door laundry under the apple trees, and Johanna on the tractor, and me with the horses. After we had spent a hot day haying and they had followed us patiently around up and down a sloping meadow, we all finally rested in the shade and drank cider.

Then the lady asked: "Baroness, how do you get all that hay up here?"

I was sure she was only teasing, and said: "Well, we always buy it from Sears Roebuck."

"No, not really! How do you get it up here?"

"Oh," I chuckled, "you buy that in powder form. In the evening you sprinkle it over the meadow, and the next morning you have the best hay."

Thoughtfully she looked into her cider, and I began to doubt—but no, it can't be!

"What do you do next with it?" she asked.

Truthfully I answered: "We feed it to the cows."

"Oh, how interesting! And how do the cows eat it?"

That was too much for me.

"You know," I said, "that is their cereal. They eat it with sugar and cream!"

When everybody laughed, she found out my joke.

"Well," she defended herself, "you see, in our zoos you find anything from elephants or lions or kangaroos down to a guinea pig, but you never find a cow."

The very same couple was to come a few years later in January to take pictures (posed) of a sugar bush in action.

While we were riding over on the sled, I remembered the cow story, and that terrific urge to find out how much she would believe took hold of me again.

"You know," I began, "it is really silly to take these old-fashioned pictures. Don't you know that nowadays one doesn't make maple sugar the old way?"

"No," she said quite innocently, "I didn't. How do they do it now?"

"Well," I said, "now they graft the trees for any shape of candy they want—a maple leaf, or little bears, or hearts; and then they simply go and pick them from the trees the way you pick apples or cherries."

"Why didn't you . . ." she wanted to say, "tell me before," but our grinning faces gave us away, and she almost pushed us off the sled.

Mr. Sears had gotten himself two helpers besides Georg, Maria, and Hedwig, and they were working on what they called "forms." They looked to me like huge wooden walls. Then these forms were put up in the cellar hole and pressed and counter-pressed by a whole forest of two-by-fours.

Then one day Mr. Sears didn't come. He didn't feel well. He

never returned. From his sick bed he still gave us advice as to what to do next. When he died, we stopped all work. We were mourning for our first and best friend in Stowe, the one who had guided our beginnings in the country with an almost paternal love. In our Sunday best we accompanied him to his last rest, and sang once more his favorite song: Brahms' "Lullaby."

Now the going was hard. We missed Mr. Sears all over the place. As if to make up for Mr. Sears' absence, Alfred was around more than before, and one day the forms were ready.

A runway was built, and Alfred said:

"Now we need a cement mixer."

We rented one from a man in Waterbury Center. Then we needed wheelbarrows. We borrowed some from the town. Then we telephoned for sand, gravel, and cement. We found we needed another carpenter who knew exactly what, when, and how to mix. The last was the hardest of all, but finally we persuaded Mr. R. In the beginning he came in the evening until he had finished another job; then he came a few days a week, and finally, he took over. Trucks came with gravel, and others with sand, and a hundred bags of cement were piled up in the horse barn. In the middle of it all stood the cement mixer, and on a bright and shining morning in August Cliff started the motor, and the mixer began to turn. Mr. R. had given us the recipe: one shovel cement, two shovels gravel, and three sand, and enough water—and he showed how much is enough; then you turn the wheel and the mixture empties into the wheelbarrow, and you start all over again. One cement, two gravel, three sand. I was at the mixer, and somehow I got the fixed idea that if you put in more cement, the cellar wall will be harder and better. So I secretly put in more cement. Whenever I look at the cracks in the cellar wall now, I know who is responsible for them. Each visiting guest was put into overalls, adorned with a shovel, and told "two gravel, three sand," while I took care of the cement.

Guests *did* come, and they were all wonderful helpers. Everything would have been just fine if it hadn't been for the cement mixer. When all was lined up: four wheelbarrows and three men (or girls) with shovels, one would hear all of a sudden a stuttering noise from the motor, and then silence. One cry, "Cliff!" and Cliff would come and try to persuade that temperamental mixer to run;

take it apart, put it together, kick it finally with his heel, and all of a sudden, without any special reason, it was on the go again. So it went off and on many times a day, and there was nothing anyone could do about it, as this was the only cement mixer available at the moment. There was no miserable death we would not have wished on that piece of machinery. We would have liked to hang it, shoot it, drown it, poison it. But even so, the walls grew, and on one of those days the cornerstone of the new house was solemnly placed by Father Wasner and sunk into the wall, together with a Latin inscription on parchment and a bottle of holy water.

Meanwhile, many letters had gone back and forth between the boys and us, and great was our joy when they came home for their first furlough, two privates, looking very handsome in their uniforms. They came just at the time when the cement was dry enough for the forms to be taken off, taken apart, and used again for the rough floor. The whole family hammered along on that rough floor, and then it was finished. There was a big party with singing and folk dancing on that new floor of our new house. We were singing in four parts again. From now on we marveled at American speed in building a house. In no time the studs were up, and the rough floor of the second floor was laid and the studs were up for the third floor; and the skeleton of the roof was going up before the boys had to leave again for Camp Hale in Colorado—they had volunteered for the mountain troops—so they got an idea of what the house would look like eventually. It was very hard to see them go again.

A real fever for work had taken hold of all of us. We were either hammering along or boarding up the walls or laying a floor, or we were in the hay or on the other side of the hill in the berry patches. There was such an abundance of berries that summer as never since. We had found an old sugaring pan. This we put up under the old apple trees beside the house. On Mondays it was used for heating water; it was laundry day under the old apple trees. On the other days it was used for canning. Guests could now choose whether they wanted to help on the building or in the hay or in the berry-picking or canning. Besides all this, the large vegetable garden needed pickers for peas and beans, and the first apples, those delicious Duchesses, were ripening.

Try as we might, we couldn't get any more men to help us. All the young men were gone, it seemed, and the older ones were already busy. The true reason, however, we would learn much later. The people in this remote mountain valley had read stories in the newspapers of fifth columnists coming as tourists into Holland or Denmark, and starting to build something, anything; a tennis court, for instance. Then at the moment of invasion these innocent-looking buildings were equipped with guns and these innocent-looking tourists were Hitler's helpers. There had come into this Stowe valley a group of foreigners, dressed quaintly, talking queerly, and they had started to build. Of course they said it was a house, but who knew whether they wouldn't one day open fire and start shooting down the valley. We were always glad and grateful that we didn't hear that story at the time when it was still believed. At that time it would have hurt us bitterly. Years later when we learned it from a laughing neighbor, we tried to picture what we could possibly have shot at, and still don't know to this day.

It was just as well that we didn't get more help, as we really didn't have any money left. The scanty amounts which we had brought along had been swallowed long since by lumber bills and cement. What we had to meet now was the weekly bill for the few men on Saturdays. That was the time when from Thursday on, one dissolved into a continuous prayer: "Dear Lord, please help!" And He always did, and we never once failed to meet the payroll. But sometimes it went just short of a miracle; like that one week when we were asked whether we could quick—quick— step in for another artist who had fallen sick, and give a concert on Friday. Yes, we could. That took care of three Saturdays. Or that other week when we were asked by people who wanted to invest money whether we would take a few thousand dollars at four per cent interest. We almost cried with joy. That took care of the rest of the Saturdays.

All of a sudden, time seemed to fly. The days grew shorter as September came around. We had to cut out several hours a day for rehearsals again. In a few weeks the concerts would start, and the roof was still not boarded up, not to speak of the shingles.

One morning Mr. R. mentioned that the people in Stowe were

in trouble. The roof of the schoolhouse was leaking, and there were no funds.

"Do you think a concert by us would bring enough?"

His face lit up.

"I guess it would."

By now we had learned that a true Vermonter will hardly ever say flatly "yes" or "no." He'll say "why not?" or, "it seems so to me," or "I guess it would." It had to be done quickly because the roof should be mended before school began. A few nights later we were standing on the stage of the Town Hall and singing our new program—the program without the boys. The concert had been sold out on the first evening after it was announced. The tourist season was over, and there were only townspeople and farmers from the neighborhood. And now something happened which will always remain unforgettable to us. After the last encore, one of the selectmen sitting in the first row got up and started to come up the stairs to the stage, and everybody else followed. The whole audience. They passed by and everyone shook hands with us in a sincere and heartfelt way, as if to say: "Now you are one of us. Welcome home!"

This was on a Wednesday. The next Saturday two pick-up trucks drove up to our place filled with young boys, each one with a hammer, led by Mr. Page, the teacher of carpentry and handicrafts in the high school.

"We have come to help *you* out now," said Mr. Page, and that was all the explanation he gave.

In the next moment he and his boys were all over the roof, and a furious hammering could be heard for the next hours. On Sunday they came again, and some more cars with townspeople with hammers, too, and next Saturday and Sunday again. At the end of each visit we served coffee, cocoa and doughnuts, and we began to believe in the old fairy tale which tells of those little dwarfs who finished a half-completed work secretly by night. Three days before we had to leave on our tour the roof was shingled, the windows and doors were in, the outside of the house was covered with tarpaper—we were ready for the winter.

While this most cruel of all wars was inflicting deeper and deeper wounds upon humanity, a group of people in a forlorn corner of the mountains had discovered how to create that good will to which is promised peace on earth: by giving and not counting; each one giving all he has; his time, his skill, his effort, leaving behind a wake of that feeling about which there is so much talked and written, but so little experienced: the feeling of true brotherhood.

Concerts in Wartime

A FEW days before we had to leave on our concert trip I went down to Stowe to the drug store. Casually I opened the latest issue of *Life* magazine and—stared myself in the face. There I was, really and truly, with Prince and Lady, and there was Georg, and there was Martina decorating the shrine of Our Lady with flowers; and there were haying pictures, and I had a vision of a hot summer day and a couple from New York, hot and exhausted, following us all over the place; and we had had no idea that this was for *Life* magazine.

When we arrived in New York at Pennsylvania Station, a redcap came running over and said:

"And how is Johannes? I saw his picture in *Life.*"

That would accompany us this whole trip. Once out in Ohio, we somehow had managed to lose our railroad tickets, but that copy of *Life,* which we had with us, served as identification.

In New York we received at the office a thick manila envelope with long strips of green and red railroad tickets and an itinerary the size of a little booklet, saying:

Leave New York, Pennsylvania Station ......
Arrive Haverford ....

Leave Haverford ....
Arrive Pittsburgh ....

Leave Pittsburgh by bus ....
Arrive Dayton ....

and so on. Between "leave" and "arrive" there were hours of time. Sometimes they were filled with a concert; sometimes we would just have to wait at a bus terminal or a railroad station. It was all new to us, as we knew American railroads only from Philadelphia to New York. It was 1943, our sixth American concert tour, and the war was at its height. The whole nation seemed under arms; on the streets, in the dining rooms, in the hotels, and on the railroads, one saw only men and women in uniform; very few civilians.

A few weeks later we felt ourselves—uniform or no uniform—members of the home front. To give our concerts was a part of the program to keep up morale, and with the very type of our music—soothing, consoling, uplifting—it had become a rather important part of that program, as dozens and dozens of letters from Army and Navy camps and all types of audiences assured us. To fulfill the assignment, by which I mean merely to move ourselves across the country, turned out to be a minor battle each day, which could be won or lost, depending on whether you made the connection between train and bus, whether you got all the members of your family in one train or, which was not less important, all the luggage. The daily battle started at the hotel with the fight for taxis. For us ten people we needed two cabs with a third one for the luggage. Although each one of us had only one medium-sized bag, there was still the spinet and three large suitcases with concert luggage and the Mass kit; in all, fifteen pieces. When we had succeeded in obtaining the taxis and landed at the station, we usually had to take the bags ourselves and ask our way through to the right platform. Although it was way ahead of train time, a huge crowd would already be assembled.

The mere looks of our costumes made somebody invariably say:

"I don't want to be inquisitive, but would you mind telling me what organization that is?"

After the mention of the Trapp Family, very often he'd say:

"Oh, I remember now. Didn't I see your pictures in *Life?*"

Other people would come over, too, and a friendly chat would take place for half an hour, an hour, or more, until we all heard the distant rumble of the approaching train. Instantly all friendly relations ceased. Everyone looked concentratedly straight ahead, his mind set on one thing only: to get into that train at any cost. While the train was slowly rolling into the station, car after car passing by, we saw with sinking hope that people were already standing in the aisles.

"Don't forget to get out at . . ." and Georg would give the name of our destination.

These were the famous last words of a father who wasn't sure whether he would meet his family soon again. The next minutes were chaos. Everyone pushed his way individually into one of the cars with one or two bags, waiting expectantly to see whether the minor miracle, a vacant seat, would happen to him. Minutes after the train had left that station and everyone had disposed of his bags somewhere, somehow, the trips of reconnaissance began, and lonesome members of the Trapp Family met in corridors and related happily whom else they had seen.

"Father is two cars to the rear with Johannes. Martina and Johanna are standing with Illi and Lorli in the ladies' room, which is jammed full. Father Wasner is four cars ahead, right behind the dining car, and the others we don't know." About the luggage no questions were asked. One just hoped. And so we hoped our way through from day to day, from train to bus and from bus to train; and after two long concert tours all over Canada and the United States, it seems almost incredible that we always arrived at the same time—all of us, family and bags.

Rosmarie and Lorli now took an important part in the instrumental section, both playing the recorders very nicely; and little Johannes was with us, too. He was just starting out to learn to play the recorder, and this important musical education would not be interrupted for six months every year. He had his lesson every day with Maria. Now he was four and a half years old. There were hours and hours of train riding at a time, and you can't tell stories forever, so Johannes had to learn to entertain himself. That way he asked his way through the numbers and letters. Once we stopped for a concert in a convent school somewhere in the Maritime Provinces in northeastern Canada. A darling Reverend Mother occupied herself quite a bit with the little boy, and afterwards she said very pointedly:

"He is a very gifted child, and you should write down everything he says and does. Who knows what will become of him some day! Notice which word he reads first, for instance. Grace sometimes announces itself in such incidents."

A few days later I was holding Johannes on my lap, and we were looking out the window. The train had stopped in a little country town, and our particular car was standing on a street crossing. It was dusk, and the neon signs began to flicker.

Johannes' attention was caught, and slowly and solemnly the promising little child spelled his first word:

"T—A—V—E—R—N."

I didn't have the heart to let the Reverend Mother know this.

This kind of traveling proved to be extremely strenuous, especially with young children. If, for instance, we had to take a train after a concert in order to reach a certain town in time for the next performance, it meant standing around on a cold, draughty platform, waiting for a train which was late, sometimes way beyond midnight. Once this happened in Illinois, and when the train finally came, it was one o'clock. Each one of us had his ticket with a Pullman reservation for his berth, and we said good-night before we entered the different sleepers, everyone set on still catching as much sleep as possible. Mine was Lower 8. I opened the curtain, took my heavy bag, swung it once, up and down, aimed, and threw it on the bed. At the same instant I heard a low moan, and out came the upper part of a man, eyes rolling wildly. His ticket also read "Lower 8" for the same car. It had been sold twice.

Another time we were heading for Scott's Bluff, Nebraska, and it was getting late, way past midnight. Everybody was tired. By-and-by we all had managed to get seats, except Father Wasner, when in a station suddenly my neighbor left, and Father Wasner sank in his place and immediately closed his eyes. At the next station there entered a little company, four soldiers and a girl, and they all must have had a lovely time together; they were in high spirits. They chuckled and giggled, and wanted us all to share their happiness; their hilarious laughter resounded in the car, little appreciated by the rest of us, who wanted to do only one thing: sleep. Fate would have it that two of the soldiers got a seat behind Father Wasner and me, and the one behind Father Wasner invited the girl to sit on his lap. I tried several times, turning around and looking pleadingly at the young lady, to check her outward cheerfulness somewhat, but had little success. Finally I gave up, snapped my seat, in which I had been reclining, upright, and grew angrier and angrier by the minute.

"Just in case I should like her to know what I think," I mused to myself, "what would I say?" and I discovered with grief that I didn't command one single strong word in this English language which would even faintly give her an idea of my sentiments.

While I was resolving to get hold of some useful expressions, I saw out of the corner of my eye that she had started playing with Father Wasner's longish hair, as if she wanted to make a braid. Now this was too much. Before I could even think, I had gotten up and straightened myself to my full height of five-foot-seven, turned, and looked at her; oh, looked———! By then our co-travelers had awakened to the fact that they were witnessing a historic moment. All talking stopped. Everyone, rapt in attention, looked at us.

And I said—searching, hunting up and down my vocabulary for the worst, the most killing word I could find:

"You—you—you—bedbug!"

This word can be recommended. It did the trick perfectly.

After a concert in Oklahoma a Colonel came backstage, almost moved to tears. With outstretched arms he congratulated us on the performance. Born in Hungary, he felt himself a close country-man to us. He took us all with him, and we had a lovely evening together. He and Georg discovered mutual friends and acquaint-ances, and when we finally, very, very late, said good-night, he had become "Uncle Ferdinand." Next day he came to the train, and just before the last good-bye, he took one of the eagles from his uniform and pinned it on little Johannes' soldier's cap, a gift from brother Rupert. Half an hour later some soldiers passed through our car on the way to the dining car. The first one, especially friendly-looking, wanting to please that little boy, stepped up before Johannes, saluted, and said:

"Colonel, may I request a furlough?"

Johannes fixed his big blue eyes on the soldier and said:

"Yes, thirty days."

The lucky soldier fished into his pocket and counted out thirty pennies for the gracious little Colonel. I went on reading in my book; then I suddenly discovered there was no Johannes next to me any longer. Alarmed, I got up and looked all over the car, ladies' room, men's room, the next car, and finally found him in the third car, busily selling furloughs all around a crowd of highly-amused privates, his little pockets full of pennies.

The train pulled into a small town in Kansas, where we were to give a concert that night. The local manager, Mr. Sullivan, was at the station with a number of strong high school boys. The hotel was just across the street, and they carried the luggage over for us. After the concert Mr. Sullivan just happened to ask:

"Where are you going next?"

"We are taking the ten-thirty bus tomorrow for Wichita, where we have to catch an express train for Colorado."

"There is no ten-thirty bus," Mr. Sullivan interrupted me.

"Oh, yes, there must be. It says so on our schedule."

"No, that has been discontinued since the war."

"But we have to catch the train in Wichita." That was all I could think of. "Then we have to take a taxi."

"There is no taxi in this town. That's why we carried your luggage to the hotel ourselves."

"Mr. Sullivan," I said, "I don't care in what we go, but please have some vehicle, whatever it is, at ten-thirty tomorrow at the hotel. Whatever it costs, we have to make that train."

And Mr. Sullivan, a typical Communuity Concert man—helpful, cheerful, and a good sport, said he would.

Next morning Agathe and I went shopping. When we came back from Main Street, there was one single vehicle in front of the hotel. Of course, that couldn't be it, but it was almost ten-thirty, and there—the bellboys were carrying out the spinet and putting it right into what was unmistakably nothing but a hearse. Bag after bag went in, then came nine chairs.

Mr. Sullivan's voice said apologetically: "That's all I could find, for an open truck would be too cold for you."

I got the best seat, next to the driver, the family got in, the double door was closed from the outside, and half the town assembled. Laughing and waving, we took off for Wichita. The unusual situation had put everybody in an unusually jolly mood. We started singing and yodeling, and kept on for the entire forty-minute drive. When we came to the outskirts of Wichita, we had to stop for a red light, cars stopping left and right of our hearse. After a second's standing there together, windows were pulled down, heads appeared, no one, obviously, had ever met the phenomenon of a singing hearse before. I tried my hardest to look straight ahead, unapproachable to questions. Just before they all burst with curiosity, the light changed, and off we went, only to repeat the same performance at the next light. So we wound our way through Wichita, and arrived at the railroad station. The large door was flanked by two tall Negro porters who, hands in pockets, stood and idly looked nowhere. In an elegant curve the driver swept around the square and landed right at their feet. He got out, opened the double door while I anxiously watched their faces. What else could they have expected to come out of a hearse but a coffin; and now there hopped out in rapid succession one—two—three—six—seven girls—the porters were almost petrified.

The concerts went very well indeed. Not that we didn't miss the boys, or that the audience didn't miss them; but we had to do without gasoline, without tires, without sugar—so we also had to do without the boys. It was a necessary lack, which would help to final victory. It would almost have been awkward to have them with us. One would have felt like explaining or apologizing to the other mothers. In the letters which went to our soldiers in Camp Hale we were glad to be able to relate some hardships, too. We wouldn't have wanted to have a high time, no complications, no deprivations, while the boys went on manoeuvres and slept in the open at thirty below, and were homesick for us, just as we were homesick for them. This way it was more just; and though we were sighing under the strain, we wouldn't have wanted it any other way.

Trapp Family Music Camp

DURING that first concert tour by railroad, we took a few weeks off around Christmas for a much-needed break, because afterwards we were to go to the West Coast and not come back until May.

What a homecoming it was! When we left the train in Waterbury, it was thirty-six below zero, to go down to forty-five the next morning. The snow was singing under our feet when we stepped out of the taxis which had carried us up the hill. Instead of the steps which now lead to the front door, there was some kind of a broad ladder; and instead of a front door, there was a thick carpet. As no inner walls yet existed, the precious curtains from Freeman's had come in handy. Alfred had draped them around the big living room. In the fireplace roared a blazing fire. The two sofas with the swansdown cushions for thirty-five dollars each were standing there on the rough floor covered with Freeman carpets. The statues of the Apostles on the mantelpiece—oh, how wonderful it all was! Everything seemed to fit perfectly into the new house. On a ladder one reached the second floor, which was a yawning hole—one large dormitory with a corner partitioned off for a temporary chapel for that winter. There we celebrated Christmas very happily in our new home; it was overshadowed only by the great yearning for the boys. This was the first Christmas that the family had not been together.

Soon afterwards we were all armed with hammers and nails again, helping to erect partitions, board up walls, and lay floors. In good weather the others would go skiing. As my back bothered me a little more as the years went by, I had given up skiing for good. One morning Mr. R. brought news from the village.

"They're going to tear down the C.C.C. camp."

That was the very camp in which we had sung for the soldiers that first summer in Stowe. When I heard that that camp which had looked so different from all the other Army camps we had visited since, was to be torn down, a pang went through my heart. The mere thought disturbed me all day, and before the men went home, I said to Mr. R.:

"Isn't it a pity to tear down the camp? What could one do to preserve it?"

"Oh, nobody has any use for the place. If you want it," and he laughed, "just make an application to the State."

When the others came back from skiing, they brought a guest along: Mr. Burt from Stowe, the man with the straw hat. They had met him at the Toll House, and he had stayed with them the whole day, showing them trails; finally, over a cup of tea at the Octagon, Martina had said to him: "Mr. Burt, you have been just like an uncle to us"—which delighted him so much that he asked whether he couldn't keep that title. So it was "Uncle Craig" from then on. I asked him to stay for supper and extend his "uncle" qualities also to me, as I had had a brainstorm. During supper I explained how much of a crime it would be, to my way of thinking, to tear down a good camp, which surely could still be used.

Uncle Craig busied himself with his plate and seemed to be thinking. Then he looked up and said quietly:

"The State Forester is coming to Stowe tomorrow. He is the one in charge of the camp. I might bring him up, and you can talk it over."

There was something so reassuring and soothing about him, the tone of his voice, the look in his eyes, something that you recognize as you get along in life as a true quality of friendship: the genuine, selfless willingness to be of service, to help. Uncle Craig became very soon a kind of encyclopedia for us. If we wanted to know: Where is there a good mason? How much does a ton of hay cost? For how much does maple syrup sell? Where does one get barbed wire when no one seems to have any? To whom should we sell Christmas trees from our farm? When were the last Indians in this region? Was Fanny Allen, Ethan Allen's wife or sister? How did the farmers remove boulders from their fields before the times of bulldozers? How do you distinguish soft maple and hard maple in winter? What is a lumberjack? What does the expression which we heard yesterday mean: "tickled silly"?—just ask Uncle Craig! In his quiet way he'd always give you an answer which

satisfied you. As a kind of exchange, he used to come in and si
at times for hours, immovable in some corner, listening to ou
practicing. When he left, his eyes would be bright and shining.

"Thanks; I feel a better man now than when I came."

Next day Uncle Craig came again and brought Mr. Perry Mer
rill, the State Forester.

First, we talked about the winter and the skiing and the new
house; and when we had reached the dessert, which was *Schmarren*
Uncle Craig said:

"Mr. Merrill, the Baroness wants to talk to you about the camp
She has certain ideas."

And then a great silence settled over the dining room. Mr. Mer
rill made some encouraging noises and looked at me; not only he
but my whole family looked at me, very interestedly and very curi
ously; and if I could have looked at myself, I would have don
the same.

"What am I going to hear now?" I was wondering.

So far, it had been an intense pity and sympathy towards tha
good little camp which was about to be torn down, the mere ide
of which hurt my heart. But now I was supposed to have certai
definite ideas. Well, let's see.

"You see, Mr. Merrill—I mean to say—what I want to explai
is this . . ."

While I was stammering, the one question zigzagged wildl
through my head: what, *what*, WHAT can one do with a camp
And there was the answer: Sing Weeks. And I listened to mysel
explaining to Mr. Merrill.

"When I was a young girl, I attended, several times, so-calle
'Sing Weeks.' We met somewhere out in the country, groups o
between fifty and a hundred, and we spent eight or ten days de
voted only to music-making and folk dancing. I haven't seen tha
done in America yet. Couldn't we start them in that camp?"

All exhausted, I put down my fork and wiped my face. M
Merrill immediately liked the idea.

"That sounds like a very wholesome recreation, and that's wha
we want to boost in our State. The type of people who might com
for such a thing are exactly the ones we want to draw to Vermont.

Now *I* was looking down at my plate, avoiding the eyes of m
family. Hadn't I started something now? Yes, I had. Here we go

"Inasmuch as there is no other party interested in preserving the camp," Mr. Merrill went on, "I can assure you that you will be granted a lease from the State of Vermont. You have to make an application, and then a lease will be drawn and will be signed by me and approved by the Governor and five other officials. You can work on your plans right away; and how about going down after lunch and having a look at the camp?"

Well, well! That camp seemed like an orphan clinging to the one person who had talked in its favor, not wanting to let go any more.

So we went down the hill, Georg, Father Wasner, and I, with Mr. Merrill in Uncle Craig's car; the rest, on skis. We met at the camp. It looked lovely in this wintry landscape. There were eight big barracks on top of the hill, one on the slope, and two more at the bottom. Although the barracks were completely empty and exactly alike, Mr. Merrill opened each single one for us. They were large and bright and airy.

"They seem to be in good condition," said Georg finally.

Greatly delighted, I noticed the undertone of satisfaction in his voice.

"This was the kitchen and dining room, and this building opposite the others was their recreation hall. Everything else was used as dormitories except the little one over there, which was the infirmary, and the extra long one on the slope, which was the guardhouse."

"The ex-guardhouse would make a fine chapel," said Father Wasner; "enough room for everybody."

"We'll get you a little steeple with a bell," promised Hedwig, the practical one.

"I don't see why we couldn't leave the arrangement as it was, with the dormitories, recreation hall, kitchen and dining room," said I.

The others had gone on trips around the buildings on their skis. Now they came back.

"Mr. Merrill," inquired Illi, "I haven't seen a single washroom in the whole camp. Where did the soldiers wash?"

"Maybe in the brook like Boy Scouts," answered Johannes.

"Yes, but . . ." continued Illi.

"Oh, I found that," said young Lorli unashamedly. "It's behind the barracks and has seventeen seats!"

Mr. Merrill and Uncle Craig suppressed a smile, and I, a blush, and then Mr. Merrill said:

"Of course, you will have to do some readjusting for your purpose. But I am sure we can find plumbing fixtures somewhere in the State for you to put in. Whatever we can do, we'll be glad to help you out."

When he saw the excitement all through the family, he smiled and said:

"Now I expect your application, and it's granted so far as I'm concerned."

"Then the camp is yours," whispered Uncle Craig.

"Look, look!" cried little Johannes.

What a spectacle! A wonderful, complete rainbow extended from the top of our hill across the camp. Funny—there had been no rain or snow that whole day. We stood and gazed: the snow-laden trees sparkling in the sun, the camp tucked in between the hills looking so homey and cozy, and over it all the rainbow, the old token of peace. I took Georg's arm and pressed it.

"Let's take this rainbow for a good sign."

Soon we were on the road again on the way out west. In New York we explained to our publicity manager in general terms that we would run a music camp in the coming summer, and would she please announce it. Soon afterwards 100,000 green leaflets went out in all directions, saying: "You are invited to enjoy a holiday of music-making with the Trapp Family Singers during the coming summer at the Trapp Family Music Camp in Stowe, Vermont." There is always a certain magic in the printed word.

During long hours riding in trains and buses I had plenty of time to consider what I had done, and what I told myself about it wasn't always flattering. There—our house on the hill was only one-third finished. An O.P.A. and a War Production Board had to be consulted for every single doorknob and every inch of pipe. Was this new project necessary? Did I have to start more trouble? More headaches all around? When I looked at my husband, I dissolved into one act of contrition. Not a single word of reproach had come from him, but when he thought himself unobserved, he looked tired and discouraged. The boys had just been sent overseas. That anxiety was wearing him down, too. We were again deep in debt, and little as I minded that, he hated debts. And now I had heaped another burden on his shoulders. We would have more uncertainty, more anxiety, and more money to borrow. That weighed heavily on him.

But the leaflets were out, and the folders were on the press, giving a description of "a typical day at the Trapp Family Music Camp" as we were planning it. Now there was no way out but through.

So far, we had always traveled by coach in the daytime, but this train from Phoenix to Los Angeles had only Pullman cars, and for a day and a half we enjoyed being together in one compartment. With pencil and paper we started: what do we need for the camp? The most important thing: hot and cold running water in the barracks for washrooms. That meant so and so many feet of pipe— or was it better to say it in miles, as the water had to come from the top of the next mountain. We were figuring on eight dormitories with three showers, four washbowls, and four toilets for each dormitory. A hundred and twenty persons, therefore, would need a bed apiece, equipped with mattress, pillow, and two blankets; the supply of bedding alone would run into a large sum. How many plates, cups, glasses, forks, spoons? Partitions would have to be made—how about the lumber? Metal of any kind was the scarcest of all. How about the pipes and fixtures? The barracks would have to be painted inside and out, and . . .

And then I was glad that we had arrived in Los Angeles and had to get out. There was not much we could do from out there anyway, except make another application to the War Production Board concerning the camp.

This was an unusually long tour. The time was getting shorter and shorter before the people would be coming to enjoy their vacations at the Trapp Family Music Camp. We had already received a hundred and four reservations from real persons who wanted to come this summer and had paid a deposit of ten dollars each.

At last we were back East. We rushed home and over to Montpelier, and Mr. Merrill handed us the lease, approved by all six important persons, and wished us the best of luck. That was May 24. As our folder invited people for July 10, that left us but little time to convert an abandoned C.C.C. camp into a homey-looking, family-style place for music-making.

Mr. Merrill had told us the good news that he had found a number of washbowls and toilets and a couple of truckloads of lumber. The rest he was sure we could get. The rest—?

There was no time to lose. To our great disappointment, the War Production Board informed us that we were not allowed to use anything new; even lumber we had to get second-hand. That was a blow. We put an ad in the paper and watched every auction, carrying home eagerly every single two-by-four we could find in somebody's attic. In the meantime some of us roamed through all the second-hand stores in Boston and New York for washbowls and toilets, for hot-water tanks and electric fixtures, but pipes we couldn't get second-hand. Another application was refused. Precious time went by. A commission came and investigated the place to see whether it was a necessity for the war effort. We tried to explain that it was necessary in the same way as good concerts, and everything which helps to keep up the morale, that the whole camp was meant to help strengthen family spirit. And so the application for the pipes was granted.

Every day the telephone was busy.

"Uncle Craig—where can I get . . . ?" and the silence on the other end of the line grew longer and longer. Finally we had the necessary men; but the painters couldn't start until the carpenters were out, and the carpenters couldn't finish because the plumbers were still working, and the plumbers couldn't do a thing right now until the pipes came from Boston or New York.

But how many other things we had to think of! Our folder promised the future campers that we would sing with them out-of-doors down at the brook under the old shade trees in the grove, where it would always be cool, even in July and August. That called for benches.

"Uncle Craig—could you possibly imagine where we could get benches for, let's say—for a large number of people?"

The faithful one could imagine. There was an auction at Mosglen Falls with benches on the list. We got them.

More and more as I came to talk with different people about camps in general I learned that such recreation spots were not at all unusual in these United States; but I was told that two things are the life-giving essentials of a camp: the camp manager and the cook. None of us had ever been in an American camp or seen one from within, so I simply took for granted all I heard, and went on another trip to Boston; this time not to visit wrecking companies, but employment agencies. Within three days I was told that I could count myself extremely lucky to have found a camp manager who was reported to be most efficient and experienced. Before he would accept the position, however, he wanted to see the place. He would come within the next few days.

They had also found a cook for me, who was supposed to be perfect in Viennese, French, American, and Chinese cuisines. She asked one hundred dollars a week, and wanted to bring her husband along. Everything was all right with me.

As I was in Boston already, I continued to hunt for pots and pans, chairs and blankets. I had to go from one store to the other, grab here a dozen blankets, there six pillows, and in a third place, a bunch of spoons, hoping to find matching forks and knives somewhere, anywhere at all.

Then came a day which I shall never forget. After I had come back from Boston, I was standing in one of the barracks, talking to Mr. Steele, our plumber. Martina came in with two visitors.

"These gentlemen are from the War Production Board," she announced.

Soon I found out that these gentlemen *were* the War Production Board, and they didn't like us at all—anything combined with the name Trapp, whether it was the Trapp Family Farm, or the Trapp Family Music Camp—too many applications.

Sternly they looked around and pointing to the newest partitions, they said:

"This is new lumber."

Well, it was and it wasn't; and I tried to explain that we had bought that lumber for the farm half a year ago, and now had bought it second-hand from the farm for the camp. But that didn't make it any better. One of the gentlemen waved a six-page folder in very small print before my eyes and said:

"Didn't you study that? Don't you know that you have transgressed the law?"

I had seen the folder before, but it was in such mediaeval English with "heretofores" and "wherewithals," references to schedules or provisions, which were "superseded by . . ." and "further amended . . ." that I never could make out what it was all about. Both gentlemen were very stern, and one said now, firmly:

"You are to stop all activities here and on the farm, and you are summoned to appear at the main office in Montpelier on Tuesday for a hearing."

With a long, sympathetic look Mr. Steele, the plumber, slipped out. That was Saturday, and it was a long time until Tuesday; a long time in which to think and be sorry, and to wish one had never heard the name Trapp Family Music Camp in all one's life.

At the main office in Montpelier I was informed that, having wilfully transgressed the law, paragraph so-and-so, I was to be fined $10,000 in cash and must serve one year in jail, and did I have anything to say in my defense?

Whereas my English, according to my own estimation, was quite good enough for most occasions, unfortunately, it grew worse and worse when I got excited, and this I was now: excited. Who would ever lend me $10,000 to pay my fine? And would Columbia Concerts ever take us back after a year in jail? And what would my family say, and Freddy Schang, and the Drinkers, and all the other friends? My imagination ran riot. The more I tried to talk composedly and quietly, the more I stuttered and stammered. I tried to explain that I had not *wilfully* transgressed the law.

"And gentlemen," I said, "I can't serve my penalty all at once. Will you allow me to do that in installments? Half a year I must have to earn the money to pay my fine. The other half I can spend in jail. I think I can do it in two years."

After this heroic speech I was all done in. One single tear stole out of the right eye and rolled slowly down my nose, and there was nothing I could do about it.

Was it the tear, or had the gentlemen meanwhile received an impression of my well-meaning harmlessness? They withdrew for a moment, and when they entered the room again, they were very different. I should relax and not get excited, and things would be ironed out. They saw that I didn't want to cheat the government, and they would be up on Luce Hill late this afternoon for another investigation. I should go ahead.

They came and were very human. We showed them all over the place, house and camp, and explained all the purposes of each.

Then it was suppertime, and we asked them to stay for an Austrian meal, goulash with beer and afterwards, *Apfelstrudel*. After they had convinced themselves that there was really no dishonesty involved, they stopped being fearful officials and were very friendly. What a revelation to us, who came from a country where every office seemed to be created to make things hard for the people, and every official seemed to be a superhuman being! Next morning we could continue our work, and I didn't have to go to jail or pay that fine, either; but the gentlemen had gone all through that leaflet of the War Production Board with us to avoid future misunderstandings.

The two boys had landed safely in Europe. They were not supposed to say too much, but from the whole tone of the letters, we could grasp that they were in Italy, and that they were enjoying it.

Amid all the hustle and bustle of the preparations for the camp, there fell one beautiful family feast: Johannes' First Communion. He was only five, but since the days of his early babyhood he had been present with us at Holy Mass in the morning, and day after day the sad moment would come when little Johannes would be the only one who did not receive the little white bread. At the age of three he started begging for it. When he was told that he must wait until he was able to make real sacrifices to show his true love, he wanted to know what a sacrifice was.

"Do something you don't want to do, like eating your spinach without yelling," explained Lorli most readily. "Or don't do something you want to do; for instance, leave those candies for me."

And the little fellow set out on the road to perfection by trying to curb his likes and dislikes. When the small chapel on the farm was installed, a new hardship had been added. Every Saturday evening the family would sit on the bench outside while one after the other went in to Confession, and Johannes was always told to keep quiet and out of the way because he was too young. But now the great day had come. He knew all he was supposed to know, and had shown good will through a lengthy period of time, and the Bishop gave permission for his First Holy Communion on Corpus Christi day. The evening before, Johannes went down to the chapel to go to Confession for the first time. This he couldn't keep to himself.

"Now it's *my* turn," and at the word "my" he beat his little breast. "Now it's *my* turn; now *I'm* coming for a change!" he hollered all over the place.

Next morning he knelt in his red altar-boy cassock and surplice at the altar steps, a burning candle in his hand, to receive his Lord and Master into his young heart. A radiantly happy boy sat in the place of honor at breakfast afterwards, his plate decorated with flowers and heaped with little gifts.

It was but two weeks before the camp was to open. Not a single house was finished. The whole family worked together feverishly. Each one wanted to have three pairs of hands and feet. The beds had been promised by a department store in Boston, and the kitchen equipment by one in New York, but nothing had come so far. Again we lived on hope.

On a rainy morning we all assembled in the camp kitchen for a family council about the rusty Army stoves and the oily, filthy cement floor which was cracked in many places. The kitchen was the sore spot of the camp. The paint had scaled from the drab, tin-covered walls. It was entirely empty except for those huge stoves and several sawhorses, on which we were perched. We didn't look very hopeful on that particular morning. We were all engaged in painting, and it could easily be told which one was painting the red floor in the chapel, or the white window sills in some of the halls, or the green flower boxes. From running to and fro through the rain our hair was wet, and for painting jobs we were all dressed in something like fatigue suits. From our seats we were looking disgustedly around the kitchen, when the door opened and one of the workmen said:

"Somebody wants to see you."

A beautifully groomed, handsome, middle-aged man lifted his hat and after a cheerful "Good morning all around," said: "Could you please announce me to the Baroness?"

Goodness—the camp manager! This camp kitchen was the last place in the world in which I wanted to meet him, but there he was, and there *I* was, and in that attire! Too late. Here was the precious man on whom the entire success of our camp would depend, as I had been told. But let's hope for the best, for his imagination, for his sense of humor—after all, there *is* a war going on, and the camp will be finished in ten days, because it must.

Courageously I stepped forward to greet and introduce him. My apologetic remarks he took most graciously, and said:

"Never mind, never mind. Could you kindly show me the camp now?"

"But this *is* the camp!" the girls chorused in amusement.

"And this is the camp kitchen!" little five-year-old Johannes cried at the top of his voice. "It isn't quite finished," he added.

"Not—quite—finished—! You—don't—mean——!"

I saw plainly that he needed a change of atmosphere, and suggested:

"Let's go over to the recreation hall."

Hedwig stopped me.

"No, Mother, I'm sorry, I'm painting there."

Where else could we go? The dormitories were out of the question, the future chapel looked like a log cabin inside out, and as for the many lovely places under the trees and at the brook— the rain was pouring down. The taxi was still waiting outside. Soon I discovered why. The chauffeur wanted to know what to do with the two elegant pig skin grips, the tennis racket, and the set of golf clubs.

I suggested that he drive up to the farm for a cup of tea. Once at the farm I changed into my best with monkey-like speed and, trying to be charming as never before in my life, I painted a picture of the future camp in ravishing colors.

He listened politely, and then he suddenly discovered that for some important reason—how silly that he hadn't thought of it before, he would have to go back to Boston on the next train!

"But you will come a few days before the camp opens, won't you?" I repeated that question now, for the fifth time at least.

"If I can possibly manage it, I shall, of course. I shall write you a note first thing when I reach Boston."

Two days later I held his letter in my hand. Among other things, he said—and I still have his letter:

"I had no idea you were not ready to operate. When I think of obtaining, shipping, installing and testing out equipment only for your kitchen by July 10—this is absolutely impossible. I strictly advise you to return your deposits and wait for next season to start *RIGHT*. To be perfectly honest, Madam, I doubt whether it is in your line to operate a camp. . . ."

Return the deposits? Impossible, Sir; every cent was spent already.

What a blow! But I couldn't get into real mourning merely for lack of time: the cook had arrived in Waterbury! This time it was a beautiful, sunny day. The lady cook showed much more understanding and real imagination than the well-groomed manager. The kitchen was freshly painted, and the stoves were just being cleaned with kerosene. After I had showed her around, continually explaining what this and that place *would* look like in eight days, we finished our business talk on the new benches under the trees at the brook. The gracious lady consented to come for seventy-five dollars a week under the following conditions: that she and her husband be given a three-room apartment close to the kitchen, that she have a large electric dough mixer, an electric meat cutter, a stainless steel coffee urn, a stainless steel sink, a gas baking oven, so and so many aluminum pots and pans. . . .

I was so grateful that she was willing to come at all, that without looking at the list, I promised that everything would be ready. Overnight I went down to New York and spent the whole next day around Cooper Square, that paradise for kitchen equipment. I didn't ask for prices any more. The main thing was—I got it all. Footsore and exhausted, I fell on my seat in the train the same evening to go back to Vermont, feeling as if I deserved the Purple Heart and the Congressional Medal.

Every day I grew prouder of my family. The girls started to paint and hammer as early as five o'clock in the morning, and worked through the day and evening until ten o'clock or later. If I wasn't in New York or Boston or Montpelier in one of the offices, or on the train, I looked over the camp anxiously and counted the objects which hadn't arrived yet. There were only five days more to go, and the beds hadn't come. Pillows and blankets had arrived, but there were no beds to put them on; and the china was standing around because the kitchen cabinets were not yet ready.

Georg was busy at the farm; the haying season was in full swing, and plumbers and electricians were working in the house. He couldn't help me much now, or so he thought; but the tight clasp of his hand once in a while and the reassuring twinkle of his eyes were the greatest help at that moment.

Father Wasner had his hands full, fixing the chapel and sacristy, ordering and copying music, numbering one hundred folders, making programs for the singing sessions of each day, and trying to obtain recorders.

The different houses at the camp had to be named. The girls suggested names of composers, the great masters. Johanna, who was very good at lettering, wrote the signs in white paint on green boards: "Mozart Hall," "Palestrina," "Schubert," "Beethoven," "Stephen Foster," "Haydn," and "Brahms Hall." Then we came to the naming of the dining room. Father Wasner opposed violently our calling it "Johann Sebastian Bach Hall"; that was a disgrace in his eyes. But it had to have a name. After the day's work was done, the girls went through a music encyclopedia, and with howls of triumph they found out that Rossini, the composer of *The Barber of Seville,* had been a baker and a cook. Not even Father Wasner could find any objection to calling the dining room "Rossini Hall."

Two days before the camp opened, half the beds were there. Two early guests came. Hastily we put them up on the farm.

July 10: The guests were expected on the evening train. The Governor of Vermont, the Selectmen of Stowe, our friend, the State Forester, and everyone from the village who cared to, were invited for the formal opening of the camp at seven o'clock in the evening, and still, half the beds hadn't come. It wasn't funny any more. Eighty-four people expected to sleep this very night, and I was still many beds short.

Among the guests who had arrived by different buses earlier in the day, there was a gentleman who noticed that I was alarmed about something. As I was running over the campus, he stopped me, put his hand on my shoulder, and said in a warm tone:

"All that matters now is that your boys and our boys come home safely. Isn't that right?"

That saved the day for me. Not only that day, but very often afterwards when I was in trouble, I repeated those words, and they worked every time.

The plumbers had gone, the carpenters had gone, the electricians and painters, too. The dormitories and private rooms looked lovely, shining with cleanliness. The chapel was finished; it even had a little steeple. In the recreation hall was the small camp store, equipped with toothbrushes, pencils, stamps, and postal cards. And last but not least, that problem child, the kitchen, had emerged from the state of an ugly larva into a most beautiful butterfly. In the shiny kitchen floor were mirrored scores of stainless steel pots and pans and ladles. There was the coffee urn, the baking oven, an oversized dough mixer, an electric meat cutter, a brand-new kitchen table seven by seven feet, and a brand-new kitchen cabinet. The large refrigerator was stuffed with hams, ducks, chickens, and veal, and the pantry looked like a medium-sized country store. In the cellar you couldn't walk any more. And in the center of the kitchen dwelt the most imposing object of all—the lady cook, with a tall, snow-white cap and the air of a Dowager Empress. Her husband was unpacking their luggage in the newly created three-room apartment furnished with maple furniture, according to their wishes. Four girls waited on the Empress. Oh, it was a delight to look into this well-run sanctuary. The heartpiece of the camp was secure.

If only that second shipment of beds would come. One couldn't even call, because they had been shipped by truck, and the truck was "on its way." For heaven's sake! During the formal opening ceremonies, while we were singing the National Anthem, Georg was supposed to raise the flag slowly—and we had forgotten to buy a flag! It was five o'clock, too late for the stores. Georg rushed down to Stowe and borrowed the one from the high school for this night.

My secretary was busy writing names on little white cards to be tacked to the room doors and over the beds in the dormitories. The express office called to tell us that a few huge packages were waiting for us. Thus the three dozen white aprons came just in time for the young waitresses, who had started to set the tables for the first meal.

Around six o'clock Governor Wills came. How I would have liked to stay with him, looking relaxed and cheerful; but a lady was looking for her luggage, which she had sent a week ago, and in the kitchen they had discovered that I had forgotten to purchase a can opener—what about the tomato juice then?

Little Johannes, sitting on a tree, watching the highway down in the valley, suddenly yelled:

"The buses are coming!"

Our guests had arrived. My husband, the girls, and I welcomed them. Then Governor Wills in his inimitably winning way opened solemnly and formally the Trapp Family Music Camp. Everyone joined in singing "The Star-Spangled Banner," and slowly the flag rose over our camp for the first time. The Governor addressed the guests and welcomed them in the name of the State of Vermont. The Selectmen followed in welcoming them in the name of the town of Stowe, and my husband welcomed them in the name of his family.

After the opening ceremonies we ushered the guests into the dining room.

"Dear Lord," I prayed most fervently, "and here they are going to stay until You have sent the remaining beds"; and I asked the waitresses to be very, very slow.

The incredible happened again. Before the juice glasses were taken off the tables, the truck arrived, and everyone helped to put the beds up; and when the guests left Rossini Hall, strengthened and refreshed, everything was ready. Camp guests and towns-people grouped themselves on the lawn around the flagpole, and we gave them a little welcoming concert under the stars. We couldn't help thinking back to that first starlight performance in the same place two years before, and as we looked up into the sky, we saw flashes of green and golden light darting upwards—northern lights. It reminded us of that crisp winter day when it all had started, and we felt as if we were still standing under the rainbow.

When I came out next morning, my secretary was already wait-ing with big eyes.

"I'm so sorry to disturb you—but we have no water in the camp. The spring has run dry; the water supply is not enough for all the people."

The guests were already streaming into the dining room. I had only two minutes' time, and then I had to "say something." With a knife I tapped on a glass, and then I announced cheerfully:

"Ladies and gentlemen, will you please get your music and also your towels ready. We want to give you this morning the sensation of a shower in the wilderness. The buses are on their way. We shall have a picnic at Bingham Falls."

And so we did. While the whole camp was enjoying a hot summer day at the cool waterfalls, making up for the lack of a morning bath, Mr. Steele, the ever-helpful, brought an electric pump, made a temporary pipeline from the brook into the houses, and supplied the bathrooms with brook water, leaving the spring water for wash bowls and kitchen.

From then on things went smoothly.

Every morning and every afternoon we sang with our guests the immortal music of the old masters down in the grove near the brook. We sang rounds and folk songs of many nations. We sang choral works of the classical masters, and it was pure joy to witness how persons who had never before sung to any extent, could derive such deep satisfaction out of learning those wonderful pieces. Every night we all danced folk dances on the lawn. For a whole day we took them up the highest mountain in the State of Vermont, Mount Mansfield; on another day we showed them one of the loveliest lakes of the neighborhood, carrying along music and food. Every excursion was a success. Every night after Benediction was over in the chapel, we sang a few motets and hymns to give those hearts present a little more chance to enter into the spirit of prayer. There was so much to pray for. So many of us had loved ones in danger: sons, husbands, brothers, fiancés. Saint James says: "Is any of you sad? Let him pray. Is he cheerful in mind? Let him sing." Many of those souls hadn't prayed for a long time. There, music acted as a magic key, to which the most tightly closed heart opened. In these moments we felt the heart-piece of our most noble vocation, as Longfellow once expressed it:

> "God sent his Singers upon earth,
>   With songs of sadness and of mirth,
>   That they may touch the hearts of men,
>   And bring them back to heaven again."

Snapshots of the Camp

THE first camp summer was over. Everything had been done now once for the first time, and we could witness how the foundation of a tradition is laid. The arrival of the guests for every Sing Week, the picnics, the typical camp routine, and the last evenings would repeat themselves year after year, until some day somebody would say: "We always used to do it this way."

The ending of the camp was very touching. There were funny surprises during the last evening meal. Little groups performed short scenes from camp life. After that, Maria's recorder class gave a short concert, showing what could be done in just nine days of teaching. We all laughed to tears when the beginners, shaking and trembling with stage fright, produced out of pure nervousness funny little shrieks while playing "Mary Had a Little Lamb."

It showed again that the recorder is the ideal instrument for any adult whose childhood musical education has been neglected. If someone discovers on his fiftieth birthday that he should have taken piano or violin lessons while in school, he will hardly want to start then, for fear of not getting very far; but he will always miss it—to be able to "make music" himself. That's where the recorder comes in handy. After six weeks of faithful practicing, even the oldest pupil can play folk tunes very nicely. The combination of soprano, alto, tenor, and bass recorders gives a lovely, mellow sound. There is no limit to the literature which can be played, beginning with easy, four-part settings and going through the vast realm of madrigals and motets. One or the other player will get even more ambitious and find out for himself about the wonderful literature written for the recorder: sonatas by Telemann, arias by Bach, etc., real virtuoso literature, too. There are untold riches in that little instrument, which can be had for less than twenty dollars.

And it really happened. People who had started out with "Mary Had a Little Lamb" in that first camp summer, and who came back year after year, are now playing Bach and Telemann, to Maria's pride and joy. They themselves have spread the enthusiasm among their friends, and the forgotten recorder is enjoying a revival all over the States.

After the recorder concert by Maria's class, we all went down to the chapel. Once more we prayed together in thanksgiving, and then we sang for our guests once more by candlelight their favorite songs: "The Children's Blessing," "The Lord Is My Shepherd," "The Virgin's Lullaby."

After that we went over to the little dell where we had given that historic concert for the soldiers, and a huge bonfire was lit.

Next morning three big buses came to take our guests to the train. When the buses were filled, they lined up abreast, facing us, and for the last time, the campus resounded with the round: *"Viva, Viva la Musica!"* each bus taking a part. Many a tear was shed. Everyone was sorry that the Sing Weeks were over.

The Trapp Family Music Camp had turned out to be the answer to the question which had been asked hundreds of times backstage after a concert, at parties, in letters:

"How could we do what you are doing: sing in our family?"

In that ten-day course we try to make the people acquainted with as much musical literature as possible, from easy beginnings to complicated cantatas and fugues. The excuse, "We couldn't possibly sing—we have no piano," is being discarded, as we usually sing down at the brook or under the old butternut trees outside of the recreation hall. Besides the singing, we also try to revive those beautiful old folk dances from all nations, and we try to show our friends at the camp that the best recreation is the kind where one does things oneself with others joining in: singing, dancing, playing games, telling stories, reading aloud, enacting those wonderful old folk customs throughout the year, following the word: "A family which sings together, plays together, and prays together, usually stays together."

Our age has become so mechanical that this has also affected our recreation. People have gotten used to sitting down and watching a movie, a ball game, a television set. It may be good once in a while, but it certainly is not good all the time. Our own faculties, our imagination, our memory, the ability to do things with our mind and our hands—they need to be exercised. If we become too passive, we get dissatisfied.

What a great joy and satisfaction it was when the campers became so enthusiastic about everything that they didn't want to wait a whole year until they could meet again. They founded the Stowe Singers, an alumni group of people who would meet once a month to sing and play the recorder together. There was a chapter in Boston, in New York, and later also in Montreal.

Funny things happened at times in the camp; for instance, that one morning when the ladies, sopranos and altos, were singing too loud—oh, much too loud, and Father Wasner, throwing up his arms, implored them:

"Reduce, ladies, reduce!"

Or that other time when the whole group of one hundred and twenty people was congregated for the afternoon singing and, while Father Wasner was detained on the telephone, a lady entertained the others with a little cloth monkey, which she made do all kinds of funny tricks. Next to her the concert pianist, Fritz Jahoda, was standing with his little daughter, Eleanor, four years old. Suddenly like a silver bell, the child's voice was ringing through the attentive silence:

"My Daddy says you look exactly like your monkey!"

In the camp we had a question box. Towards the end of the Sing Week one evening would be devoted to answering and discussing questions.

"What do you think about popular music?" was one of the most frequent questions.

Father Wasner would attend to the questions concerning music. With emphasis he would declare:

"The mere word 'popular' means 'of the people,' but these tunes going under that name have nothing at all to do with the people. They are artificially made up by some individual, put on the market with the aid of great publicity, but after two years they are completely forgotten, which only shows how little popular they have been. Neither the words nor the music express the true sentiments of the people. That's why they have no strength to survive." And then he always pleaded: "But there is such genuine folk music in this country, real pearls of folk songs throughout the hills and dales of New England and down the Appalachian Mountain range, the cowboy songs in the West and the Negro spirituals in the South. These are the ones which deserve the word 'popular,' as they come out of the people, and will live through the centuries."

Another much-asked question was:

"Why does the Trapp Family not wear American clothes?"

We explained that after the First World War the people in Austria returned to wearing their national costume for economic reasons. It is so much less expensive. You have two or three wool dresses for the winter and three or four cotton ones for the summer, and that lasts you for years and years. You change the white blouses and the colored aprons according to weekdays or holidays. In a family with seven daughters that makes a great difference. When we arrived in America in our national costume, it was for years out of the question to buy what we call "civilian clothes" merely for reasons of money. When it would have been possible, however, we bought a farm instead. Meanwhile, the people got used to our looks. We love our dresses for still another reason besides the money question, and that is that we don't have to bother with the fashion of the day; whether frog-green or cardinal-red is the latest rage, or which pocketbook matches which color stockings doesn't bother us in the least. This way no nightmarish evening gowns which suffer from lack of material somewhere can haunt us. It has become an all-around agreeable and practical situation for us, saving money, time, and peace of mind.

"And what are you going to do about your girls' marrying? Do they meet young men? Do they have boy friends?" was the third of the most popular questions.

As far as marrying went, my husband and I had started way back in Europe to say one Hail Mary together every day for each one of our children in order that they might find the right mate in life. As for meeting people—who met people more than we with all those parties and concerts, invitations, and now with the camp? But things were altogether different over here from what they had been in Europe. I had always felt sorry for my girls because they didn't have that wonderful experience I had had when I was young and in our Catholic Youth Movement. Those large groups of young boys and girls meeting together for singing and folk dancing and long hikes and discussions—what pure joy, what a wonderful thing! Such groups didn't seem to exist here, and we didn't care for the "going steady" system. Youth always meets youth in the things they have in common. There is definitely nothing wrong for a girl to be invited by a boy to go to a movie and afterwards sit at a drug store counter over an ice cream soda with two straws—the trouble is only that you'd enjoy so much more going with nine other girls and ten boys, playing volley ball for a couple of hours, then singing to your hearts' delight motets, madrigals, and folk songs, then doing some of those beautiful ancient folk dances, always all of you together, and ending up perhaps with a short night prayer when the stars are coming out. There are individuals here and there, young boys, young girls, all over the United States, who feel exactly like that, and would call such entertainment ideal. Let's hope and pray that out of their numbers may come one day a leader to unite them all in a movement which may sweep like a forest fire from coast to coast, burning in its flames all this unhealthy sophistication and filling home and church with a new generation.

One day seven young men walked into the camp and introduced themselves as students from the University of Montreal. They had heard us in a concert there and wanted to meet us all again. The very moment I saw them, I was startled. In their shorts with their brown knees and rucksacks, they reminded me very strongly of that type of boy I had always wished my girls to know. They happened to come in a desperate moment when we were short of help all around the camp. Would they have time to stay and help us out? Four weeks later when they finally had to go home after their long weekend with us, I realized with a heart most touched and moved how true the word of Our Lord is: "Whatsoever you shall ask the Father in My name, that will I do." "Whatsoever," He had said, and He meant it. A mother had asked for the right company for her children, and there it was. Singing, dancing, hiking, camping, discussing, and praying together had filled all the spare time of the last weeks. The young men still come back time and again. They bring their friends. We have met their families, and some of them have stayed on our hill and become members of the larger family.

It was during the second camp summer, 1945, that one day in August we were notified over the telephone that the war was over. One of us ran down and rang the bell of the chapel, and when all the people had gathered outside on the lawn, we told them. I shall never forget how impressed I was that there was no great shouting, no loud rejoicing, but one by one, they all filed into the chapel to give thanks.

Then came a telegram that our boys were coming home from Italy. Not only the whole family, but also the whole camp participated in arranging their welcome. These boys had become a sort of symbol for all the others who were expected home now, sooner or later. They had become "our boys." The large hay wagon was decorated with garlands and flowers. Georg drove the team. Little Johannes was riding ahead on his pony, Popcorn, the girls and I in our feastday best, on the wagon. So we awaited the boys at the edge of the camp property. There they had to get out of the car and into the wagon and, accompanied by all one hundred and twenty camp guests, they rode on in triumph. What a day! Only then I saw how much Georg must have suffered in silence and secret all these anxious years of uncertainty, now when the burden had dropped off his shoulders.

After the gale of the first joy and happiness of being together again had quieted down, the boys began to make plans. Rupert had put aside his personal plans for so many years, had sacrificed his medical career for the mere necessity of keeping the family going with our concert work; and we had always appreciated it deeply. The war had shown that he was not indispensable in that work any more. Now he could think of getting his American degree as an M.D. He enrolled at the University of Vermont and went to school again.

Werner, within whom the farmer and the musician were always fighting, decided to stay in concert work and work on the farm between times.

Once we had three girls in the camp. They came from a family of ten children. They became such close friends with our girls that they came back the very same summer, together with Father, Mother, and the rest of the family. They were wonderful people, and we had so many things in common! Later somewhere on our concert tour I got a letter from Rupert in which he complained how lonely he was, and wasn't there anyone I knew whom he could visit.

"Yes," I said, "I do know somebody. Why don't you go and see the Lajoies in Fall River?"

The next thing was an overjoyed, beamingly happy announcement of his engagement to Henriette Lajoie, which we received while on tour in Seattle. Three cheers for the camp!

Trapp Family Austrian Relief, Inc.

WHEN Joseph, the young son of Jacob, was taken into Egypt, it was against his will. There his beginning was very hard; but after years of much trouble, he succeeded in winning the confidence of the people and their king, and his exile turned into glory. Oftentimes he may have wondered for what this new name and new fame were given him, until one day he learned through travelers that a famine was raging in his homeland, and his people were starving to death. Now he understood, and with the help of his new countrymen, he could use his new power to help his people at home.

Something similar happened to us. *Our* beginning in *our* Egypt was a hard one; *we* also succeeded in winning the confidence of the people in the new country; and as we built up a new name and new fame, also with *us,* exile turned into glory. Also *we* wondered at times what it all meant, until one day we, too, learned that in the old homeland a famine was raging, and the people were starving to death. That was the answer, and most happily could we turn now towards the old home and with the aid of the new countrymen, help the old ones.

It happened like this.

In January, 1947, a few days before we had to leave for the West Coast again, a letter arrived, addressed to the Trapp Family Singers. It came from the General of the American Army of Occupation in Austria, and the letter described briefly how terribly hard, how heartrending the suffering of the Austrian people was. And then the letter pleaded: Could the Trapp Family Singers perhaps do something for Austria during their concert tours?

This was a call, a summons. The letter was read aloud in the family, and a council was held. For this we would have to incorporate. The very next day we went to our capital, Montpelier, and founded the Trapp Family Austrian Relief, Inc. A paper with the seal of the State of Vermont and signed by the Secretary of State testified that this corporation was founded for the purpose of "general help and relief to poor, displaced, and unfortunate people of all nationalities and creeds in the United States and elsewhere," and that it was "not organized for profit, but is organized exclusively for charitable purposes." The first meeting of the association was held at the law office of Mr. William N. Theriault. At this meeting by-laws of the corporation were discussed and unanimously adopted, and the board of trustees was duly elected by unanimous vote: President, Georg von Trapp; Vice-president, Maria Augusta von Trapp; Treasurer, Reverend Franz Wasner; plus two additional officers: Secretary, Johanna von Trapp; Clerk, Werner von Trapp. It was also voted that the corporation procure a corporate seal and a rubber stamp.

Now we were permitted to collect food and clothing and money from coast to coast, and *contributions could be deducted from the donor's income tax*. That impressed us. We had been told that big firms, factories, and also individuals made at one time terrifically large contributions to charities for that very reason. We saw ourselves heading for millions in collections. We also had a leaflet printed, which we intended to distribute among the audiences of our concerts. In this we said that our native country, Austria, which so many Americans know and love, was in gravest danger.

"The country which gave to the world a Haydn, Mozart, Schubert, Johann Strauss—a 'Silent Night'—may perish if we don't all help together and act right now"; that "everybody is informed about conditions in the larger European countries, but hardly anybody knows what is going on in Austria . . . where her people are just about to give up courage and hope." We told them that "all over Austria the population suffers from lack of practically everything; especially food, clothing, and fuel. Moreover, thousands of people arrive daily in freight cars at different stations. In Vienna conditions have reached a climax of misery." Then we said: "Let a social worker tell you about her daily attempts to do the impossible"—and we quoted from actual letters we had received.

"Our railroad stations have been shattered by bombs. In the ruins live thousands of displaced persons, waiting for trains to take them no one knows where, while hundreds of new ones arrive daily. The dying and the dead, the badly sick with high fever, and little children are lying together between the pieces of the walls. We have no barracks, of course no hospital room, for these poorest of the poor. When the new transports arrive, we usually find little babies with diapers frozen to their emaciated bodies, children dressed in newspaper or old rags kept together by string and pieces of broken wire, and the grownups in all stages of exhaustion and starvation. Usually these people have been in that box car for two weeks or longer without any care. It is absolutely impossible to describe the condition in which they arrive. We would need food, clothing, and first aid materials for thousands, but we hardly have enough for a few hundred.

"We can't get needles. We have to rent a needle for a Schilling a day, and woe if you should break it."

A university professor of Vienna says in a letter to us: "Personally, I do not mind the hunger so much, but it is so very embarrassing that I cannot get shoe laces and have to walk around without."

Then the leaflet went on.

"The urgent necessity for help is also felt and stressed by the authorities of the U. S. Occupation Army. A high American officer and an American Army Chaplain, in cooperation with local agencies in Austria, sent us recently more than 5,000 addresses of the most needy people."

Then we told them that we had founded our corporation and called it the Trapp Family Austrian Relief, Inc., in order that our name might warrant that every cent, every item, would reach its destination: a needy person in Austria. "We have no overhead expenses; we do everything within our family."

Then we suggested ways to help Austria:

1. Send to the *Trapp Family Austrian Relief, Inc., Stowe, Vermont,* any clothing or non-perishable foodstuffs you can spare. We

can use everything: shoelaces, pencils, needles and thread, woolen blankets. . . .

2. Contribute by donating funds. Make checks payable to the 'Trapp Family Austrian Relief, Inc.,' Stowe, Vermont. YOUR DONATION AS A CHARITABLE CONTRIBUTION IS DEDUCTIBLE FROM THE INCOME TAX.

3. Write to us and ask for addresses of needy families or individuals if you prefer to take care of someone yourself.

And the leaflet ended:

"The other day we came across the words of St. Ambrose, one of the greatest men of the fourth century, spoken at the time of a famine: 'If you know that anybody is hungry or sick, and you have any means at all and do not help, then you will have the responsibility for each one who dies, and for each little child who might be harmed and crippled for life.' Let us also remember that other word: 'As long as you did it to one of these My least brethren, you did it to Me.'"

Thus fortified with stationery with a letterhead, these 100,000 leaflets, a rubber stamp, and the best will not to spare ourselves, we set out for the West Coast.

We had never done anything like it before, but had we ever run a music camp, or a handicraft exhibition, or thought of giving concerts, or started to build a new house? These big assignments had been hurled at us without allowing even enough time to buy ourselves a handbook to look up the "how to."

We tried everything we could think of. Upon arriving in a town, some of us went to the local newspaper to give an interview on starving Austria, while another group did the same on the local radio station. From both parties we usually received the greatest understanding and cooperation. At the beginning of the concerts the leaflets were handed out, and during intermission I made an appeal to the audience. I used to say:

"If you want to avoid making packages, our big blue bus will be tomorrow morning in front of the hotel——" (and then I almost invariably named the wrong hotel, usually the one from the day before—but the people always found the right place).

The next morning I would stand outside of the bus with a couple of the girls, and—what a touching sight—the people would flock to the bus from all directions, carrying bundles or heaps of clothing in their arms. In smaller country towns pickup trucks would drive up behind the bus and empty their contents on our seats.

It was in March and somewhere in the Southwest when, after a concert, a lady stopped at the bus, took off her winter coat, and said:

"It's my only one, but I don't need it any more this year. Could you please send it to a teacher over there? I'm a teacher myself."

In another place a mother came to see me in the hotel, her face tear-stained, her hands twisting a handkerchief. A few days before she had lost her only daughter in an accident. After she had heard the appeal in last night's concert, she had worked half the night to collect all the girl's things. Now she brought them in five big boxes together with a photograph.

"Look at her," she said, "and pick me out a girl of her age in Austria, who will write to me."

When we came to the border of California, our bus was filled to the brim. At the border we were stopped and asked to show our luggage. Eyes turned to heaven, we silently pointed to the bus: "Look at the luggage!" But law is law, and the officer of the State Board of Health, or whatever it was, had to demand that we empty our warehouse. Rows of tables were arranged there for the travelers' convenience in showing their suitcases. We drove to the last row of these tables, and while emptying the bus, put everything in bags and boxes. After two hours forty-six large pieces were packed, to the admiration of the staff of that Health Board.

It was in California, in Ventura. Our appeal for Austria was received as never before. The whole town responded. We were asked to come back in a week. Different organizations made clothing drives, and when we came back to collect the contributions, our bus was almost too small. It was packed to the last seat up to the ceiling, and we all had to stand in the aisle as far as Santa Barbara. The very kind Superior of the Franciscan Fathers helped us all he could. On the grounds of the Old Mission the things were packed and shipped in numerous large crates.

Meanwhile, word had gotten around about the relief work which we were combining with our concerts. In the majority of places the people loved and appreciated this idea.

"We live in extraordinary times; that's why we have to do extraordinary things," the Mayor of a small town assured us.

But some people objected, and a few objected violently. They insisted that they went to hear a concert and didn't want to be reminded of the suffering going on in the world. They wanted to relax and not be called upon again. Well—that's another point of view, and we tried from then on to respect that. We always asked the local people, the ones in charge of the concert, what they thought about this relief work, whether the people would mind it. Sometimes we omitted it, and in the places where we did make our appeal we had no difficulty.

We were perfectly overwhelmed with the way the American people in general reacted to our petition. And this after many years of constant drives. Starting with Finnish and Greek relief, there had been an uninterrupted chain of appeals and campaigns, and on top of that—we came along with our unprofessional relief organization, which consisted of a rubber stamp, a leaflet, a letterhead, and one family which was burning to help. And the miracle repeated itself after every concert. After we had said we needed food and clothing for the starving Austrians and we needed money to send it to them—the people went home, got food and clothing and also some money and, like the widow's cruse, the big blue bus never went empty.

This happened to be the longest concert tour we ever had. We covered almost thirty thousand miles and gave one hundred and seven performances. On the West Coast we once had seventeen concerts in succession without a break. We had large distances to cover every day, and the days looked like this: For an hour every morning our bus was filled up with gifts for Austria by the townspeople who had been at last night's concert. When it was high time for us to leave, Rudy, our driver of that year, and incidentally of Austrian parentage himself, would blow the horn furiously.

"Three hundred and fifty miles today!" he would shout.

After heartfelt thanks to the generous givers, we took off, and immediately started on the daily routine. In grocery stores we had asked for empty boxes; in granaries, for empty feed bags. These were now packed systematically by Martina, Hedwig, Rosmarie, and Lorli. When the boxes and bags were filled, they were handed up front to the men. Georg and Werner tied them with double string. Agathe wrote the labels. Johanna and Maria typed lists of contents and letters announcing the parcels. They had found out that if you squeeze a typewriter between your knees at a certain angle, you can write quite well in a moving bus. Meanwhile, I was reading. The letters came in at first by the dozen, but soon by the hundred. When enough finished packages were piled up so that Rudy was all walled in and no traffic between front and rear was possible any more, Rudy used to pull up at the next post office in a small country town, and the postmaster would have a red-letter day in his life: that big blue bus with the word "Chartered" in front and "Trapp Family Singers" on the sides pulling up almost to his window, girls in quaint dresses hopping out, and packages, boxes, bags piling up on his counter—why—that's like Christmas! They helped weigh the load, and at the end they asked for a thousand 3-cent stamps, and off they went again. The next half hour in the bus was passed in complete silence, everybody licking stamps, pasting them on envelopes—the leaflet was being sent to long lists of addresses. Then the packing was resumed, and after two hours, another pile of twenty or thirty bags was dumped at another post office. And so on.

Reading the hundreds of letters was a hard task. There were letters from people who had seen better times and never in their lives had thought that they would one day have to beg. These letters were usually very long and wordy. After having talked about anything under the sun, music or pre-war memories, at the very end came a final remark such as:

"My old wife and I are sitting on the floor of our completely empty room. Even the doors with the door frames and the windows with the window frames have been stolen." (The climate in an Austrian winter is little different from Vermont.) "We have nothing to eat, nothing to heat with, nothing to wear. Sincerely yours."

There were the most touching thank-you letters coming in, like this one:

"But the most precious gift was the pound of coffee you sent me. With this I have paid my debts at the shoemaker's, grocer, milk store; I paid the rent for our room for half a year in advance; I could exchange some flour, jam, and a little butter for it; and some of it I still keep in case some one of us should get sick. How can I ever thank you enough?"

The two Catholic Army Chaplains in Vienna and Salzburg had

most generously offered their help at the very beginning. Permission was given for us to ship everything right to them. They handed it over to a small staff of volunteers, who checked on the cases and handed the goods out. In that way it was possible to avoid having the things go to the black market or into undeserving hands. Through the untiring efforts of Colonel Nuwer, Chaplain in Vienna and Major Saunders, Chaplain in Salzburg, help could be brought to the spot in an incredibly short time. Both Fathers, and also General Collins, who had instigated the whole program, became honorary members of the Trapp Family Austrian Relief, Inc. Naturally, we got more mail from Salzburg, as everybody in that countryside knew us personally, and so our dealings with Father Saunders were more extensive. Although we have never seen him, he has become very close to us.

As the trip went on, we got more and more tired, but we learned that one can be happily tired, and the element of happiness can outweigh that of tiredness. When, on the way back, we stopped in St. Paul, the seminary there had collected in the gymnasium hundreds of pairs of shoes, heaps of cassocks, suits, etc.; and on top of it all, the seminarians helped to pack the gifts and send them to the seminary in Salzburg. Finally they took up a collection and even paid the transportation.

Long after we were back from our trip, and on and on during the months, boxes and bags with food and clothing arrived in Stowe. It was more than we could handle every day, and we started to store it in one of the buildings in the camp. When camp started that summer, that long barrack was full to the ceiling with clothing. What we needed was hands, volunteers to help. Like a godsend came a friendly lady one day from Rochester, New York, and simply took over. She recruited volunteers in the morning and another crew in the afternoon. She started in and made sure that every left shoe had its right one. And under the able direction of Mrs. Harper the huge job of packing thirty thousand pounds of material was achieved in a few weeks.

All these are only highlights. We could go on and on quoting names, names of towns, and names of people, who answered the call: "Please help!" Half a year later the big barrack in the camp was full again; but we were absolutely out of funds, and it does cost money to send quantities of goods abroad. What should we do?

In our library at home we had a book about the Leopoldine Society of Austria. That was founded in 1829 and through it the Austrian clergy and people contributed almost a million dollars to Catholic missions in America. There was the idea. We wrote a short letter, explaining our desperate situation: that we had many thousands of pounds of goods and couldn't send them for lack of money, and then we sent one such letter to every priest in America. The whole family was occupied for two solid weeks in folding these 40,500 letters, putting them into envelopes, and classifying them according to States. Again the miracle happened. Money came flowing in, mostly in one dollar and five dollar checks, and it amounted to exactly the sum which we needed.

One day a big manila envelope arrived. Through General Collins, public charities in Austria approached us with some five thousand addresses of the most destitute and needy families, and would we or could we find American families who would take over one such address and send food and clothing from time to time?

On our little mimeographing machine we brought out small forms. The first page had the address of the needy family, and in three sentences, the most necessary information. The second page had suggestions for four different packages: (1) "To keep them alive"; (2) "To keep them clean and neat"; (3) "To keep them warm"; (4) "To make them happy." The third page said: "Detach this side and return to our office with your signature."

In this way we can keep track whether the oral offer, "Oh give me ten names, I can easily take care of them" happened to come with the high spirits right after a concert, or whether the person really took care of the adopted brother. To date around fourteen thousand families have been placed with generous Americans.

Meanwhile, things became a little better in the old country. The show windows are not empty any more. But the question is, what is harder: not to be able to buy anything because the stores are empty, or not to be able to buy anything because the prices are miles beyond your budget? You can only look at what you cannot get—and that makes a people restless, and that is always dangerous. Compared with what they were two years ago, conditions in Austria are a good deal better; compared with what they were efore the war—conditions in Austria are still unbearably hard. Therefore, our small relief association, which has managed with the grace of God to send around three hundred thousand pounds of goods in a little over two years, will continue to work as long as there is anyone left in need of relief and as long as used clothing, old toys, canned goods, etc., find their way to us. Everything which is now sent serves a two-fold purpose: first, it relieves the dire material need; and second, it helps to keep up hope, without which one cannot live.

"Many a one has lost his faith in God because he first lost his faith in man; and again, many a one has found his faith in God again because he met a good man who took the bitterness out of his heart," says Cardinal Faulhauber.

A Letter

IN THE summer of 1947 there went out to all our friends in America and Europe the following letter:

Dear Friends:

In the many letters arriving daily from far and near, for which we thank you from our hearts, recurs that one anxious question: "But how was that possible—was he sick—just what happened?" And so we want to tell you how it happened. If it were a story, it would have to be called: "A Hero's Life and a Hero's Death." But this is not a story. It is only a sad letter.

Our last concert tour was very long and strenuous. As usual Georg accompanied us. While driving up the West Coast from Los Angeles to Seattle, I noticed how pale he looked, but he insisted he felt perfectly all right except for a growing tiredness.

"But we're all tired, you as well as I," he said.

In Seattle he began to cough. I implored him to fly back to New York to see a doctor who had once helped him wonderfully through bronchitis.

"I'm not sick; I want to stay with you," he begged.

But the cough got worse, and in Denver, Colorado, we put him on the plane.

When I didn't get any news from him for five days, I was worried. Unfortunately, just at that time there was a telephone strike all over the United States. I couldn't call him. I telegraphed to the doctor, and the answer came back:

CAPTAIN VON TRAPP RECOVERING RAPIDLY FROM PNEUMONIA.

When I finally got Georg on the telephone, he said:

"I'm already much better, but here in the hospital it's terrible. Do come, and then let's go home. I want to go home."

But we still had concerts, and another week went by. I received two letters and a report from the doctor, and it all sounded reassuring. But an inner unquiet had gripped me, which would not be soothed away, and finally I flew the last 1,500 miles to New York.

As I entered the hospital room, Georg sat up in bed, stretched both arms wide, and said only: "Come!"

I held him long, pressed close to me, to gain time to pull myself together. My heart almost stood still with fright at the appalling change which in two short weeks had taken place in him. Sunken, hollow cheeks, deep-set eyes circled with dark shadows, bluish lips —his dear face was almost unrecognizable, and he was as thin as a skeleton. A frightful thought rose in my mind: perhaps it was not all so simple as it had sounded in the letters.

But Georg was very happy now.

"Thank heaven you're here! Now see to it that you get me out of here fast. Then let's go straight home."

At his wish I took, right away, the telephone on his night table, called the doctor in charge, and asked when I could take Georg home.

To my amazement, the answer was: "Any time, tomorrow or day after tomorrow." I should come to the doctor's office that evening. He wanted to talk to me.

That reassured me again. Surely it couldn't be so bad if he was permitted that long trip of 330 miles. As soon as we were at home on our mountain, the good air, the heavenly quiet, the spring sunshine, together with his favorite dishes and all that love and care can think of, would soon bring him back to health again.

So we spent a cozy day. I had to tell him every detail of the last two weeks. Then we made plans.

"You know, I have no pain, there is nothing the matter with me any more, only I am so terribly tired and weak."

These were the last carefree hours of our life together. But we didn't know it. Or did we suspect it somehow? Each time when I stood in the doorway with a last, cheerful good-bye, something "important" occurred to one of us: "Just this I must really tell you." Georg was so jovial and happy, and, "Actually he doesn't look so terribly bad, only a bit under the weather," thought I to myself as I sat in the taxi and rode to the doctor, who would, o course, give me prescriptions for diet, medicine, etc.

"Thank goodness, the pneumonia is well over," I said to th doctor, as I sat opposite him in his consultation room. Somewha hesitatingly he answered.

"Yes, but the X-ray picture shows a large shadow in the lung which indicates a tumor."

"Well, then, we must cure that tumor," I said, looking confi dently and encouragingly at the doctor.

"But it is not a benign tumor," he answered in a muffled voic without looking up. I didn't understand him, and was only aston ished. Then suddenly like lightning, an appalling thought wen through my head.

"For heaven's sake, Doctor, it can't be cancer?"

Silently he bent his head low over his folded hands, and a heavy silence settled over the room. . . .

New York is a very large city, and within the limits of this city live more people than in all Austria. But for me in that sinister night it was worse than a wilderness. In the wilderness at least I would have seen the starry sky, but in New York the little sky which one might still see between the skyscrapers is veiled in smoke. In my desperation I didn't even think of taking a bus or a taxi. Mechanically I simply walked on in the direction of the hotel for two and a half hours; and not a single church did I pass on the way. Quite automatically I had put my hand in my pocket and started to say the rosary. Once again this ancient prayer, which has borne up to heaven so much human suffering and heartache proved to be a good, strong friend in need.

In my room I literally hung on the telephone. The friends on whose help I counted most had gone away. The next friends' only child was sick, and before I could say anything of my trouble, they described to me their own. How I would have liked to tele phone the children or Father Wasner; but they were on the way home, and I had no idea in which city they were stopping that night. Meanwhile, it was past midnight, but there was no question of sleeping. My room was high up on the twenty-seventh floor. Through the open window I looked out over the sea of buildings. As the church steeples are much lower than the surrounding sky-

scrapers, one doesn't see them. Even this consolation is denied. My God, how lonely one is in a big city!

At last that night was over. At five o'clock in the morning I finally found an open church. At seven o'clock I took a taxi to go back to the doctor to see if there wasn't something, anything we could do. I remembered having heard that recently Thomas Mann, at the age of seventy-five, had successfully undergone an operation for cancer of the lung.

"Even that we have already thought of," said the doctor. "There is a marvellous specialist in this very rare and exceedingly difficult operation here. But the tumor is located in a place where one cannot operate."

"Well, what else can we do then?" I choked through my tears.

"Unfortunately, nothing."

"But I can't just let him die like that!"

Silence.

And now I had to go to the hospital to get a completely unsuspecting Georg, and could give no sign that the doctor had given him about three months to live.

He was so glad to be out of the hospital that he paid no attention to my face.

The next day we went home. Georg was rather talkative. Interrupted by violent coughing, again and again he wanted to tell me of earlier times. Then for a longer time he was silent and gazed earnestly ahead.

Suddenly he said: "See, now it is that way again. From time to time there comes such a picture. I see you all on the farm, working and getting tired out, and then I look for myself, and I'm not there any more."

Was that a premonition?

We arrived in Waterbury, Vermont, the nearest railroad station to Stowe. As the train came slowly in, I saw Rupert's laughing face greeting us through the window. He was home for a short holiday before starting his interneship. The poor fellow knew nothing yet. But as he helped Georg down the steps of the train, his laughter gave place to real alarm.

Arriving in his bedroom, Georg said with a sigh of deepest satisfaction:

"We have the most beautiful home I can imagine. Here it is best."

And now he could not do enough to assure me how good he felt. While he was resting from the exertions of the trip, I told Rupert everything. On the very same day we asked a good friend of ours, a well-known doctor in the university town of Burlington, to come over. Shocked, Dr. R. heard the diagnosis of the New York doctors. Then he went over to Georg.

Long, anxious minutes slipped by. When Dr. R. finally came out of the room, I could hardly believe my eyes, so—almost pleased he looked.

"You cried too soon," he said to me. "I am absolutely unable to share the opinion of my New York colleagues, and I don't find him so bad at all. As far as cancer goes, I don't believe it. The pneumonia took a lot out of him, and now he needs quiet—much quiet. It will be weeks before he's back to normal again!"

One can also cry for joy. I could not grasp my happiness at all. I felt as if I had escaped from a concentration camp. I rushed to the chapel for an ardent prayer of thanksgiving, and then to Georg!

So—quiet, much quiet. If only there were not this racking cough, which stirred him again and again out of his sleep.

If during the past nights I had been unable to sleep for grief and affliction, now happiness kept me awake. In this night I thought of the many convents, in whose churches and chapels we had sung for cloistered nuns and monks to the greater glory of God. They were our most grateful audiences. And they had not forgotten us; at Christmas, Easter, and on feastdays came greeting cards with assurances of prayer. These friends we needed now! In a short letter I told of "the Captain's illness," and asked for prayer. This letter went to all those convents and monasteries, as well as to all our friends in Europe.

A few days went by. Georg was tired and happy. He didn't want to talk much. He liked it best when I sat at his bedside, held his hand, and read aloud to him. Sometimes he fell asleep during the reading; then with my left hand I got out my rosary. It was strange: Georg, who was always so concerned for others and never claimed a service for himself, now did not want to let me out of his sight for a minute. Not even at night. He was afraid of the

*night. When the convulsive coughing had again shaken him
awake, he often said: "Pray something out loud!" Our Fathers
took turns with short ejaculations or with the ancient prayer which
I still knew from Nonnberg:*

> *"Oh God, we cry unto Thee,
> In the Name of Jesus,
> Through the Blood of Jesus,
> Through the most Sacred Heart of Jesus.
> Most wonderfully Thou canst help us.
> Holy God,
> Holy, strong God,
> Holy, immortal God,
> Have mercy on us!"*

*Again and again the anxious heart appealed to Our Lady:
"Maria, cure of the sick, consoler of the afflicted, pray for us." A
gentle pressure of the hand indicated to me: so, now that's enough;
now let's sleep again a little.*

*Georg's faith was just like himself—child-like and uncompli-
cated. The Lord God, Our Lady, the dear Saints and the Poor
Souls, were all one big family, to which we also belonged. He
didn't get very far with prayer books. He presented his petitions
to his God in his own way: "Look, dear God, it's thus and so;
please help us."*

*An almost personal friendship bound him with Our Lady. When
two good Austrian Carmelite Fathers came to visit us one day and
told enthusiastically about the "Saturday Promise" of Our Lady,
he was immediately very much interested and wanted to know
details. They told him that several hundred years ago Our Lady
had appeared to a Saint of the Carmelite Order, given him a piece
of her robe, and solemnly promised:*

*"Whoever dies clothed in this garment, I shall take to heaven on
the first Saturday after his death."*

*From this resulted the so-called Confraternity of the Scapular.
Everyone could avail himself of the benefits of this promise by
being admitted into this Confraternity. The scapular is two small,
brown patches which, attached by strings, are worn over the shoulders, next to the body. Georg was very much impressed by this
promise. He was admitted into the "Scapular" and always faith-*

fully added to his night prayers the three Hail Marys which the priest assigned to him at his reception.

I repeat this here in such detail because Georg once said to me from his sickbed: "We should tell everybody about the scapular; it is such a consolation."

On the doctor's advice, Georg sat for a while in the afternoon in a comfortable armchair. He longed for the return of the children. When Dr. R. called again, he was very much satisfied. Since he had to go to Chicago for ten days, he gave us the telephone number of a Dr. W., just in case, and when Dr. W. came, he, too, spoke most hopefully about Georg's condition.

In spite of the confidence of both doctors, I could not rid myself of a secret fear. To prepare me for what was to come, the doctor in New York had pointed out to me that Georg would become visibly weaker, finally a serious shortness of breath would set in, and if heart failure did not intervene, he would slowly suffocate. Like my own death sentence these words still sounded in my ears.

Then Dr. W. himself was suddenly taken ill, and recommended to us a particularly capable internist from the university clinic in Burlington, Dr. F.

Outside the wind howled and tossed spongy, wet snow against the window. Georg asked more and more often about the children, who were still on concert tour. The big house was so lonely and quiet. Finally, the blue bus came panting up the hill. The poor children, they only knew that Papa was much better. Happily they pressed all at once into the sickroom and then—how suddenly they were struck dumb, with what difficulty they held back their tears. The horror which rose in their eyes made me once more aware of the ghastly change. I had just wanted to ask: "Doesn't Papa look much better already?" but the question remained unasked. Quietly I slipped out of the room, out of the house, and behind the big poplar tree I wept bitterly.

The children's return worked like a strong medicine. Georg would have liked to have them around him all the time. He had them tell about the last concerts, about the success of the collections for Austria, wanted to see the current mail, to read letters from Austria himself, and began again to talk of the old times.

How stubborn the human heart is! Since it cannot live without hope, it hopes still against all hope. It clings to each tiny straw, *and until the last moment, will not believe the awful truth. The new doctor, Dr. F., was much more confident than the first two doctors.*

I felt a heavy responsibility weighing on me. I knew that Georg continually repelled the idea of his own death because of my apparent hope and confidence. What should I do? Should I remind him to make a will, ask him how he wanted this or that arranged, just in case . . . Beyond that, I could not think. Great as my apprehension was, there was still the testimony of three first-class doctors against that of the New York doctors. Even Rupert was full of confidence.

Meanwhile, from all over this country and Europe came answers to my plea for prayer. A real army of allies stormed heaven.

Then came a good visit from an Austrian Jesuit Father, who is now a pastor in Boston. As I couldn't help reading the deep emotion in Father Weiser's face, I said to Georg:

"Look, in the New Testament it says clearly: 'Is any man sick among you? Let him bring in the priests of the church and let them pray over him, annointing him with oil in the name of the Lord.' Let's ask Father Weiser for the Last Sacraments; that will certainly do you good."

Father Weiser was his good friend. Georg agreed immediately.

"All right, tomorrow morning."

We had all gathered in the chapel. While Father Weiser was hearing Georg's confession, we recited the rosary. Then came Father Weiser to fetch the Holy Eucharist. With burning candles we went before our Saviour, singing, into the sickroom. It was a solemn and festive occasion. Georg was so happy and peaceful; loudly and clearly he answered, together with us, the priest, who said all the prayers in Latin and German. What strength and confidence flowed forth from these prayers! Something of Georg's peace and joy touched all our hearts. When the holy act was over, the children kissed their father and quietly went out.

Afterwards I was alone with Georg. "I feel so much better," he said softly, taking my hand in his, and fell asleep. Quietly he slept for several hours. Even the cruel cough was still. Right away my heart began to sing: maybe—maybe. That was the Wednesday before Pentecost.

It was the calm before the storm. The following Saturday short-

ness of breath set in. Painfully he squeezed out the words: "What's this, do I have to die now?" And he looked at me anxiously and imploringly.

We telephoned Dr. F. immediately. He reassured us. It was only an attack of asthma; Georg was most probably allergic to some of the pollen from those many flowers his children had brought with them upon their homecoming. He gave him an injection against asthma, and we cleared the pelargonias and petunias out of the room.

When the new doctor saw our dreadful anxiety, he took the whole afternoon and stayed in the sickroom to observe the patient. Before he left, he gave Rupert different medicines and assured us over and over again that no one ever died of asthma, that Georg would soon be much better. His general state of health was completely satisfactory. How eagerly and gladly does one believe what one wants so much to believe!

The next day was Pentecost Sunday. With hearts filled with anxiety we prayed to the Holy Ghost, Who is also called the "Comforter."

It was the beginning of a martyrdom. Panting heavily and struggling for breath, Georg sat among the pillows. The greatest variety and the most modern asthma medicines brought no relief, and even the morphine dose had to be increased more and more to give him a little rest at night.

Since the beginning of the shortness of breath on the Saturday before Pentecost, the family had multiplied their prayers. Every hour the chapel bell called us. Day and night we took turns before the Blessed Sacrament.

Thursday after Pentecost came. In the afternoon Dr. F. had again spent several hours with the patient. The shortness of breath was mysterious to him.

"If it weren't for his breathing," he said, "the Captain could sit out here in a chair, and in a week, on the balcony." He described his general condition, heart, lungs, etc., as substantially better than a week ago. He did not think it was cancer, and as for the breathlessness, he thought it might be attributed to a nervous condition. He went away more confident than ever.

Then everything was as it had been in the last days, supper, evening prayer. At eleven o'clock I noticed a difference in his breath-

ing. Suddenly I knew with absolute certainty: This is now the end. I called Rupert and waked all the children except little Johannes. Father Wasner came also. After one look at the sick man he left, returning immediately with the stole and the book of Prayers for the Dying.

To assist Rupert we called the nearest doctor in Stowe, a white-haired elderly lady. She came, made a quick examination, said only, "The heart," and gave him a couple of injections. Then she sat down in the back of the room. We knelt around the bed. Slowly and solemnly the words of the Prayers for the Dying sounded through the room. We prayed the rosary together. No, many rosaries, how many, we don't know. After every single decade we said a few ejaculations aloud slowly. He was fully conscious, and in the midst of a violent struggle, he repeated from time to time: "My Jesus . . . Mercy!"

It was long after midnight when the doctor listened again to his heart.

She said in an undertone: "I'm afraid this is the end."

I knew what I had to do. Many years before, we had promised each other that the one would tell the other when the end was coming. Up to this moment I had waited for a miracle and clung to the confidence of the doctors. But now the word of a doctor had destroyed the very last hope. It had to be.

I got up from my knees and said very close to his ear: "Georg, the end is coming."

A terrible sob shook the breast fighting for air, and with a last effort he put his right arm around my neck, his hand sought my forehead. A farewell blessing. But that was not yet all.

"Georg, my dear Georg, you accept death willingly from the hand of God, don't you?"

That was the important, the all-deciding question which we had promised each other to ask. And in the violent spasms of his final struggle for breath, a hero to the last, he gasped, "Yes."

That was the last word of the dying father. Indelibly it was burnt upon our hearts.

A Saint once said: "The most beautiful word which a man can say to his God is the little word, 'yes.'"

Once more Father Wasner brought Holy Communion. In full

consciousness Georg received his Master and Saviour, his Commander-in-Chief and Best Friend.

And now it was really there, the end. It was a hard, cruel battle. A hero's death.

How terribly still it was in the room when the last deathrattle was silenced. The poor breast had its peace now, the brave heart stood still. In this holy silence Georg suddenly opened his eyes. The tortured features became calm and with an expression of endless wonder Georg gazed into another world. What may he have seen there? It must have been something indescribably beautiful. After about two minutes he nodded his head a little, and the dear eyes closed forever.

It was Friday, May 30, 1947 at 4:30 A.M.

We said the rosary again beside the deathbed, and then went over to the chapel for the first Requiem Mass.

Little Johannes had been sleeping soundly in the next room with the door open. When he awoke around eight o'clock, his first question, as usual, was:

"How is Papa today?"

When he heard the sorrowful answer, his face lit up with joy.

"That's good that Papa died on a Friday; now Our Lady will take him to heaven soon!"

We were prepared for tears and great sorrow, but not for that. The child had immediately remembered what his father had told him about the scapular.

After Holy Mass we stood a moment together in the hall in front of the chapel, weary with a night's watching, shivering, sorrowful and lonely. A despondent voice asked:

"What shall we do now?"

Then suddenly a scene arose before my inner eye, and I said:

"Children, I know exactly how your father wants to have it."

Sitting around the black breakfast coffee—no one could eat anything—I told them:

"When we were in Vancouver Island a year and a half ago, a guide described to us the customs of the Vancouver Indians in burying their dead. Do you remember his describing how they crammed their dead into a little wooden box and put this box on a forked branch in a tall tree? That was their funeral. Then

Papa turned to me and said in a sly undertone: 'But I don't *want* to be buried that *way!*' Half joking, half serious, Papa enumerated his wishes. 'You know, when I'm dead, you mustn't begrudge me my rest. Since my Cadet days I've never had enough sleep. Then I'll really be able to catch up. You mustn't cry and lament, but you should be glad for me, for then I'll have gone home, and you'll soon follow. This lying in state and those black sheets I *can't* stand. Let me sleep a day or two among you in the living room. You sit around me, praying and singing. You must sing all my favorite songs for me again. And flowers I want, a whole room full, but they must not be bought. They must all be grown on our grounds.' The conversation obviously amused him, and he said impulsively: 'You know, I've already found a little place for myself not too far from the house so you can come and visit me often. Do you think I'll have enough friends that they can carry my coffin over on foot? I can't stand these rubber-wheeled things. On the way to the grave you must sing 'Andreas Hofer's Farewell to Life' and 'Meerstern, ich Dich Grüsse,' and 'Innsbruck, ich muss Dich lassen.' On the way back there really should be an Austrian military band playing a lively march. But I guess I have to do without that,' he said quite resigned. Then we both had to laugh heartily."

Never again had I thought of this conversation, and now this scene came so vividly to my mind that I almost thought I could hear his voice. And so our dear dead one had not yet laid down his command. It was up to us to fulfill his last wishes and commands.

First we applied for permission from our Bishop. Most willingly, kindly, and full of sympathy, he gave Father Wasner the authority to consecrate a cemetery on our own grounds. Before he could do that, however, the area had to be fenced in. All the children went to work immediately to build a beautiful wooden fence. Storms and rain were over; a brilliant blue spring sky arched over the world. We thought of the flowers. In the middle of the woods, where once a little farm had stood, we knew of a few wild apple trees. The boys brought a whole wagonful of enormous branches, and the living room was converted into a garden in bloom. In front of the chimney we hung a red brocade curtain. Then we brought our father down, dressed in his Austrian gray wool suit.

Of all his decorations, he had taken only the Maria Theresien Cross with him. This we placed on his breast. Over his knees we spread his old U-Boat flag. Above him on the mantelpiece stood the old wooden figures as usual, Our Lord and His Apostles, smiling down on the silent sleeper, surrounded by candles and flowers. His face radiated such sublime dignity and beauty that one could not look long enough at it. It reminded one of the Apostle's words: "I have fought a good fight; I have finished my course; I have kept the faith. As to the rest, there is laid up for me a crown. . . ."

Meanwhile, telegrams had gone out all over the world to relatives and friends. Answering telegrams came in. Two of them, particularly touching, spoke of the "brave knight of the Theresien Order, Baron Trapp." One was signed "Zita," and one, "Otto"— Empress Zita of Austria and her oldest son, Otto. I laid them beside his Maria Theresien Cross.

Throughout the whole day there were always at least two of us with him. At seven o'clock in the evening the whole family in Sunday best gathered around their father. Friends had arrived by airplane. "Pray and sing," he had wanted. From seven o'clock until midnight we prayed the rosary and after each decade we sang one of his favorite songs. At midnight we got up from our knees, solemnly Father Wasner intoned the Te Deum, and we sang, "Holy God, We Praise Thy Name." According to the promise of Our Lady, she must have taken him to his eternal home, and with this his birthday in heaven had begun. Filled with deep, solemn joy, we ended the death watch.

Next day the cruel reality overwhelmed me again. Weeping bitterly, I knelt at his side.

By chance, Johannes came in, waited a while, and then, a little reproachfully, said:

"But Mother, you mustn't disturb Papa in heaven. Didn't you tell me how beautiful it is there? How can you cry so?"

Finally, the day dawned, which was to take him from us forever: Trinity Sunday, the funeral day. Long before daybreak I was awake. Suddenly I heard the tapping of little feet; Johannes clambered up into bed with me.

Full of joyous excitement, he said:

"Mother, I dreamed something so beautiful, I had to come and tell you right away. I dreamed that the funeral was already over, *but we only buried an empty coffin, and our* Papali *himself carried the Cross ahead of the procession; he was tall and shining, and just beautiful. Mother, isn't that fine?"*

And the little fellow snuggled up to me happily. Johannes is not a child given to fantasy, he never invents stories, and never tells dreams. I was quite moved, and not for a moment did I doubt that this childish dream was more than a dream.

It appeared that he had more than enough friends to carry the coffin on their shoulders past the apple trees in bloom to the small mountain cemetery. We walked behind and sang the beautiful old songs. All our Guardian Angels must have helped us to be able to do it.

By the open grave Father Wasner told of Georg's heroic life and pious death, he explained the touching ceremonies of a Christian burial, and finally said that, according to an Austrian custom, we give our departed friend as a last gift a handful of blessed earth and a few drops of holy water. Everyone present was cordially invited to participate in this custom. It was truly touching, how everybody rendered this last, loving service, while from the edge of a near-by woods the doleful, heartrending trumpet call sounded: Retreat.

Dear friends, you may wonder that we told you all this in such detail, but we are convinced that he *would have it so. He was a man whose taste was for the fundamental, the genuine, and the important things. What is more important than the ability to die well? In that he gave us a shining example that we cannot keep for ourselves. He wants to welcome all of us, his family and you, his dear friends, there where he has gone before us.*

It seems to have been cancer after all. A few weeks after his death I heard of a doctor who, in his own practice, had had seventeen cases of cancer of the lungs, of which every single patient was a U-Boat man from the First World War. Thus it would not be impossible that "the Trapp," died a hero's death, true

TILL THE LAST FLAG WAS FURLED.

The Memorable Year

"THERE was a man in the land of Hus, whose name was Job: and that man was simple and upright, and fearing God, and avoiding evil. . . . Now on a certain day, Satan was standing before the Lord. And the Lord said to him: Whence comest thou? And he answered and said: I have gone round about the earth. . . . And the Lord said to him: Hast thou considered my servant Job, that there is none like him in the earth, a simple and upright man, and fearing God, and avoiding evil? And Satan answering, said: Doth Job fear God in vain? Hast not thou made a fence for him, and his house, and all his substance round about? blessed the works of his hands? . . . But stretch forth thy hand a little, and touch all that he hath: and see if he blesseth thee not to thy face. Then the Lord said to Satan: Behold, all that he hath is in thy hand; only put not forth thy hand upon his person. And Satan went forth from the presence of the Lord.

"Now upon a certain day . . . there came a messenger to Job, and said: The enemy rushed in and took thy oxen and asses and slew the servants.

"And while he was yet speaking, another came and said: The fire of God fell from heaven, and striking the sheep and the servants, hath consumed them.

"And while he also was yet speaking, there came another and said: The enemy hath fallen upon the camels and taken them.

"He was yet speaking, and behold another came in, and said: The house fell upon thy children; and they are dead.

"Then Job rose up . . . and said: The Lord gave, and the Lord hath taken away. As it hath pleased the Lord so is it done. Blessed be the name of the Lord."

"The Trapps—everything they undertake seems to turn out a

success. And how closely they live together, the parents with their ten children. There seems never to be a fight, hardly a misunderstanding. What an *exceptional* family! Of course, in real life things don't happen that way. Any normal family at one time or another has to cope with sickness, breakdowns, even death; with family clashes and endless quarrelings and the neighbors' gossip. They are rather a picture-book family!"

How many times has that been said about us and written up in newspapers and magazines, and how hard did we try to correct this impression, try to prove that we are not exceptional, but that our times are; that only one generation ago, families still used to live in a close unit, working, playing, and praying together; that ours is not only a success story, but we have our trials and troubles, too.

But somehow, that didn't sound convincing. There we were: prosperous—healthy—lucky—united. Until the year which will be unforgettable to us, our memorable year.

It began in May with a fresh grave on our hill and its merciless "never again."

In early June while I was on business in Boston, the message reached me: "Come home at once. Rosmarie has disappeared." The burden had become too heavy for the sensitive young soul: a most strenuous concert tour, combined with concentrated preparatory work for high school graduation, the anxiety during the beloved father's sickness, and finally his death. For three days and three nights we searched the countryside, the rivers, ponds, and woods. The people of Stowe offered their cars, their time, their sympathy. The Mystery of the rosary: The Finding of the Child Jesus in the Temple, has a new meaning as one's heart goes through that same agony of the search before the finding. After three days the story had to be given to the radio and newspapers. With our name that meant nation-wide publicity, reporters crowding on the porch, searching stubbornly for the romance, the only explanation for the disappearance. Then she was found while crossing a pasture in the woods. Months filled with untold anxiety and prayer had to pass until God sent the helper, a priest who was also a doctor and a psychiatrist and helped the young soul to find its way back to God and society.

One morning in June, little Johannes woke up at five o'clock.

"Mother, I'm so hot, and my neck aches and my legs and my arms."

His temperature was 104°, and the doctor said over the 'phone: "Oh, oh, I'll be right up."

The newspapers had mentioned several cases of infantile paralysis in the State. When the doctor finally came and discovered that it was "only" rheumatic fever—what a relief! For seven long weeks a lively little boy had to be kept quiet on his back.

This was in the early summer.

Then Hedwig developed a severe backache and was brought into the hospital by the doctor for observation. After another most anxious week, it appeared that it was not that grim sickness that the doctor had feared at first.

Then came the summer camp. People arrived and were shown to their quarters. The program went on as usual. You try so hard to do your best. You come and go. You smile, you talk—but all the time you feel like a machine which has to be wound up. All you do is automatic; at times, even your prayer. Of course, your will is turned in a general way towards God. You are resigned, you don't want to argue. You repeat over and over again: "Thy Will be done." But what you *feel* is that terrible emptiness. The sun has set in your life; it is getting cold. The hundreds of people around you cannot console you for the loss of the one.

It was in August once when I stood outside on the kitchen square in the camp and watched aimlessly a pickup truck and a car back up towards each other. At this moment Lorli came running to take something off the pickup. I screamed as loudly as I could. It was too late, the drivers didn't see her. How lucky we were—only a couple of ribs were broken.

When in September another baby had come and gone, not able to live on account of my bad kidneys, I didn't seem able to recover. When the whole family went to Fall River, Massachusetts, for Rupert's wedding, I was deep in bed, too sick to be even sad or sorry or worried. I was only relieved: now I wouldn't spoil his great feastday with my tears. When I had recovered to a certain extent, I wanted to take part in the concert tour, and left together with the others in November. After a few weeks long fainting spells set in, accompanied by convulsions and high blood pressure. The doctor diagnosed it as a euremic condition, and I was put into a hospital in the Middle West. I was seriously sick. After the best doctors had tried everything, I was told that all there was left for me to do was to pray. On Christmas Eve I received the Last Sacraments. In January I improved slightly and was allowed to travel home. There was nothing medicine could do for me now. I could only wait. It might take many more months.

After the "seven fat years" the "seven lean years" had come upon the Trapp Family, all compressed in ten months. Now they had to cope with sickness, breakdowns, death. At times it looked hopelessly complicated.

But must it not have looked that way to Job, the man in the land of Hus who had lost all his material goods, his children, his health, his good name, and the confidence of his friends? And what did Job do? After he had said: "The Lord gave and the Lord taketh away, blessed be the name of the Lord," he prayed for the friends who had turned against him.

And how does Holy Scriptures usually end a story which is written as an example for us? "Go and do thou likewise."

Cor Unum

THERE is a beautiful story in the Gospels: There was once a man who was paralyzed; and that's all we know of him. We don't know whether he wanted to be cured, whether he ever asked for it. We don't know what his thoughts were. But this man had friends, and they had made up their minds to have him cured. They put him on a litter and carried him over to the house where on that day the famous prophet, Jesus of Nazareth, was preaching. There was such a crowd around the house, that they couldn't get in. But they were so determined that nothing could make them change their plan. They climbed up to the flat roof with their sick friend, and through an opening, they let down the litter directly at the feet of Our Lord. Then the Gospel says so beautifully: "And when Jesus had seen *their* faith, He said to the sick one: 'Arise, take up thy bed and walk.'"

This is one of the most consoling stories, as it shows what we can do for our friends, and what our friends can do for us. When the news of my serious sickness had gotten around, letters and telegrams came in great numbers from all over Austria and America, assuring us that many people were storming heaven. And again it happened: When He saw *their* faith, He said to the sick one: "Arise . . . and go." Against all hope, I recovered fully. According to the doctor's words, this cannot be attributed to medicine. Whatever the paralyzed man's thoughts may have been before— when he took his bed and went home, he knew that through the faith of his friends, he had been cured. How he must have loved them ever after!

Then came the big day in May when we were summoned to the courthouse in Montpelier—the five years of waiting were over. It happened to be the Feast of Corpus Christi, and since early morning we had been in a festive mood. What a mixed group it was, waiting there in the courtroom: Italians, Croatians, Syrians, English, Irish, Polish people, and we Austrians. The clerk called the roll. Then the judge entered the room. We all rose from our seats. Then we were asked to raise our right hand and repeat the solemn oath of allegiance to the Constitution of the United States of America. After we had ended: "So help me God," the judge bade us sit down, looked at us all, and said: "Fellow citizens." He meant us—now we were Americans. The individual flags of seven different nations had been lowered. Only the Stars and Stripes were waving in the breeze. It was a big day.

After Armistice Day when the boys were still in Europe, they had gone for a short visit to Salzburg and found that our old home there had been confiscated by Heinrich Himmler personally; that it had been made the headquarters for the last period of this cruel war; that the chapel had been turned into a beer parlor; parents' rooms into Himmler's private suite; and what had been Father Wasner's room had become Hitler's quarters when he came visiting. Gruesome stories they heard, like this one:

One day when Hitler was visiting there, chauffeurs and orderlies were waiting outside on call. One of these soldiers hummed the melody of a Russian folksong. Hitler heard this, jumped to the window and yelled:

"It is beneath the dignity of a German soldier even to hum a Russian folk song"; and he had them all shot on the spot, without taking the trouble to find out who the singer was.

That house was haunted for us all. How could we ever live harmoniously on such bloodstained ground? When it was given back to us after the war, we prayed that we might be able to sell it. Our prayer was answered. The house was sold to a religious order in America which wanted to establish a seminary in Europe. The place is now called Saint Joseph's Seminary. It has a chapel again.

With the money we paid our debts, mortgage and all. What a feast that was! With the rest we wanted to build two additional wings on the house, one with a large chapel, and the other with enough room for guests so that eventually we could have our Sing Weeks at home, winter and summer.

After having learned the hard way how not to build a house, we engaged a contractor this time. All we had to do was sit back and watch those powerful bulldozers eat their way into a deep cellar twice as long as the one we had dug inch by inch, and in one-tenth of the time. With grim satisfaction we watched the hard-pan trying to be really hard, but being chewed up like soft butter by those blades. When the new wing was roughly finished, the family and the men who had worked on the house had a big steak dinner. Then we had to stop building for the time being because the money was used up. Some day there will be another steak dinner when the new wing is completely finished.

Martina had a bosom friend, Erika, from whom she was inseparable all during her school years. Ever since we had come to America, it was understood that Erika would sometime come to visit. This plan, interrupted by the war, was resumed right afterwards, but it took years until finally Martina stormed through the house waving a telegram and shouting:

"Erika arrives by plane in Boston tomorrow!"

Two weeks later a happy young couple entered my room—it was Werner and Erika, who wanted to go on through life together. There was a beautiful engagement feast. The newspaper man, when he learned in an interview that Father Wasner had in his speech compared Erika to Rebecca, who had also left her home and her family to follow a beloved husband into a strange country, said dreamily:

"Rebecca—oh, yes, I saw the movie—" wherewith we hastened to explain that it was Rebecca of the Old Testament, who had married Isaac.

The wedding shortly after Christmas was celebrated in the new chapel. When the bride threw her bouquet over her shoulder, Martina was the lucky one who caught it, and there is one of the Canadian boys who agrees most heartily that for this reason Martina has to be the next bride.

One day last year we felt very strongly that our home had to be given a name. We all sat down together and tried to work it out right away. At first, it seemed to turn into one of those evenings where you can't stop laughing. The suggestions got funnier and sillier all the time: "Snowplow's Turn," "Musical Tavern," "Heaven's Lobby," "The Lord's View." An old Chinese proverb says: "Every minute you laugh prolongs your life an hour." If this is true . . .

Father Wasner, who had joined us, finally said:

"The new name should have a meaning. It should stand for what the place wants to be." That made us serious again, and it made us contemplate: what *does* the place want to be? Father opened his Latin copy of the New Testament, and his eyes fell on the words of the Acts of the Apostles which describe the life of the first Christians in Jerusalem: "They were one heart and one soul"—"*COR UNUM ET ANIMA UNA.*" This Father Wasner read aloud to us, and there was a great silence. It was the answer to what we had been looking for: our new name and our new motto.

In their coat of arms the Trapps had the words: "*Nec aspera terrent*"—"Let nothing difficult frighten thee." That seemed quite appropriate to have been used by us so far. We needed it through the perilous cruise across dangerous waters. When we acquired our new citizenship, we gave up our title and the coat of arms, and somehow, "*Nec aspera terrent*," which had served very well, was not so necessary any more. A new word to live by from now on had been given us now: "*Cor unum.*" The goal is that the world should be able to say: "Look how they love one another. They are one heart and one soul."

We all felt the greatness of this hour, and willingly we accepted the new challenge. Werner, who usually rather listens than speaks, took the word then and summed it up for all of us.

"Let us take this first Christian community for our example. Let us have no private property, but share everything together as they did. And let us feel obliged, every one of us, to keep a quiet half hour in which we shall daily meditate on the life of Christ, that we may imitate it better and better."

That was the beginning of "Cor unum," and the end of the "Trapp Family" as an entity. It was a great and memorable moment in which we learned that the Trapp Family Singers had by now become an institution whose existence does not depend on the members of the closest family any more. It had been our mission to present a certain type of the best unknown music performed in a certain way to the multitudes near and far. More and more often it had happened that people, older ones and younger ones, who liked that particular spirit, wanted to be "adopted" into the family. The family ties have proved to be elastic, and so the family has grown and is still growing. If it now happens that one of these new members can even contribute with his voice, so much the better.

Our hill has become a holy hill for us since it contains that hallowed space with a lone grave, covered with flowers, framed by mountains, overshadowed by a large wooden Cross. From there silently, but still so eloquently, the head of the family watches over his own.

There we go through the year together, celebrating the feasts and the fasts as we were used to doing in the old home. Many of the old folk customs have been transplanted to the new world, much to the joy of the friends of Cor Unum.

As the weeks, the months, the years go by, we see more and more that only one thing is necessary to be happy and to make others happy, and that one thing is not money, nor connections, nor health—it is love. That love about which Saint Paul breaks out in his famous canticle of praise:

"Love is patient, is kind. . . . It does not envy . . . is not ambitious, is not self-seeking, is not provoked, thinks no evil . . . bears with all things, believes all things, hopes all things, endures all things. Love never fails."

And the author of *The Imitation of Christ* continues:

"Love is an excellent thing and a very great blessing, indeed. It makes every difficulty easy. It bears a burden without being weighted, and renders sweet all that is bitter. Love knows no limits, feels no burden, thinks nothing of troubles, attempts more than it is able, because it believes that it may and can do all things; for this reason it is able to do all, performing much where he who does not love fails and falls. Love is watchful. Sleeping, it does not slumber. Like a living flame, a burning torch, it tends upward and passes unharmed through every obstacle."

Whatever faults may be committed, big or small, whatever clouds may pile up on the horizon, dark and threatening, love will overcome all.

"Who seeks for heaven alone to save his soul,
    May keep the path, but will not reach the goal;
    While he who walks in love may wander far,
    Yet God will bring him where the blessed are." *

Herein lies the hope of all those who belong to
                    Cor Unum.

* From *The Story of the Other Wise Man* by Henry Van Dyke. Reprinted by permission of Harper & Brothers.